Samuel Beckett and the Second World War

Historicizing Modernism

Series Editors
Matthew Feldman, Professorial Fellow, Norwegian Study Centre, University of York; and Erik Tonning, Professor of British Literature and Culture, University of Bergen, Norway

Assistant Editor: David Tucker, Associate Lecturer, Goldsmiths College, University of London, UK

Editorial Board
Professor Chris Ackerley, Department of English, University of Otago, New Zealand; Professor Ron Bush, St. John's College, University of Oxford, UK; Dr Finn Fordham, Department of English, Royal Holloway, UK; Professor Steven Matthews, Department of English, University of Reading, UK; Dr Mark Nixon, Department of English, University of Reading, UK; Professor Shane Weller, Reader in Comparative Literature, University of Kent, UK; and Professor Janet Wilson, University of Northampton, UK.

Historicizing Modernism challenges traditional literary interpretations by taking an empirical approach to modernist writing: a direct response to new documentary sources made available over the last decade.

Informed by archival research, and working beyond the usual European/American avant-garde 1900–45 parameters, this series reassesses established readings of modernist writers by developing fresh views of intellectual contexts and working methods.

Series titles
Arun Kolatkar and Literary Modernism in India, Laetitia Zecchini
British Literature and Classical Music, David Deutsch
Broadcasting in the Modernist Era, Matthew Feldman, Henry Mead and Erik Tonning
Charles Henri Ford, Alexander Howard
Chicago and the Making of American Modernism, Michelle E. Moore
Ezra Pound's Adams Cantos, David Ten Eyck
Ezra Pound's Eriugena, Mark Byron
Great War Modernisms and The New Age *Magazine*, Paul Jackson
James Joyce and Absolute Music, Michelle Witen

James Joyce and Catholicism, Chrissie van Mierlo
John Kasper and Ezra Pound, Alec Marsh
Katherine Mansfield and Literary Modernism, Edited by Janet Wilson, Gerri Kimber and Susan Reid
Late Modernism and the English Intelligencer, Alex Latter
The Life and Work of Thomas MacGreevy, Susan Schreibman
Literary Impressionism, Rebecca Bowler
Modern Manuscripts, Dirk Van Hulle
Modernism at the Microphone, Melissa Dinsman
Modernist Lives, Claire Battershill
The Politics of 1930s British Literature, Natasha Periyan
Reading Mina Loy's Autobiographies, Sandeep Parmar
Reframing Yeats, Charles Ivan Armstrong
Samuel Beckett and Arnold Geulincx, David Tucker
Samuel Beckett and the Bible, Iain Bailey
Samuel Beckett and Cinema, Anthony Paraskeva
Samuel Beckett's 'More Pricks than Kicks', John Pilling
Samuel Beckett's German Diaries 1936-1937, Mark Nixon
T. E. Hulme and the Ideological Politics of Early Modernism, Henry Mead
Virginia Woolf's Late Cultural Criticism, Alice Wood
Christian Modernism in an Age of Totalitarianism, Jonas Kurlberg
Samuel Beckett and Experimental Psychology, Joshua Powell
Samuel Beckett in Confinement, James Little
Katherine Mansfield: New Directions, Edited by Aimée Gasston, Gerri Kimber and Janet Wilson
Modernist Wastes, Caroline Knighton
The Many Drafts of D. H. Lawrence, Elliott Morsia

Upcoming titles
Samuel Beckett and Science, Chris Ackerley

Samuel Beckett and the Second World War

Politics, Propaganda and a 'Universe Become Provisional'

William Davies

BLOOMSBURY ACADEMIC
LONDON • NEW YORK • OXFORD • NEW DELHI • SYDNEY

BLOOMSBURY ACADEMIC
Bloomsbury Publishing Plc
50 Bedford Square, London, WC1B 3DP, UK
1385 Broadway, New York, NY 10018, USA
29 Earlsfort Terrace, Dublin 2, Ireland

BLOOMSBURY, BLOOMSBURY ACADEMIC and the Diana logo are trademarks of
Bloomsbury Publishing Plc

First published in Great Britain 2021
This paperback edition published in 2022

Copyright © William Davies, 2021

William Davies has asserted his right under the Copyright, Designs and Patents Act, 1988,
to be identified as Author of this work.

For legal purposes the Acknowledgements on p. xii–xiii constitute an extension of this
copyright page.

Cover design: Eleanor Rose

All rights reserved. No part of this publication may be reproduced or transmitted
in any form or by any means, electronic or mechanical, including photocopying,
recording, or any information storage or retrieval system, without prior
permission in writing from the publishers.

Bloomsbury Publishing Plc does not have any control over, or responsibility for, any
third-party websites referred to or in this book. All internet addresses given in this
book were correct at the time of going to press. The author and publisher regret any
inconvenience caused if addresses have changed or sites have ceased to exist,
but can accept no responsibility for any such changes.

A catalogue record for this book is available from the British Library.

A catalog record for this book is available from the Library of Congress.

ISBN: HB: 978-1-3501-0683-3
PB: 978-1-3501-9657-5
ePDF: 978-1-3501-0684-0
eBook: 978-1-3501-0685-7

Series: Historicizing Modernism

Typeset by Deanta Global Publishing Services, Chennai, India

To find out more about our authors and books visit www.bloomsbury.com and
sign up for our newsletters.

For Alan Railton Wells, in memory.

Contents

List of Figures	x
Editorial Preface to *Historicizing Modernism*	xi
Acknowledgements	xii
List of Abbreviations	xiv
Introduction	1
1 Beckett and the Second World War	15
2 Beckett, War and the Everyday	51
3 Revolution and Revulsion: Beckett and Vichy France	77
4 Beckett and Irish Neutrality	117
5 The Language of Recovery: Beckett and France after the Liberation	147
6 Beckett and War Writing	173
Epilogue	209
Bibliography	215
Index	231

Figures

1	'Le Juif et la France', September 1941	30
2	Beckett's *sauf-conduit provisoire*, 1942	40
3	Beckett's *maquis* identity card, 1944	47
4	'Marche Noir', 1943	74
5	*Révolution nationale*, R. Vachet. n.d., *c.* 1940	81
6	'Image d'Épinal', artist unknown, n.d., *c.* 1941	84
7	'Laissez-nous tranquilles!' (Leave us in peace!), G. Mazeyrie, Té, 1941	107
8	'Saint-Lô: Bombardement de 1944'	131

All effort has been made to contact copyright holders where necessary. In some cases, no copyright holder was found. If this information becomes available, the author would be happy to acknowledge copyright in future editions of this book.

Editorial Preface to *Historicizing Modernism*

This book series is devoted to the analysis of late nineteenth- to twentieth-century literary modernism within its historical contexts. *Historicizing Modernism* therefore stresses empirical accuracy and the value of primary sources (such as letters, diaries, notes, drafts, marginalia and other archival materials) in developing monographs and edited collections on modernist literature. This may take a number of forms, such as manuscript study and genetic criticism, documenting interrelated historical contexts and ideas, and exploring biographical information. To date, no book series has fully laid claim to this interdisciplinary, source-based territory for modern literature. While the series addresses itself to a range of key authors, it also highlights the importance of non-canonical writers with a view to establishing broader intellectual genealogies of modernism. Furthermore, while the series is weighted towards the English-speaking world, studies of non-Anglophone modernists whose writings are open to fresh historical exploration are also included.

A key aim of the series is to reach beyond the familiar rhetoric of intellectual and artistic 'autonomy' employed by many modernists and their critical commentators. Such rhetorical moves can and should themselves be historically situated and reintegrated into the complex continuum of individual literary practices. It is our intent that the series' emphasis upon the contested self-definitions of modernist writers, thinkers and critics may, in turn, prompt various reconsiderations of the boundaries delimiting the concept 'modernism' itself. Indeed, the concept of 'historicizing' is itself debated across its volumes, and the series by no means discourages more theoretically informed approaches. On the contrary, the editors hope that the historical specificity encouraged by *Historicizing Modernism* may inspire a range of fundamental critiques along the way.

Matthew Feldman
Erik Tonning

Acknowledgements

This book would not have been possible without the friends, family and colleagues who have endured my preoccupation with Beckett's war years for so long. I am profoundly grateful to Steven Matthews, who guided the early version of this project as a doctoral thesis and has provided boundless support for my work on Beckett and beyond. For their encouragement and kindness, I thank Jim Knowlson, Mark Nixon and John Pilling, from whom I have learnt so much as Beckett scholars and as friends. I thank Jim too for his permission to reproduce documents from the Knowlson Collection at the University of Reading and for his help in all things related to Beckett and the war. I am fortunate to be surrounded by many fine scholars and Beckett enthusiasts at the University of Reading. My thanks to all of them. I thank Hannah Simpson, who read the manuscript cover to cover, gave tremendously helpful feedback and has seen me through its writing with emotional and scholarly support. The book would also not have been possible without the warmth and friendship of Doug Atkinson, James Brophy, Gareth Mills, Michela Bariselli, Helen Bailey and Zoe Gosling. There are countless more people I am lucky to have come to know through Beckett, and I thank them all.

I thank Stephen Thompson, David Brauner, Conor Carville and Paddy Bullard for their helpful comments on parts of the book, and Mark Nixon and Andrew Gibson in their capacity as examiners on the doctoral version of the project. Thanks to those who have participated in discussions at conferences and seminars over the years where several parts of this book have been presented. In particular, I am grateful to Mark Nixon and Anna McMullan for the invitation to speak at the 2019 Beckett International Foundation seminar; a good portion of Chapter 2 benefited from being aired there. For their assistance on the topic of Beckett and Saint-Lô, I thank Phyllis Gaffney, the staff at the Royal College of Surgeons in Ireland, Eoin O'Brien, James Little and Stan Gontarski. For his assistance with Francis Stuart's war years, I am grateful to Geoffrey Elborn for his time and kindness. Mark Nixon and Dirk Van Hulle oversaw the publication of an early version of part of Chapter 4 in the *Journal of Beckett Studies*. I thank them for permission to reprint the work. Thanks to Hannah Simpson in her capacity as co-editor with Megan Girdwood of two special issues in which parts of this book have appeared in earlier forms: part of Chapter 3 appeared in the 'Writing Bodily Resistance in World War II' issue of *Twentieth-Century Literature*, and a section of Chapter 6 is derived from an article published in the 'Global Perspectives on the Body and World War II' issue of the *Journal of War and Culture Studies*. My thanks to the editors of these journals for their permission to reprint my work here. I thank Edward Beckett for taking an interest in my research. Excerpts from Samuel Beckett's manuscript of *Watt* are reproduced by kind permission of the Estate of Samuel Beckett c/o Rosica Colin Limited, London. I thank the staff at the Harry Ransom Center for their support during my fellowship in 2016, the staff at the University of Reading Special Collections throughout my research and the staff at the National Archives, Kew. I am grateful to Matthew Feldman and Erik Tonning for taking on the book for the *Historicizing Modernism* series, and to the staff at Bloomsbury Academic for guiding it through to publication.

I thank Tom Saville, JJ Coates, Tom Bowden, Thomas Purbeck, Matt 'Glenn' Lloyd, Nathan Morley and Andy Macdonald for their years of friendship, Sipan Shahnazari, for my first Beckett encounter, and Sophie Payne, Yanos Soubieski, Verity Burke and Carl Gibson, for seeing me through from the front lines. Rebecca Erratt built me a table right before I finished this book; it is perfect for Catan. To my family, words of appreciation are not enough. Janet, Ella, John, Scooby and Rufus, thank you. This book is dedicated to my grandfather. I hope he would have been proud.

Abbreviations

Works by Beckett

CDW	(2006), *The Complete Dramatic Works*, London: Faber & Faber.
CIWS	(2009), *Company / Ill Seen Ill Said / Worstward Ho / Stirrings Still*, ed. D. Van Hulle, London: Faber & Faber.
CP	(2012), *Collected Poems of Samuel Beckett*, ed. S. Lawlor and J. Pilling, London: Faber & Faber.
CSP	(1995), *The Complete Short Prose 1929–1989*, ed. S. E. Gontarski, New York: Grove Press.
Dis	(1983), *Disjecta: Miscellaneous Writings and a Dramatic Fragment*, ed. R. Cohn, London: John Calder.
Dream	(1993), *Dream of Fair to Middling Women*, London: John Calder.
E	(2009), *Endgame*, preface by R. McDonald, London: Faber & Faber.
ECEF	(2009), *The Expelled / The Calmative / The End / First Love*, ed. C. Ricks, London: Faber & Faber.
HII	(2009), *How It Is*, ed. M. O'Reilly, London: Faber & Faber.
LSB I	(2009), *The Letters of Samuel Beckett, vol. 1: 1929–1940*, ed. M. Dow Fehsenfeld and L. More Overbeck, Cambridge: Cambridge University Press.
LSB II	(2011), *The Letters of Samuel Beckett, vol. 2: 1941–1956*, ed. G. Craig, M. Dow Fehsenfeld, D. Gunn and L. More Overbeck, Cambridge: Cambridge University Press.
LSB III	(2014), *The Letters of Samuel Beckett, vol. 3: 1957–1965*, ed. G. Craig, M. Dow Fehsenfeld, D. Gunn and L. More Overbeck, Cambridge: Cambridge University Press.

LSB IV	(2016), *The Letters of Samuel Beckett, vol. 4: 1966–1989*, ed. G. Craig, M. Dow Fehsenfeld, D. Gunn and L. More Overbeck, Cambridge: Cambridge University Press.
M	(2009), *Molloy*, ed. S. Weller, London: Faber & Faber.
MC	(2010), *Mercier and Camier*, ed. S. Kennedy, London: Faber & Faber.
MD	(2010), *Malone Dies*, ed. P. Boxall, London: Faber & Faber.
MPTK	(2010), *More Pricks Than Kicks*, ed. C. Nelson, London: Faber & Faber.
Mu	(2009), *Murphy*, ed. J. C. C. Mays, London: Faber & Faber.
TFN	(2010), *Texts for Nothing and Other Shorter Prose 1950–1976*, ed. M. Nixon, London: Faber & Faber.
U	(2010), *The Unnamable*, ed. S. Connor, London: Faber & Faber.
W	(2009), *Watt*, ed. C. J. Ackerley, London: Faber & Faber.

Other works

BC	J. Pilling (2006), *A Samuel Beckett Chronology*, Basingstoke: Palgrave Macmillan.
DDY	J. Guéhenno (2014), *Diary of the Dark Years: 1940–1944*, trans. D. Ball, Oxford: Oxford University Press.
DF	J. Knowlson (1996), *Damned to Fame: The Life of Samuel Beckett*, London: Bloomsbury.
GD	M. Nixon (2011), *Samuel Beckett's German Diaries: 1936–1937*, London: Continuum.
PI	E. Morin (2017), *Beckett's Political Imagination*, Cambridge: Cambridge University Press.

Archives

BDMP   Beckett Digital Manuscript Project, University of Antwerp.

HRC   Harry Ransom Humanities Research Center, The University of Texas at Austin.

JEK   James and Elizabeth Knowlson Collection, University of Reading.

KEW/KV   National Archives, Kew, London.

UOR   Beckett International Foundation, University of Reading.

Introduction

In June 1946, Samuel Beckett signed and submitted for broadcast a radio typescript entitled 'The Capital of the Ruins'. The text recounts, at times somewhat elliptically, the experience of the Irish Red Cross in the town of Saint-Lô in northern France and their attempt to build a provisional hospital. Saint-Lô and the surrounding area had experienced some of the worst bombings of the D-Day campaign two years prior. The city was 'bombed out of existence in one night', Beckett writes. This fact alone clearly left its mark on the author, and he concludes the draft script by questioning the optimism of recovery which accompanied the hospital project:

> One may thus be excused if one questions the opinion generally received, that ten years will be sufficient for the total reconstruction of Saint-Lô. But no matter what period of time must still be endured, before the town begins to resemble the pleasant and prosperous administrative and agricultural centre that it was, the hospital of wooden huts in its gardens between the Vire and Bayeux roads will continue to discharge its function.... 'Provisional' is not the term it was, in this universe become provisional. (*CSP*: 277–8)

The text situates the local circumstances of the project within the 'universe'-altering effects of total war and the 'provisional' condition it created in its wake. Beckett closes by reflecting on the potential legacy of the Saint-Lô project, the Irish contribution to French reconstruction and the question of 'humanity' itself in the aftermath of the war:

> I think that to the end of its hospital days it will be called the Irish Hospital, and after that the huts, when they have been turned into dwellings, the Irish huts. I mention this possibility, in the hope that it will give general satisfaction. And having done so I may perhaps venture to mention another, more remote but perhaps of greater import in certain quarters, I mean the possibility that some of those who were in Saint-Lô will come home realising that they got at least as good as they gave, that they got indeed what they could hardly give, a vision and sense of a time-honoured conception of humanity in ruins, and perhaps even an inkling of the terms in which our condition is to be thought again. These will have been in France. (*CSP*: 278)

Beckett's recourse to the notion of the 'provisional', to flux and instability, amid the arresting image of 'humanity in ruins' after the war anticipates the writing he produced over the following two decades during the turbulent period of European recovery. Yet this well-worn story of Beckett's time with the Irish Red Cross also reveals how he had assimilated, even revised for his own means, the language and imagery of war and reconstruction, and developed a clear conviction that war had in some way changed the very 'universe' that surrounded him.

This book addresses the historical conditions which drew Beckett to the notion of the 'provisional' and considers how we can situate his writing in the historical and political circumstances of the war and its aftermath. In war, provisionality is an enduring condition. How and when something will occur – when food will arrive, how a destination will be reached – are never certain. Uncertainty drives the lived experience of war.[1] In wartime, safety is provisional, and, in the Second World War, this was as true for civilians as it was for soldiers. Cities could be bombed from increasingly long range, and ever deadlier air raids meant each day was shadowed by death and destruction.[2] The Second World War saw the home front become lethal in its own right, a new form of 'total war' which created a multitude of combat zones around the globe and collapsed the safety of the civilian 'universe'. Across this book, different forms of the provisional are identified and examined for their effects on Beckett's experiences of war and the writing which followed, from the provisional of the everyday to the provisionality of governments and even the provisionality of peace.

In the shadow of the war and its aftermath, Beckett produced some of the most compelling and challenging work of the twentieth century, famously in prose and drama but also in poetry and criticism. Yet his writing from the 1940s onwards rarely involves overt historical or geographical settings. As a result, Beckett scholarship for a long time paid little attention to the historical and political dimensions of his work beyond the incidental circumstances of its composition. Often, the war has featured as a part of the scholarly appreciation of Beckett's work in relation to the Holocaust and theories of trauma and testimony, prompted most readily by the 1982 translation of Theodor Adorno's reading of

---

[1] The uncertainty of combat situations is famously known as 'fog of war'. 'Uncertainty' and the provisional nature of information have also been identified as key factors in conflict management and civilian responses to war. See Ramsay (2017).
[2] Laura Salisbury (2020) has conducted fascinating research on the psychological effects of civilians waiting for aerial bombardment and its relation to 'lived time'.

Endgame and addressed recently in extended studies by David Houston Jones (2012) and Joseph Anderton (2016), but these theoretical approaches have remained less interested in the direct material and political conditions that inform Beckett's writing. Historically and politically sensitive readings of Beckett's texts have largely focused on Ireland, with work by Emilie Morin (2009), Patrick Bixby (2009) and Seán Kennedy (2010, 2015, 2020), among others, revealing the significance of Beckett's formative experiences in Ireland during the first three decades of the twentieth century, notably in terms of the politics and propaganda of the Irish Free State. However, in-depth accounts of Beckett's engagements with the wider political realities that surrounded him by Emilie Morin (2017) and James McNaughton (2018) have revealed much about the 'radical political intelligence' of Beckett's work (McNaughton 2018: 34). Morin's illumination of numerous archival sources and historical documents has also brought much needed clarity to Beckett's attitudes to censorship, freedom of movement and the mechanics of propaganda. Nevertheless, while scholars such as Laura Salisbury (2013, 2014), Andrew Gibson (2010a, 2010b, 2013, 2014, 2015) and Anna Teekell (2018) have offered various historically attuned approaches to Beckett's war years, a book-length study has yet to examine Beckett's work in relation to the Second World War and the aftermath of European recovery.

Underpinned by a materialist and historically orientated war studies methodology, this book analyses Beckett's writing in the context of the Second World War by drawing on war studies' focus on the elements of war that often go 'ill seen' or 'ill said'. This book pays particular attention to the everyday circumstances of war, responding most readily to the prospect that, as Kay Boyle put it, 'Beckett's casual remark that he stayed in Paris until 1942 covers more peril, more pain, and more actual hunger than many of us have ever known' (*LSB III*: 56). Many of Beckett's works evince the wartime reality of food scarcity which Boyle describes. Likewise, preoccupations in his writing with travel, freedom of movement and the documentation of identity recall the quotidian conditions of the war, and the frequency of physical violence and violent thoughts in many texts point to the climate of terror that war creates.

The effects of propaganda are also central to this book. Specifically, I trace how Beckett's work recycles and inverts images resonant with the dominant propaganda in France in the 1940s. Jacques Ellul's famous definition of propaganda is useful here. Modern propaganda is, Ellul writes, 'a matter of reaching and encircling the whole man [sic] and all men [sic]', furnishing them 'with a complete system for explaining the world' that imposes 'a complete range of intuitive knowledge, susceptible of only one interpretation, unique and one-sided, and precluding any divergence' (1973: 11). Beckett's 'German Diaries' from his 1936-7 trip to Nazi Germany reveal that he was all too aware of propaganda's influence on thought and language. He is often humorously dismissive of what he calls 'the Nazi litany' and 'NS Gospel' recited by German citizens (*GD*: 86). This book explores how Beckett's works treat the techniques and ideals of the propaganda he encountered in both the 1930s and 1940s to such methods of inversion, parody and revision. It identifies how, because of the effects war and its various propagandas have on language and the creation of meaning, these literary processes are not just aesthetic or formal but political. In the aftermath of the Blitz, Stephen Spender recognized that the 'task of the poet is to organize words in such a way' that resists 'the propaganda of political parties' (1941: 137). Such a 'task' is achieved both through the depiction of the intricacies of war and political ideas and, more broadly, through the creation of literature which invites critical, interpretative thinking. Spender's is not a call for simple mimesis. Rather, it is an articulation of what Adam Piette calls the 'ethical demand' that war makes on literature, the demand that 'the extreme historical moment is recorded' with attention to 'the affect and sensations of those undergoing war's transformations' (2016: 2). Marjorie Perloff proposes that the war and its conditions demonstrated the ethics of writing to Beckett: that, following Wittgenstein, 'aesthetics and ethics are one' (2005: 102). In documenting how Beckett's texts record in their own way the 'extreme historical moment' of the Second World War, this book develops Perloff's proposition by emphasizing that 'ethics' contains the political and everyday pressures of war which demand literary response; that, in effect, the war confirmed for Beckett that aesthetics and politics are also one.

Beckett's 'German Diaries' also reveal that he saw an overlap between the structures of thought which underpinned Nazi propaganda, rationalist philosophy and the tradition of the *Bildungsroman* novel. Across these three, he identified a common pattern of thought centred on an anthropocentric logic of progress. After reading Friedrich Stieve's pro-Nazi history of Germany, *Abriss der deutschen Geschichte von 1792-1935* (Outline of German history 1792-1935), Beckett raged against the attempts to construct a narrative of Germany that imagined Hitler's regime as the inevitable outcome of the nation's past.[3] In his diary, Beckett condemns Stieve's 'history book' and describes his distaste

---

[3] The revision of German and European history involved attempts to erase significant events in the development of European democracy, particularly in France and Germany. 'Nazi historians', Claudia Koonz writes, 'predicted that the day on which Hitler became chancellor, January 30, 1933, would eclipse July 14, 1789, as a historical watershed' (2003: 10). This propaganda was not limited to historians, though. For a discussion of various instances of complicity with the regime across the German academy, see Bialas and Rabinbach (2007).

for the conception of 'history' as the rationalization of existence through teleological narratives:

> What I <u>want</u> is precisely a Nachschlagewerk [reference book], as I can't read history like a novel. . . . I say I am not interested in a 'unification' of the historical chaos any more than I am in the 'clarification' of the individual chaos, & still less in the anthropomorphisation of the inhuman necessities that provoke the chaos. What I want is the straws, flotsam, etc., names, dates, births & deaths, because that is all I can know. . . . I say the background & the causes are an inhuman & incomprehensible machinery & venture to wonder what kind of appetite it is that can be appeased by the modern animism that consists in rationalising them. Rationalism is the last form of animism. Whereas the pure incoherence of times & men & places is at least amusing. Schicksal [Fate] = Zufall [Chance], for all human purposes . . . the expressions 'historical necessity' & 'Germanic destiny' start the vomit moving upwards. (15 January 1937; qtd. in *GD*: 87, 177–8; underline in original)

For Beckett, the sweeping narrative of German history created by Stieve is 'vomit'-worthy precisely because it emphasizes and presumes progress as a traditional novel might, presenting a beginning, middle and end in which the Aryan state fulfils its destiny as the supreme European power. Such condemnation follows his dismissal of what Mark Nixon identifies as '[t]he only book of overt nationalistic persuasion' that Beckett bought during his travels, Hans Pferdmenges's *Deutschlands Leben* (1930; Germany's life). Beckett called it 'NS Kimmwasser' (National Socialist bilge) (4 November 1936; *GD*: 91). As Adam Piette writes, 'Nazi propaganda was primarily a form of dramatic technique, a grandiose fictionalizing of what might happen to you and me' (1995: 142). It is this dramatic, fictionalizing impulse at the heart of Nazi propaganda which Beckett's language of 'bilge' and 'litany' is directed against, a method of diminishing the bombast of Nazi's fascist vision to the level of tiresome rubbish. Such ultra-nationalist propaganda prefigured the rhetoric and imagery of the Vichy regime which Beckett would experience during the war.

The encounters with Nazism were formative for Beckett, notably on the topic of the absorption of art into political discourse. Nazism used its denigration of 'degenerate art' through the 1930s to solidify its position among Germany's conservative elite, all the while promoting nationalist and fascist artists who complied with the regime's 'system for explaining the world' (Ellul 1973: 11). After his trip to Germany in 1936–7, Beckett was more sensitive to the same process as it manifested in modern Ireland. This led to increasing tensions with his friend Thomas MacGreevy, especially on the topic of Jack B. Yeats's relationship to Irish history and politics:

> I understand your anxiety to clarify his pre and post 1916 painting politically and socially, and especially in what concerns the last pictures I think you have provided a clue that will be of great help to a lot of people, to the kind of people who in the phrase of Bergson can't be happy till they have 'solidified the flowing', i.e. to most people. . . . You will always, as an historian, give more credit to circumstance than I, with my less than suilline interest and belief in the fable convenue, ever shall be able to. (Beckett to MacGreevy, 31 January 1938, *LSB I*: 599)

Beckett's German tour clarified his position on the incorporation of art and culture into political discourse, be it the democratic nationalism of the Irish Free State or the National Socialism of Nazi Germany. Such experiences equipped him with a more focused sensitivity to the processes of propaganda and official language, a sensitivity that was tested most fully in the invasion and occupation of France in the 1940s.

While this book builds on the advances made by Emilie Morin, James McNaughton and others in reading Beckett in his historical contexts and the analysis of the political intelligence of his writing, it also approaches Beckett through a war studies lens that has been little applied to his work. War studies is concerned with examining military conflict through a diverse range of approaches drawn from social studies, culture studies and historical analysis. This field maintains that documenting the circumstances of and responses to war is necessarily complex, chiefly because any attempt to reconstruct the conditions of warfare will always remain partial since war is not experienced uniformly, nor is it responded to the same way twice. To meet such challenges, contemporary war studies combines the 'cultural turn' in the field in the mid-1990s, particularly as arose from the Group for War and Culture Studies at the University of Westminster, and the focus on the everyday by scholars such as Vivienne Jabri (most recently in the 2016 project *Traces of War*) and Shannon L. Fogg (2009), the latter's work on Vichy and the everyday having energized scholarship devoted to the regime's regional activities during the Second World War.

The everyday has become a particularly important avenue of inquiry in contemporary war studies, shifting emphasis from the extraordinary and the spectacular to what James Procter identifies as the political and ethical imperatives of the 'everydayness of the everyday' (2006: 78). In the peculiar conditions of war, the spectacular or extraordinary can become the everyday – when the bombing of cities becomes daily, say, or when violence and reprisals become habit. 'No entries in this diary for days', Jean Guéhenno wrote in his Paris occupation diary in October 1940, '[s]ilence and misery over the city. When calamity becomes habitual, it, too, can be uneventful' (4 October 1940, *DDY*: 27). In war, and under occupation more so, daily life can also become menacing as the possibility of escape from the everyday diminishes. This critical framework of war and the everyday attends to how war structures the circumstances from which culture emerges. It acknowledges that literature that does not directly refer to warfare can still be shaped or contaminated by both the material conditions and the sociopolitical and cultural climates that war and its aftermath generate. As such, in this book, Beckett's works are treated more explicitly as war writing than is commonly found in Beckett scholarship.

There is, of course, a well-established tradition of reading Beckett's work in relation to the horrors of the mid-century, but it is one that has largely remained within the terms first set out by the 1969 Nobel Prize committee who described his writing as:

> not about the war itself, about life at the front, or in the French resistance movement . . . but about what happened afterwards, when peace came and the curtain was rent from the unholiest of unholies to reveal the terrifying spectacle of the lengths to which man can go in inhuman degradation – whether ordered or driven by himself – and how much of such degradation man can survive. (Gierow 1969)

For the editors of *The Faber Companion to Samuel Beckett* (2006) war is 'latent in much of SB's work, as subtext, the unstated, the absent'; it is 'another example of the human predicament, an emblem of a ruined humanity'. 'The war background is not indispensable', they suggest, 'precisely because of SB's successful transformation of his material, his undoing of his creative origins' (Ackerley and Gontarski 2006: 626). While this description recognizes the importance of the war's shaping effect on Beckett's work, the focus on Beckett's creative 'undoing' occludes the exploration of Beckett's texts as war writing, a framing likely forgone for fear of confining his work to its historical circumstances, undoing that process of 'undoing'. War studies is little concerned with this prospect, since it takes war to be a multi-directional, multifaceted historical force, and recognizes how culture and intellectual thought can be shaped by war in myriad ways, even long after the conflict event itself has formally ended. Literary war studies specifically attends to how war imprints itself on literature, notably in its disruptive effects on language and cognition, from the repetition, contradiction and doublespeak of propaganda and official rhetoric,[4] to the psychological symptoms of indecision and dislocation resulting from the fear of attack, shell shock and aerial bombardment.[5] War also creates a plethora of imagery which can both consciously and unconsciously inform literary creation, from bleeding soldiers and dead bodies to the images and symbolism of the political ideologies in conflict during war.

Throughout the book, I pay attention not only to Beckett's use of various wartime allusions and images but also to how Beckett both acknowledges and refuses history in his writing. In doing so, I explore how Beckett's work treats history, and war in particular, through its referential rather than representational methods. C. D. Blanton identifies the rejection of representation as a late modernist approach to the conditions of modern warfare. Blanton argues that the hallmarks of modern war – mechanized violence and cycles of comprehensive propaganda campaigns – forced many writers in the 1930s and 1940s to adopt 'an elusive poetics devised under the force of the injunction to include history but caught simultaneously in a history too complex and often too menacing to include straightforwardly' (2015: 4). While 'the great experimental modernists, like Joyce and Woolf, ... fractured narrative to achieve a new form of mimetic fiction' (Teekell 2018: 137), late modernists like Beckett were faced, under the imminent and then realized threat of a second global war in half a century, with the break-up of the very idea that life could be represented; mimesis was no longer possible in the face of such 'menacing' history. Seán Kennedy has documented this referential literary mode in Beckett's work in relation to Ireland, arguing that the author's fleeting historical references after 1945 suggest that Beckett registered that history can 'neither be expressed nor escaped' (Kennedy 2015: 187). For Andrew Gibson, Beckett's habits of referentiality are symptomatic of the history he encountered:

---

[4] As Marina MacKay writes, 'the prosecution of war, infamously, depends on a referential minimalism akin to [George Orwell's] newspeak – "casualties", "collateral damage", "strategic withdrawal", and "displaced persons" are among the many phrasings we use to name and avoid the unbearable' (2009: 5). Before *Nineteen Eighty-Four*, Orwell elaborated on the notion of wartime 'newspeak' in his essay 'Politics and the English Language': 'Defenceless villages are bombarded from the air, the inhabitants driven out into the countryside, the cattle machine-gunned, the huts set on fire with incendiary bullets: this is called *pacification*. Millions of peasants are robbed of their farms and sent trudging along the roads with no more than they can carry: this is called *transfer of population* or *rectification of frontiers*' (1981: 166–7; emphasis in original).

[5] As early as 1916, indecision and geographical dislocation were two often-cited symptoms of shell shock (Mott 1916: vi), now referred to as Post-Traumatic Stress Disorder (PTSD) or Combat Stress Reaction (CSR).

> If Beckett's works cannot simply be 'matched up' with historical contexts . . . they are streaked by historical turmoils and the emotions provoked by them. Historical symptoms and effects weave their way across the rocky, unforgiving Beckettian surface like intermittent lodes of ore. (2010a: 22)

In Gibson's analysis of Beckett, 'the emphasis chiefly falls on discrete and discontinuous historical particulars', a methodological move that resists the very totalizing impulses that Beckett saw in the 'monde romancé that explains copious[ly] why e.g. Luther was inevitable without telling me anything about Luther, where he went next, what he lived on, what he died of, etc' (15 January 1937, 'German Diaries'; qtd. in Gibson 2010a: 22). The Beckettian aesthetic, at least that of the work written during the war and in the decades that followed, makes use of history 'in fits and starts, as appearances and disappearances', Gibson writes, as 'historical spasms, seizures, flushes and shivers, fevers and cold sweats'; the 'Beckettian ague in large measure corresponded to the great agon of the world contemporary with it'. However, 'agues can be almost sprightly,' Gibson concludes. 'They have their own intense, hectic vitality' (2010a: 22). By more closely analysing the implications of these historical 'fits and starts' in relation to the war, I reveal how we can more seriously consider Beckett as a writer of the Second World War.

While this book does not deal directly with theorizing modernism per se, it operates out of the scholarship of Blanton and others that emphasizes the reconceptualization of modernism's temporal boundaries, particularly descriptions of late modernism and its relationship to the Second World War. Shane Weller identifies late modernism's signature features as 'parataxis, repetition, fragmentation and, above all, linguistic negativism' (2015: 100), modes of writing which grapple with the unspeakability of a modernity defined by the specific horrors of the Second World War.[6] By understanding Beckett as a late modernist writer aesthetically and historically, we also open up his writing to the critical work on late modernism and war by scholars such as Marina MacKay (2007, 2009, 2017), Gill Plain (2015, 2019) and, in an Irish modernist context, Anna Teekell (2018). This scholarship recognizes late modernist writing as that which takes up modernism's notion of 'modernity as crisis' (Cleary 2014: 5), but begins from the historical minutiae of war itself, particularly the everyday and the evolving relationship between front and home front across the twentieth century, so as to establish 'the ways in which the political conditions of the

---

[6] For a wide-ranging examination of Beckett's relationship to modernism, see Olga Beloborodova, Dirk Van Hulle and Pim Verhulst's edited collection *Beckett and Modernism* (2018).

Second World War produced acutely self-aware literary forms' (Teekell 2018: 5). On this count, detailing Beckett's status as a war writer is also to expand our notion of his relationship to modernism.

War studies also offers a more nuanced approach to temporal designations, specifically those of wars themselves. In the case of the Second World War, the period 1939–45 represents the official commencement and cessation of hostilities (and so determines 'prewar', 'war' and 'postwar'). However, the formal documentation of a war is not its limit point. As Gill Plain argues, the social, political and cultural effects of the Second World War 'cannot be contained within the temporal limits of 1939–45', since 'wars do not simply end' with an armistice or peace treaty (2015: 10). 'The social, psychological and logistical "hangover" of conflict can continue for years after hostilities have officially ceased,' Plain suggests; equally 'postwar' does not 'wait for the signing of a treaty', and 'the cultural symptoms of war's end are manifest in advance of its actual conclusion' (2015: 10). As Adam Piette contends, the post-1945 moment in Western Europe was riven by anxieties over just what 'peace' in a post-Holocaust, post-atom bomb age could be, as well as by the knowledge that any collective European consciousness in the post-war years was still haunted 'by the nothing-generating spirit of destructiveness' at the heart of fascism (2019: 168). In these terms, Beckett's war comprises the long process of pre-war build up with the rise of European fascism (taking in his trip to Nazi Germany, for example, or his response to the Spanish Civil War[7]) and the even longer return to 'peace' after the war's end. This latter phase includes Beckett's return to Ireland in 1945, his work in Saint-Lô, the political tensions and relative poverty of still-recovering Paris in the late 1940s and early 1950s, and the Cold War. Understanding how 'being in the war' meant a much looser sense of beginning and end, of time itself, helps us to better grasp Beckett's own habits of historical reference. As I show in this book, this is particularly crucial for the ways in which he compresses multiple historical moments or references into particular allusions. Likewise, it sheds new light on how we might conceptualize certain aspects of the war itself. Beckett and Déchevaux-Dumesnil's decision to return to Paris in 1940 indicates that some notion of 'postwar' was already present in France, or at least that 'war' moved from active conflict to accommodating the realities of occupation. In turn, their membership of Gloria SMH shifts 'war' from occupation to refusal and resistance. The trials and purges of the postwar also bred conflict, and for a

---

[7] On being solicited by Nancy Cunard for a response to the conflict in Spain, Beckett replied with '¡UPTHEREPUBLIC!'. See also Beckett's letters to MacGreevy and Joseph Hone in June in June 1937 (*LSB I*: 508–11).

time it appeared that it was not peace that would come to France after 1945 but civil war. For many people, the war existed well beyond 1945, and Beckett was not alone in his concern in the October of that year that he might be 'bottled in a warring Europe for another 5 or 10 years' (*LSB II*: 24). The expectation of further conflict is another multifaceted aspect of war, and, as Marina MacKay notes, '[t]he different kinds of war that World War II encompassed affect its literature in profound ways' (2009: 2). This book examines the 'kinds of war' that Beckett experienced and the effect it had on the work he produced.

Despite the methodological acknowledgement of war's temporal fluidity, war studies has seldom responded to Beckett's writing, and his inclusion in scholarship devoted to the intersections of literature, culture and war is somewhat rare. Beckett's name is absent, for example, from MacKay's edited *Cambridge Companion to the Literature of World War II* (2009) beyond the date of the first staging of *Godot* in the *Companion*'s chronology. This is indicative not of a fault with the volume but that, when it is addressed in war studies, Beckett's writing is designated most often as related to the war's aftermath, specifically the Cold War and the fallout of the atomic bomb. In *Modernism, War, and Violence* (2017), MacKay locates Beckett in a continuum of modernist responses to violence, identifying 'the suspenseful dread of Samuel Beckett's Atomic-Age limbos' as a variation of modernism's 'transformations of established conventions of representation', particularly vis-à-vis the trauma of warfare and the broader sense that modernity is defined by certain kinds of mass industrialized suffering (2017: 2). Though MacKay does acknowledge the biographical detail of *Watt*'s composition during the conflict (2017: 112), there is a general disconnect that ties Beckett not just to the aftermath of the war but to the 'Atomic Age', to the Cold War, particularly identified through the apocalyptic tones and setting of *Endgame*. MacKay is undoubtedly right to identify the startling ways in which Beckett's work appears to acknowledge that 'the Second World War shaded into the Cold War in 1945 and 1946' with a terrifying seamlessness (2017: 135). Yet to understand Beckett's work in relation to the Cold War, we must consider not only his experiences of the 1940s but also the impact of events through which he lived such as the First World War and its legacy, the Irish struggle for independence and the rise of European fascism. In doing so, we can then see how these might continue to reverberate in his writing as recovery and the Cold War set in with their own kinds of propaganda and political rhetoric. By bringing together the advances made in both war studies and Beckett studies, I hope to establish war studies as a field that can nourish the ever-growing scholarly understanding of Beckett's work, and to demonstrate how war studies itself benefits from readings of Beckett's texts, particularly when it comes to engagements with non-representational and experimental war writing.

The chapters presented here combine three approaches to unpack the effects of the Second World War on Beckett's writing. First, they elaborate on the historical circumstances of Beckett's experiences of wartime and of post-war recovery. To do so, they conduct materialist analyses using archival and historical sources combined with a war studies emphasis on the everyday nature of warfare, particularly on the topics of propaganda, food, travel and socioeconomic conditions. Second, they identify hitherto ignored historical allusions and images related to the war in Beckett's texts. Third, they engage in historically informed interpretative readings of Beckett's works in relation to the war and its aftermath. This involves mapping how his works recall and engage with different aspects of the war through both their form and content. Such a process requires examining how Beckett's works deploy active rhetorical and formal strategies which reveal a range of responses to the war, its everyday pressures and its governing ideologies, from how the meaning-making potential of language is altered by propaganda and official vocabularies to how the imaginary implications of motifs like hungry tramps or wounded bodies are altered in the politics of war.

Chapter 1 gives a historicizing account of Beckett's war. It offers a description of the events and situates his experiences within the political and historical contexts of occupied and Vichy France. The chapter also examines Beckett's later apprehensions about his Resistance activity via analysis of the wartime complexities of the Resistance itself; later chapters also explore the 'Resistance myth' that existed in France in the post-war years. Many readers will be familiar with the biographical story of Beckett's war years, told as it has been by Deirdre Bair, Anthony Cronin, James Knowlson, Lois Gordon, Andrew Gibson and Emilie Morin, among others. What Chapter 1 offers is further contextual emphasis along the lines of Gordon, Gibson and Morin, as well as new emphasis on the material conditions of the war and observations on the wider political implications of Beckett's experiences. The details set out in this chapter are intended to orient the reader and also provide new or reemphasized perspectives, particularly Beckett's foreign status in terms of administration and food access. This leads into Chapter 2's discussion of the pressures placed on everyday activities during wartime, which are explored through a close reading of the recurrence of habitual, quotidian concerns over food and hunger in *Waiting for Godot*.

Chapter 3 conducts an analysis of Beckett's wartime novel *Watt*, his novellas of the late 1940s and his novel 'trilogy' of the 1950s – *Molloy*, *Malone Dies* and

The Unnamable – in the context of the propaganda campaigns of Vichy France. Beckett's membership of the Resistance meant not only the defence of the cosmopolitan, liberal Parisian way of living with which Beckett identified in the 1930s but also a resistance to the ideologies of the Vichy regime and the occupying Nazi force. Chapter 3 demonstrates that Beckett's texts continued to confront the values and ideals that fuelled Nazism and Vichy's authoritarian vision of France well beyond the official end of the war.

Chapter 4 surveys Beckett's return to Ireland in 1945 and his involvement with the Irish Red Cross in Saint-Lô. This chapter examines the received understanding of Beckett's relationship to Ireland's neutrality and questions the accepted critical position that Beckett rejected Ireland's neutral stance outright, emphasizing that Ireland's neutrality was militarily and politically necessary yet enforced through an agenda focused on censorship and moral hygiene. The chapter explores Beckett's post-war relationship with Thomas MacGreevy and his experiences in Saint-Lô to further elaborate on this topic. It then analyses 'The Capital of the Ruins' as both Beckett's most direct piece of war writing and as a response to Irish neutrality politics.

In Chapter 5, I turn to the intellectual milieu of post-war Paris. Focusing on the extent to which humanism pervaded post-war French intellectual life, this chapter evaluates Beckett's engagement with the cultural reconstruction of France in both his critical and creative writing. This context informs a close examination of the recurring themes of assimilation and anthropology in Beckett's prose with reference to Jean-Paul Sartre's controversial *Réflexions sur la question juive* and Sartre's extended discussion of 'assimilation' in French society.

Finally, Chapter 6 looks to war memory and the genre of war writing to examine the ways in which Beckett's post-war texts often negotiate the more direct horrors of warfare – bodily disfiguration and the necessity of violence – through reference to other wars, notably the Boer War, the First World War and the Irish fight for independence. This chapter puts these elements of Beckett's work into dialogue with other writers more often explicitly identified as authors of war books or war writing. The book concludes with an epilogue that considers the longer-term effects of the war on Beckett's work and its shift towards a focus on memory and grief. The chapter closes by reflecting on the avenues the book has opened up for further analysis of Beckett's writing in a war studies framework.

1

Beckett and the Second World War

France and Britain declared war on Nazi Germany on 3 September 1939, following the invasion of Poland on 1 September. Beckett was in Ireland at the time. Five months prior, he had written to Thomas MacGreevy from Paris that '[i]f there is a war, as I fear there must be soon, I shall place myself at the disposition of this country' (*LSB I*: 656). By 4 September, Beckett had travelled via England to France to rejoin his friends and his partner, Suzanne Déchevaux-Dumesnil, in Paris. Within the month, Beckett had applied for papers to allow him to stay in France. He also offered to drive ambulances for the city.

'Under the blue glass': The declaration of war and the invasion of France

While the declaration of war came rapidly after the invasion of Poland, Beckett's life in Paris between September 1939 and May 1940 involved few major upheavals. That is not to say the war was not felt in the city, particularly with the mobilization of French soldiers and increasing media reports on the German advances. Nevertheless, Beckett's life and work continued apace: he persisted with his translation of *Murphy*, finishing most of it by the end of the year; he saw James Joyce and helped him in various capacities; and he continued to meet friends and artists in the city. Yet if there were no major changes to Beckett's routines, small changes were indicative of the uncanny nature of this phase of the war. Where before Alfred Péron had been on hand to assist in the *Murphy* translation, now Beckett was alone, Péron having been mobilized with his regiment (26 September 1939, *LSB I*: 668). Georges Pelorson, another candidate for translation assistance, was also on hold for his regiment at the time (Cronin 1999: 310).

Behind the veneer of normality, however, France underwent significant changes. With the declaration of war, the French government put into effect legislation to intern German foreigners, formally designating them as 'hostile' on 10 September 1939. The altered implications of a 'foreign' status in wartime France were palpable only a few days after Beckett's return to Paris, as was the degree to which administration and bureaucracy had already come to define many of the everyday aspects of the war. 'Being foreign' gained a heightened tension, though at this point Beckett's Irish nationality was of little concern compared to those with German connections who were declared *étrangers non désirables*. Approximately 12,000 Germans and 5,000 Austrians were sent to French camps, many of which had been built before the war as provisional holding centres to contain the tens of thousands of Spanish refugees who had fled Franco's victory. The French government's internment policy unwittingly pre-empted the practices of the Nazis and the Vichy regime once arrests of Jews and 'other perceived enemies' commenced (Riding 2011: 29). Indeed, accounts of Le Vernet camp from before the fall of France, used by the Vichy regime to hold suspected 'dissidents' and later by the Nazis to hold Jewish detainees destined for Dachau, suggest that hunger and the degrading use of forced nudity were commonplace in the camps interning Germans and other 'enemy' foreigners (Riding 2011: 31).

Throughout the early stages of the war, Beckett continued to make it known to his adopted country that he was willing to help should Paris come under threat (*LSB I*: 668). Paris now had to be maintained and defended against not only physical destruction but Nazism itself. If the true horrors of the regime's racist policies were yet to be recognized, Beckett was already aware of the exclusionary and essentialist politics of the Reich to which his relatives the Sinclairs, particularly Boss, had been subjected (*DF*: 183). He had also encountered first-hand Nazi Germany's repression of 'degenerate' artists during his travels in 1936–7. For Beckett and the circles he moved in, Paris was a liberal, artistic and multinational melting pot.[1] However, with the threat of invasion, Beckett's relationship with the city was unavoidably modified. Paris no longer represented a space of sanctuary and artistic opportunity. When Nazi forces were progressing closer to France with each passing day in early 1940, this life

---

[1] Beckett's experiences in Germany in the late 1930s revealed the militarized sensibilities of the nation: 'They must fight soon (or burst)' (*GD*: 7). For many intellectuals and artists in Paris in 1939–40, though, war seemed a distant possibility. Stéphane Hessel, the son of the German writer Franz Hessel, noted of the Parisian intellectual circles close to Beckett that 'When [Franz] saw how these intellectuals were reacting, that is when [he] understood they were not worried by the war[.]' 'Protected by the Maginot Line, they thought Germany would not invade, that Germany would collapse with economic problems, that the French and British fleets still ruled the world, that the United States would enter the war sooner or later, that even the Soviet Union would not stay out. So intellectual life flourished around people like Joyce, Breton, Duchamp' (qtd. in Riding 2011: 35).

would have seemed increasingly precarious, distant though the German soldiers remained from the city itself. Yet if a certain Parisian life was under threat at the time, Paris itself was relatively safe from physical harm compared to cities like London. In preparing for invasion, Joseph Goebbels argued that Paris should be preserved as he planned to use the French capital as a seat of cultural power in the new Nazi empire, the city's heritage supplying the cache that some believed German cities lacked (Riding 2011: 51).

The significance of Beckett's foreign status in a country at war was made apparent to him when he did not receive travel documents at the beginning of 1940. His lack of 'safe-conduct' pass prevented him from travelling to see the Joyces in Saint-Gérand-le-Puy. France had yet to be invaded, but Beckett's freedom of movement was already radically altered by wartime legislation. The requirement that one had the right document on hand for travel, collecting rations or even simply walking the street quickly became a hallmark of life during the war. As we will see, Beckett's works repeatedly register the anxieties, frustrations and dark comedy of a life of documentation and hunger.

Eventually, in March 1940, Beckett was able to join the Joyces and Jolases for Easter. His return to Paris from Saint-Gérand-le-Puy at the beginning of April coincided with the fall of Norway and Denmark to German forces. On 10 May 1940 (Saint Joan of Arc's Day), the Netherlands, Belgium and Luxembourg were invaded, clearing a path for the German army to enter France through the Ardennes, emerging in Sedan. Though Beckett remained safe in Paris, the failure of the Maginot Line was a significant blow to the city's morale. The arrival of the invasion through the eastern forests was also symbolic, as Sedan and the Ardennes are sites with long military histories. The Battle of Sedan in 1870 ended with the defeat of Napoleon III, the last emperor of France, and ushered in the Third Republic, the very institution which was to be overthrown by Vichy and the occupiers. It was also a key site in the Ardennes battle in 1914, which saw the French repelled by superior German forces. The Ardennes and Sedan resonate so widely with French military history that they press themselves on the memories of Nell and Nagg in *Endgame* (*E*: 13).[2] This is a site of significant French war memory, recurring in a series of major French military defeats that each precipitated great change for the nation.

Though most of the letters written by Beckett from the period include little direct commentary on the events of the war and invasion, their language is

---

[2] James McNaughton identifies Nell and Nagg's 'sites of kindling' as 'locales of massive military-historical confrontations', though he notes only the German significance of the 1870 battle, identifying it as the event that 'made the Second German Reich possible' (2018: 158).

marked by the sense of incomprehension and apprehension which many shared in France and across Europe at the time. Nine days after the invasion of France, on 21 May 1940, Beckett could only register the war in ellipses in a letter to George and Gwynedd Reavey: 'I have had several visits from Péron, on leave. He was in good form. But now . . . ?' (*LSB I*: 680). Those three dots suggest an acknowledgement of the possibility of imminent change in the country; they also mark the threshold of unknowability and ineffability that the invasion represented. We see a similar sense of the unspeakable in the 10 June 1940 entry in Agnès Humbert's occupation diary: 'We have to get used to this appalling possibility: Paris may fall. It's one thing to think it, but it's quite another to say the words out loud: "Paris may fall." I'm stopped by a superstitious dread: I can't do it. Some things should never be said out loud, for fear they may come true . . . ' (2009: 3). Two days prior, Humbert had recorded her concerns in proto-'Beckettian' terms: 'The silence is deadly. There is nothing to do but wait' (2009: 2).

Throughout the early stages of the invasion of France, Beckett continued to work in Paris. He tried to place his translation of *Murphy*, attempted a 'sketch' for *Paris Mondial* that was 'cancelled because of recent events' (*LSB I*: 678) and had another attempt at his play, 'Human Wishes', based on the life of Samuel Johnson (*BC*: 86–7). Again, in the letter regarding *Mondial*, as in his letter to the Reaveys, the war remains an unspoken thing, an 'event' present but not fully realized. By May 1940 cultural activity in Paris had stalled to a halt with the closure of concert halls and theatres, the suspension of activity at institutions such as the Conservatoire de Paris, and the shutdown of major periodicals.[3] With the increasing occupation of northern and eastern France and the bombing of Paris and its suburbs on 3 June – notably the Citroën factory and the airport – the possibilities of fleeing the country quickly shrank.

On 28 May, Belgium surrendered and, by 4 June, almost all British forces in France had fled via Dunkirk. Like millions of others, Beckett was forced to confront the real possibility of an utterly changed Europe and, perhaps more importantly, a changed notion of what France represented for natives and foreigners alike.[4] In the first two weeks of June, France collapsed against the

---

[3] Take *Le Ménestrel*, an influential journal of music which published its final issue on 24 May 1940 with the acknowledgement that the German invasion would prevent further issues.

[4] Jean Guéhenno records in his occupation diary an acute concern with this imminent change to the idea of 'Europe': 'It is painful to think that the same people among us who worked the most consciously toward the creation of Europe yesterday should be the most disorientated today, at the very moment when Europe, they say, is being forged. Europe? No, but a *certain* Europe. Not the just Europe we wanted. What means do we have to promote justice and reason once again? We were "European" against the nationalism of separate nations. What will we be against this false

German military. The invasion of Paris loomed. In a letter to Marthe Arnaud on 10 June, Beckett followed a despairing 'where would we go, and with what?' with an account of looking at one of his cherished van Velde paintings:

> Under the blue glass Bram's painting gives off a dark flame. Yesterday evening I could see in it Neary at the Chinese restaurant, 'huddled in the tod of his troubles like an owl in ivy'. Today it will be something different. You think you are choosing something, and it is always yourself that you choose; a self that you did not know, if you are lucky. Unless you are the dealer. (*LSB I*: 684)

The 'blue glass' is the blackout solution that was applied to windows in Paris (*LSB I*: 684, n.4). It is the lens through which the people of Paris witnessed the fall of France. Beckett did not yet know that he was only two days from 'choosing' to depart Paris to escape the invading forces, but his tone is melancholic, reflective, already starved of the light he imagines emitted from his van Velde piece. In the scene from *Murphy* that Beckett recalls, Neary sits in near silence, in a Chinese restaurant, 'sad with the snarling sadness of the choleric man' (*Mu*: 74). For Beckett, the war meant reckoning with a new status, that of a foreigner in an occupied nation he had chosen as his permanent home. Very soon, France would be re-conceptualized by the collaborationist Vichy regime as a nation fit to join Hitler's Nazified Europe.

On 12 June, Beckett and Déchevaux-Dumesnil escaped the city with two million other refugees. Their train, like many that left the city during this time, had no fixed destination. They reached the Joyces in Vichy the same day. German forces entered Paris two days later, after the French government had fled the city. Vichy was the government's destination too and, on reaching the spa town, they declared that there would be no organized resistance to German forces in Paris. Following the resignation of Paul Reynaud on 16 June, Marshal Philippe Pétain announced in a radio broadcast that hostilities were to cease;[5] Charles de Gaulle flew to London the following morning. This was Pétain's first broadcast as the head of what was now the *État français*, a nation soon to be divided in two: the north administered by the Germans, the south by the government in Vichy, or the 'Nono zone', as Beckett called it (*LSB III*: 56). Though the Vichy regime did not have governing control over the north, they could broadcast to it, hold rallies there and disseminate propaganda literature.

Europe? Are we doomed to be in the opposition forever?"' (24 September 1940, *DDY*: 25; emphasis in original).

[5] After the Germans entered France at the beginning of June 1940, Pétain had been made deputy prime minister by Reynaud. For a discussion of Pétain's political profile, see Chapter 3.

In mid-June 1940, the French government announced that 'all centres of population above 20,000 were to be declared open cities' and the Germans were to be welcomed (Jackson 2004: 180). The brief, devastating conflict cost France the lives of 50,000 soldiers at a conservative estimate, and somewhere in the region of 1.5 million soldiers were taken prisoner.[6] It was these losses and their apparent implications for the French race, alongside a cult of Pétainism steeped in the marshal's own military record, which underpinned the Vichy government's drive for a new, authoritarian vision of France. As we will discuss in later chapters, on Pétain's coming to power, Vichy's *Révolution nationale* (National Revolution) was disseminated across the country in a flurry of radio broadcasts, propaganda documents and community initiatives devoted to Vichy's ideal of national spirit.

The material hardships of war and occupation

Between 14 and 22 June 1940, the Nazi occupiers and the Vichy regime drew up their armistice agreement and division of the nation. During this time, Beckett had his last meeting with the Joyces in Vichy, also attended by Georges Pelorson (Cronin 1999: 316). Joyce gave Beckett a letter of recommendation to Valery Larbaud who 'saved' him from penury with a loan of 20,000 francs (*DF*: 299). On 23 June, Beckett and Déchevaux-Dumesnil took a train to Toulouse on which refugees and fleeing soldiers – many still in their uniforms (*DF*: 299) – were hoping to put distance between themselves and any further conflict, even if it meant homelessness and hunger. The sight of fleeing soldiers had a notable effect on France's morale at this crucial stage of the war. Agnès Humbert recorded on 20 June 1940 that her encounter with 'six haggard soldiers' in 'shreds' of uniforms 'haunt[ed]' her (2009: 5). According to René Remond, historian and young witness to the events of 1940, the image of enfeebled soldiers left 'a deep and lasting traumatism in everyone' (qtd. in Shennan 2000: 165–6). Any notion of French military power had shattered, and the commonplace sight in 1940 of the defeated French soldier took over any narratives of military prowess, all of which aided Pétain in capitalizing on his own service record to aid his rise to power.[7] As we will see in Chapter 6, such images of distressed,

---

[6] Almost half of those captured were done so between Pétain's broadcast and the signing of the armistice. The figure for those killed is generally given as between 50,000 and 90,000, a revision from the earlier estimate of between 90,000 and 120,000. As Jackson notes, these are heavy losses either way (2001: 180).

[7] In 1939, France had one of the largest militaries in the world. With 'just under 5 million soldiers, [France] was thought by many – among them Stalin – to be the best [military] in the world, heavily

troubled or wounded soldiers recur in Beckett's post-war writing, often refracted through reference to other wars or the haze of memory, as in Nell and Nagg's reminiscences of Sedan.

In Toulouse, Beckett was again confronted with the realities of his non-citizen status. Knowlson's moving account of Beckett and Déchevaux-Dumesnil's experience is worth quoting in full:

> In Toulouse, they were directed to a refugee centre. As an alien, Beckett had been trying for many months to get his papers processed in Paris in order to show clearly his neutral status as an Irishman and as a freelance writer. But, since the papers had never come through, he felt that he could not risk any encounter at this stage with hypersensitive officialdom; once caught up in the system, he felt that it might become difficult to avoid being detained indefinitely as an unregistered alien. So they slept (or at least attempted to sleep) out on a bench. It was, as Beckett put it elliptically, 'awful'. (*DF*: 299)

As explored in Chapter 2, an anxiety about proving one's identity is replete in Beckett's writing in the immediate years after the war, often transformed into moments which halt a character in their wandering.

Attempting to reach Mary Reynolds and Marcel Duchamp on France's west coast, Beckett and Déchevaux-Dumesnil headed towards Bordeaux. However, as would become the norm with public transport during the war, their train stopped without reason at Cahors and everyone was forced off (*DF*: 299). Stranded in the pouring rain, the couple eventually found a shop floor to sleep on. Beckett told Stuart Maguinness in 1958, 'The last time I wept was in Cahors, in 1940. Well, nearly the last' (qtd. in *DF*: 300). Eventually, the couple reached Arcachon, where Reynolds helped secure them a room. For the next few months, Beckett worked intermittently on the translation of *Murphy* and, later in the summer, wrote to George Reavey in Madrid, who mediated contact with Beckett's family in Ireland to secure the small monetary allowance that Beckett could try to access in France.[8]

Beckett and Déchevaux-Dumesnil returned to Paris in late September or early October 1940.[9] The city appeared unscathed, but the swastika flying over the Eiffel Tower signalled that France was now a very different nation under very different governance. The German occupation in Paris had an immense absurdity to it, one in which life in some ways seemed strangely unchanged,

---

armed and well-equipped and led by highly acclaimed veterans of the victorious army of 1918' (Kedward 2005: 316).

[8] Cronin gives the allowance of 2640 FF as approximately £15 (1999: 317).
[9] The exact date of their return remains in question. Bair gives October (1980: 261), as does Cronin (1999: 319), while Knowlson suggests early September (*DF*: 302).

particularly when exhibitions and performances restarted. However, accounts suggest the city was haunted by an eerie silence which accompanied the everyday difficulties of rationing and limited fuel supplies during the first of several cold winters, as Jean Guéhenno recorded: 'cold and hunger for many people. Dire poverty. And this frightful silence' (20 December 1940, *DDY*: 44). Food shortage, collaboration and the threat of denunciation soon became part of daily life in the city.

The documents confirming Beckett's occupation as a writer and his status as a citizen of neutral Ireland only arrived at the end of November 1940. With this paperwork, Beckett could claim Parisian citizen-level rations. The conditions of wartime Paris during this period were mixed. On the one hand, the city had not suffered terrible bombings or structural damage. On the other, food and fuel shortages left the city at risk during the bitter winter of 1940. Further rationing came into effect after significant crop failure. Such practicalities were the primary concern for people like Beckett and Déchevaux-Dumesnil during the period, particularly as they did not earn enough or have the right connections to benefit from importing food packages or engaging in the black market. Harsh winters were a feature of life across the war, exacerbating the oppression of occupation. 'Nothing can express the monotony and the resigned stupidity of life in Paris. It is very cold,' lamented Guéhenno, who described the conditions of the city as 'scientifically designed scarcity' (14 February 1942, *DDY*: 144).

All the while, the cultural and social upheavals of wartime Paris would not have escaped Beckett's notice. In May 1940, Beckett had hoped that Jean Paulhan, editor of the leading French cultural magazine *La Nouvelle Revue Française*, would take his translation of *Murphy* (*LSB I*: 679–8). In December 1940, Paulhan was replaced by Pierre Drieu La Rochelle, a leading fascist writer who steered the magazine towards collaborationism and used it to further his support for the Nazi vision of Europe.[10] The end of 1940 saw some normality return to Beckett's life in Paris with the reappearance in the September of the demobilized Alfred Péron. Péron resumed teaching at the Lycée Buffon and helped Beckett with the translation of *Murphy*, which continued into the early months of 1941. The life Beckett knew in France before the war became even more remote, though, with the death of James Joyce on 13 January 1941 from a duodenal ulcer. Amid all this, Beckett found the impulse to begin the creative project that would eventually become the novel *Watt*.

---

[10] For an in-depth discussion of Drieu La Rochelle's politics, see Tucker (1965).

Watt: Beckett's 'escape operation'

In February 1941, Beckett began work on *Watt*, the novel that he later described to Sighle Kennedy as his 'escape operation' from 'the horrors of that hateful time' (15 May 1977, *LSB IV*: 460). The first loose sheet of the manuscript indicates that Beckett began in the evening of 11 February, and these early notes start with Beckett setting out the basic questions of factual determination required to build a story – 'who, what, where, by what means, why, in what way, when' – to which he attributes elements derived from the Aristotelian categories for describing being: substance, quantity, space, instrument, cause/purpose, mode and time (HRC *Watt* MS, Loose sheet 3; qtd. in Ackerley 2004: 24). In one sense, this is a simple creative exercise before writing has properly commenced. In another, however, it is a list designed to 'get the story straight', to get the facts in order before proceeding, a process of utmost importance in the lockdown conditions of wartime occupation. Watt's process in the published text of overdetermining the potential facts of a given matter is derived from this initial drafting, and the parodic, hyperbolic process of stating every possible outcome or variant of a given situation – Mr Knott's appearance, for example – has something of the interrogative mode which was part of the daily cycle of encountering officials during the occupation. Beckett worked on *Watt* throughout the war, both in Paris and later when hiding in Roussillon, refining the text and zeroing in further and further on Watt's 'anthropomorphic insolence' (*W*: 175) and his desire to rationalize his experiences – intellectual manoeuvres which Beckett found to cause 'vomit' in his trip to Nazi Germany and which the war seemed to exacerbate further.[11]

The manuscripts of *Watt* contain a handful of direct traces of the war. The first notebook, filled in Paris, contains a profile doodle of Pétain with striped kepi and bushy moustache (HRC *Watt* NB 1: 50r). In the second Paris notebook, there are drafts of letters in French (NB 2: 5v; NB 2: 32v) and English (NB 2: 84v). The first French letter thanks an unknown recipient for a bottle of whiskey that kept Beckett warm during the cold winter. The letter refers to Canadian rye, a detail included in the early draft of Mr Knott's pot (NB 3: 71r; TS, 246). The English letter is a draft missive to Beckett's family, thanking the sender for news and lamenting the difficulties of communication. The third notebook, which contains sections written in Paris, Vanves and Roussillon, includes one of the sayings of Monsieur Aude, a farmer Beckett worked for in Roussillon:

---

[11] For a discussion of the relation between Beckett's visit to Nazi Germany and *Watt*'s parody of the rationalist tendencies of realist fiction, see Davies (2020), which develops McNaughton's work (2018) on the formal dimensions of the novel.

'Et les caisses se touchent dans le vigne Aude Sept. 29, 1942' (And the crates are touching in the vines) (NB 3: 190v; qtd. in *DF*: 325). In the fourth notebook, written entirely in Roussillon, Watt ponders paintings 'now burnt', locked away 'in a lumber-room' or simply 'sent away', reminiscent of Nazi cultural cleansing (NB 4: 2–3; qtd. in *GD*: 160).

The drafts of the novel – commonly referred to as the *ur-Watt* – directly address the Ireland of Beckett's early life and that of his parents' generation. Seán Kennedy (2014) identifies this turn to Ireland during the war in Europe as a kind of historical suspension whereby Beckett satirizes fascist and authoritarian thinking through the lens of the Irish Big House genre and the rhetoric of degeneration espoused by figures like W. B. Yeats. The first and second notebooks are mostly preoccupied with detailing the 'nothingness' experienced by James Quin (precursor to Mr Knott) who is 'still standing among the ruins ... the last to dissent ... the last to relent' (*Watt* TS: 1r). Quin is a figure of a bygone world largely now in tatters. Beckett writes with the memory of his own family home in Cooldrinagh in mind (a house near the trainline), turning to an Ireland of old mansions and tenants to comically treat the Big House tradition to a 'kind of epitaph' (Moynahan 1995: 245–52). Much of the draft is also dedicated to long sections describing the health of Quin and his familial decline, as well as detailed descriptions of the habits and lineages of the Lynches, a family of peasant tenants, who occupy the surrounding lands of Quin's estate. In Chapter 3, we will explore how the focus on the cultural practices of the Lynch peasants in the manuscripts echoes the preoccupations of Vichy in its attempts to revitalize the nation along ruralist, nativist lines, and the overlapping conservative nationalist agendas of Vichy and the Irish Free State.

The published *Watt* contains fewer overt references to the war, but that does not mean the conflict does not mark the text. The barbed wire fencing that separates Watt and Sam's pavilions recalls the camps that populated the region around Roussillon (Curtis 2002: 156), signalling as it does a violent separation between parties with barriers designed to repel as much as they are to enclose. That the fences are not new but well worn also evokes the pre-Vichy state of the camps; Sam describes the fences as 'greatly in need of repair, of new wire, of fresh barbs' (*W*: 133). Like the civilians recruited to guard the camps throughout Vichy (Curtis 2002: 156), Sam occupies a liminal state between civilian and officialdom. He seeks to breach the barrier but wants to find a hole in the fence that will allow him to move without 'hurt' or 'damage' to his 'pretty uniform' (*W*: 137).

Other traces of wartime vocabulary occur sporadically in *Watt*. Watt describes birds as 'missiles' flying overheard (*W*: 124), and, as Mark Nixon has observed (*GD*: 88), Beckett uses the language of life in Nazi Germany at scattered moments; referring to the feat of finding the 'cube root of a number of six figures', for example, Mr O'Meldon remarks that it has only once been achieved by a horse in 'an episode in the Kulturkampf' (*W*: 162). The novel also contains less direct evocations of the war's conditions, particularly the catalogue of food in Mr Knott's pot that reads like a wish list under rationing. Moreover, the novel is filled with the sense that reason itself has become truly maddening as Watt tries to apply lists and permeations to survive the Knott household, a house much like a world at war, seemingly impervious to logic, where information is paramount for getting out alive.

By August 1942, Beckett had completed two notebooks of material and begun a third. At this stage in the drafts, the 'Nothingness' at the heart of the character Quin's existence forms the (absent) heart of the planned novel, and his preferences, predilections, family history and personal ailments comprise the content. A 'Johnny Watt', narrating as 'we' (qtd. in Ackerley 2004: 231), has begun to emerge at this juncture. That Beckett had some sense of completion to this first phase of the novel is suggested by the diary entry and subsequent recollections of Francis Stuart. In his diary, Stuart wrote on 8 August 1942 – published first with the date of 9 August (*Journal of Irish Literature*) and later with 5 August (*The Irish Times*) – that he had received a 'letter from Sam Beckett in Paris, which I was glad to get' (1976: 88). Stuart later remarked that Beckett had mentioned finishing a novel in the same letter (*LSB II*: xvii) and clarified in an article for the *Aer Lingus* inflight magazine that he understood Beckett to mean he had finished the novel 'in the mind' (1986: 38). Stuart's claims are not wholly accepted (W. J. McCormack suggests that Beckett's name was added to Stuart's entry for the American market in the 1980s), though Beckett wrote to then doctoral student John Wheale in 1981 (in a letter not in *LSB IV*) that though he did not remember writing to Stuart, he did not dispute the claim (JEK A/2/278).[12]

Watt was written against a historical backdrop that saw reason and logic, the tools Watt deploys to negotiate Mr Knott's house, used to persecute those deemed by Vichy and the Nazis to be 'undesirables'. When Beckett and Déchevaux-Dumesnil returned to Paris in the autumn of 1940 after their first

---

[12] In a note on one of the drafts of Stuart's part in *Beckett Remembering*, Knowlson writes that he believes the diary entry to be genuine regardless of Beckett's haziness on the matter in 1981 (JEK A/2/278). Stuart's biographer Geoffrey Elborn suggested to me in a personal correspondence that Stuart was not given to the kind of deception McCormack and others suggest, deplorable as some of his political choices may have been.

exodus from the city, they did so in the belief that Paris was a city relatively untainted by German occupation: 'Reports reaching the couple from the capital suggested that the Germans had been behaving fairly decently' (*DF*: 302). While it was true that Paris had emerged from the invasion without much damage, it was a city caught in the grip of an occupying force attempting to normalize the imposition of censorship,[13] the implementation of statutes against Jews and other 'undesirables', and the remodelling of culture in the city to suit the occupiers. These authoritarian changes were largely unopposed by a beleaguered French populace still reeling from the defeat of the army, so much so that Pétain's rise to power was met predominantly with relief (Gildea 2015: 22) and many of the *statuts de Juifs* went essentially unchallenged (Ousby 2000: 178–9). Some more right-wing sections of the populace, and even certain moderates, welcomed these changes (Gildea 2015: 22).

The persecution of 'undesirables'

The introduction of antisemitic legislation in 1940 was systematic and 'came from within' Vichy, preceding Nazi law so efficiently that the Nazis rushed to put out ordinances to give the impression that 'the regulation of the Jewish question appeared to emanate from the German authorities'; there is even some suggestion that Vichy's antisemitic policies precipitated those the Nazis would later introduce (Marrus and Paxton 1995: 12–13).[14] On 27 September 1940, following the denaturalization of approximately 6,000 Jews in July and the repeal of anti-hate speech legislation (*la loi Marchandeau*) on 27 August, Germany barred all Jews who had escaped the occupied zone during the invasion from returning. Those who remained in the occupied zone were required to register with local authorities and to carry papers marked to identify them as Jewish. Communists were also at risk of persecution, as were Freemasons, gypsies and 'undesirable' foreigners. Déchevaux-Dumesnil's connections with Communist friends became a problem under these conditions, particularly as

---

[13] Humbert notes that on 7 August 1940 a 'list of banned books' had 'already been drawn up' for destruction (2009: 12).

[14] Marrus and Paxton also go so far as to state that, in their examinations of wartime archives, there is 'no trace of German orders to Vichy in 1940 to adopt antisemitic legislation' (1995: 5). After 4 October, Vichy introduced various extensions and subclauses to its definition of 'foreign Jew' along idiosyncratic lines pertinent to the specific make-up of France's population. In turn, the narrative that Vichy protected French Jews has also been dismantled. '[I]t is hard to attribute much credit to the Pétain regime itself' for those who survived being deported to the camps, write Marrus and Paxton (1995: 363).

arrests and executions were a regular method of combating the Communist hostility to Vichy and the occupiers. However, Vichy also exaggerated the scale of civil unrest fermented by Communist activity so as to conceal 'the power struggles, and factional infighting' of the government (Jackson 2001: 155). One of the larger of the early clashes between the Nazi occupiers and Parisian Communists came when 300 protestors were arrested by German police at the beginning of October 1940, just as Beckett and Déchevaux-Dumesnil returned to Paris.

The first nationwide *statut de Juifs* instituted on 3 October 1940 prevented Jewish people from public service and high-ranking military positions, as well as 'professions that influence public opinion' such as teaching or journalism. On 4 October and 7 October respectively, legislation gave French prefects the power to intern foreign Jews, and Algerian Jews were stripped of their French citizenship (Marrus and Paxton 1995: 3). Vichy's law for the internment of foreign Jews in the unoccupied south was so rapid that it 'went beyond anything yet legislated in the Occupied Zone' (Marrus and Paxton 1995: 12). By the end of 1940, Vichy's *Révolution nationale* propaganda campaign was also underway in both the south and the north. While the Nazi occupiers in Paris had been 'behaving fairly decently' (*DF*: 302), Vichy's authoritarian agenda was already in full operation. In Paris, theatres, cafes and museums reopened, giving the city an air of normality, though many venues were required to feature events and performances devoted to Vichy and Nazi sensibilities (Riding 2011: 55–6).

Between 1940 and 1942, the grip of the Vichy regime – functionally based out of the spa town but operating throughout the newly declared French 'state' – intensified as the regime's *Révolution nationale* rolled out across France. Supporters of the regime's propaganda agenda were planted in vital cultural institutions. In August 1940, 'volunteers' appeared at Agnès Humbert's museum 'out of thin air' claiming to be 'close to the marshal' and 'prattl[ing] about Vichy and a new France, strengthened and revitalized by her ordeal' (18 August 1940, 2009: 15). Fuelled by a comprehensive propaganda programme, the 'revolution' sought to revivify France along racial lines. Vichy declared the Third Republic a decadent institution that sheltered 'undesirables', namely Jews, Freemasons, Communists, Protestants, gypsies and the disabled, all of whom were deemed by the logic of the regime's vision of 'true' France to require exclusion and, with the help of the Nazis, extermination. Vichy wanted to refashion French society in a new social and cultural structure based around the key principals of work, family and devout patriotism. 'Travail, famille, patrie' became the official motto of the French state during the war. Child patriotism and revised school curriculums were key to this nationwide project. Beckett's friend Georges Pelorson (later Georges Belmont) worked for Vichy and oversaw many of the propaganda initiatives directed at children. Beckett does not appear to have ever openly condemned Pelorson's wartime activities. This may well be out of embarrassment, even sympathy, at a friend who took a 'turn', as Beckett put it (qtd. in Dowd 2013: 86), but this remains speculation. Others from Beckett's circles were actively bitter towards Pelorson, particularly Maria Jolas. Vincent Giroud (2000) makes it abundantly clear that Pelorson had turned to fascist thinking well before the war. After the war, Pelorson was cagey about his war years, referring to his position as 'my side' and Beckett's as 'his', and in his memoirs he avoids speaking explicitly about the period (JEK A/7/13). Suffice to say that Pelorson was heavily involved with several different aspects of Vichy and was clearly motivated by pre-war fascist sympathies as he pursued his career with the regime. He also worked for Vichy for far longer than the nine months he reported to James Knowlson in a late interview ('Interview with Belmont, Georges', JEK A/7/13).

Under the rule of the occupiers and Vichy, extremist groups also became much more visible and vocal in France. In February 1941, the Vélodrome d'Hiver played host to Jacques Doriot and between 30,000 and 50,000 members of his ultra-nationalist and collaborationist Parti populaire français (PPF; French Popular Party). Though he began his career as a Communist, Doriot was one of the most hard-line public supporters of Nazism in France by the war. He frequently criticized the Vichy regime for not going far enough in its collaborationist activity, campaigning for severer antisemitic policies (Jackson 2001: 192–4). Beckett was reading Hitler's *Mein Kampf* with much disgust at the time (Bair 1980: 314; *DF*: 303), and groups like the PPF represented a microcosmic instance of violent Aryan idealism coming to France.

The full implementation of Vichy's *Révolution nationale* campaign included stricter and stricter rules over the activities of Jews and other 'undesirables'. Nazi control in France strengthened during the period, but Vichy went further than just complying with dictates coming from the Führer. Pétain frequently took to the radio to denounce the Third Republic – a 'great enterprise of rottenness', he called it (qtd. in *DDY*: 68) – and to spread messages of support for the ideals of rural labour and domesticity in the nation. On 2 May 1941, Jean Guéhenno recorded with disdain the newly established annual celebrations of Pétain:

> Yesterday the first of May and Saint Philip's Day. That is our Marshal's first name. . . . A decree turns the first of May into the Marshal's Day and Labor Day. . . . The domain of the military and the domain of the worker coalesce

in his person: the marshal of troops and the shoer of horses. These are the Jesuitical idiocies Vichy propaganda was developing all day long yesterday. This is the stupidity into which we have fallen in eight short months. All the walls are plastered with posters. One can make out, delicately set across a blacksmith's anvil, the blue baton with the seven stars of the Head of State. An edifying image! (*DDY*: 80–1)

The 'flabby, quavering' speeches of Pétain (*DDY*: 73) preceded the round-up of 5,000 foreign Jews in Paris on 14 May 1940. Parisians were already aware of the deportations and concentration camps, though specific details were hard to come by. Such a scale of arrest, though, made the peril for 'undesirables' in France all the more tangible. As Guéhenno records, new vocabulary, the language of Nazi and Vichy racism, entered circulation: 'Yesterday, in the name of the laws of France, 5,000 Jews were taken away to concentration camps. Poor Jews from Poland, Austria, and Czechoslovakia, humble people with modest trades who were greatly endangering the state. They call this "purification"' (*DDY*: 83). Conditions in the camps were already terrible, even deadly; between 1940 and 1942, an estimated 3,000 deaths occurred in French internment camps from malnutrition, sepsis and other environmental illnesses (Marrus and Paxton 1995: 176). In the same month, a celebration of Pétain on a French holy day and the arrest of scores of Jews in Paris took place. Vichy's agenda was clear: the creation of a Pétainist cult of personality which could legitimize an exclusionary regime, one which made it easy for the French state to comply with, and even anticipate, the Nazi's 'Final Solution' policies.

Two major events typify the methods used by Vichy in their persecution of 'undesirables'. The first was a 'scientific' exhibition named *Le Juif et la France* (The Jew and France; see Figure 1) held from 5 September 1941 to 15 January 1942 on the Avenue de l'Opéra (Bach 1999). The event was organized by the Institut d'étude des questions juives (Institute for the Study of Jewish Questions) and included scientists from the Paris School of Anthropology. It received Nazi funding.

Official records indicate a million visitors attended the exhibition, though Debbie Lackerstein suggests it is more likely half that figure with many citizens suspicious of the German influence over the event (Lackerstein 2012: 263). Advertised on newsreels, on posters, in pamphlets and via two large loudspeakers on Avenue de l'Opéra, the exhibition did not need to be attended for its presence to be felt. It was an indication of official rhetoric in the French state at the time. As one of the most overt antisemitic cultural initiatives during the period, the exhibition represents the scale of Vichy and the Nazi's attempts to 'bludgeon' the French populace into fully embracing antisemitic views (Kedward 1993: 5).

Figure 1 'Le Juif et la France', September 1941, Propaganda-Ausstellung gegen die Juden in Frankreich, German Federal Archives Collection, Bundesarchiv, Bild 146-1975-041-07 / CC-BY-SA 3.0. https://creativecommons.org/licenses/by-sa/3.0/de/deed.en.

If the exhibition and similar events were often derided by the populace, or at least had their popularity and significance inflated by Vichy propaganda, Vichy-led roundups and deportations revealed the sinister, ultimately murderous underbelly which underpinned the Pétain regime's antisemitism. Most famous is the Rafle du Vel' d'Hiv in the summer of 1942, the event which coincided with the end of Beckett's work with the Resistance cell Gloria SMH, discussed later. The event was preceded by government legislation forcing Jews to wear the Star of David (29 May) and introducing strict curfew (8 July). On 16 and 17 July, 13,000 Jews were gathered in the Vel' d'Hiv and detained before being sent to concentration camps. French police carried out the arrests with the help of members of Jacques Doirot's PPF party.

By the end of August, 30,000 Jews had been detained in Paris (*BC*: 90). Despite the scale of arrests and the use of camps and prisons around Paris and throughout France between 1940 and 1942 (*PI*: 160–1), still little was known about what took place in them at the time. Extreme uncertainty, itself a method of control implemented during the war, persisted across the weeks that followed the Rafle du Vel' d'Hiv. Despite common descriptions of the round-up, the Rafle was not a single event that took place over twenty-four hours. Transports containing those from the round-up destined for Auschwitz left Drancy and other camps steadily over the subsequent days and weeks. Jewish children, separated from their parents, were not transported to Drancy from their provisional holding centres until the last fortnight of August (Fontaine 2007). In his interviews with James Knowlson, the roundups were foremost in Beckett's memories of the war, and he equated them with his membership of the French Resistance: 'Péron was the one who got me involved in the "Gloria" Resistance group. It was at the time when they were rounding up all the Jews, including all their children, and gathering them in the Parc des Princes ready to send them off to extermination camps' (Knowlson and Knowlson 2007: 79). Beckett's works remember the deportations and the camps in fragments. *Eleutheria*'s Victor wakes from his sleep muttering of 'the eyes – a thousand ships – the towers – circumcised – fire – fire' (1996: 118), while *Endgame*'s Clov turns his telescope on the audience and declares that he sees 'a multitude ... in transports ... of joy' (*E*: 20). Both are chilling, the former taking place in a post-war Parisian family home and the latter in a bare space surrounded by 'zero'. Such scenes disclose both horror and fascination with the sights of crowds 'in transports', and it was with the deportations in mind that Beckett remembered his membership of the Resistance later in life.

Beckett and the Resistance

The political and material conditions of France in 1941 make up the backdrop against which Beckett joined the Resistance group Gloria SMH on 1 September (*DF*: 763).[15] Founded by Polish resistors, Gloria SMH was originally devoted to helping British airmen out of the occupied zone. Once under the stewardship of the British Special Operations Executive (SOE), the cell was focused on gathering details of German naval and troop movements. Run by Jeannine 'Gloria' Picabia and Jacques Legrand, both of whom Beckett had known before the war, the cell included some eighty members who possessed a wide variety of skills suitable to

---

[15] On dating Beckett's Gloria SMH membership, Knowlson observes the following: 'A document of the 6th Bureau of the Ministry of the Armed Forces dated 7 March 1955, confirms that Beckett had been an agent P. 1 (which counted as active military service) in "Gloria SMH" from 1 Sept. 1941 (Lindon). This was not a particularly late entry into the cell. One of the most active members, Suzanne Roussel, joined only in June and quite a few of the other members were not recruited until several months after this. This information comes from the official liquidation papers of the cell drawn up by Suzanne Roussel' (*DF*: 763).

couriering information through France and back to London (*DF*: 305). Beckett's role was to retype and sometimes translate information brought from across France, condensing the details down to a single piece of paper and taking it to 'the Greek', who would create 'match-box' sized photographs of Beckett's sheets which were then transported into the 'so-called unoccupied zone', as Beckett called it (*DF*: 282). Often, Jeannine Picabia's mother Gabrielle took the documents across the occupation line herself using transport provided by a network of garages, many of which outfitted cars to take Allied soldiers and prisoners into southern France where they could be extracted to safe or neutral territory (*DF*: 308). Through this system, the information that Beckett worked on would make its way to London. It needs stating that Déchevaux-Dumesnil was equally involved in these activities, as demonstrated by several documents held in the James and Elizabeth Knowlson Collection at the University of Reading. Among the Knowlson files, a copy of Jeannine Picabia's record of Gloria SMH's personnel produced for the SOE during her debriefing lists both Beckett and Déchevaux-Dumesnil as operating in the 'Photography' arm of the cell (JEK A/3/77/10). In an unpublished letter written by Beckett from Saint-Lô on 14 October 1945 to officials in Paris, he asks for permission for Déchevaux-Dumesnil to be allowed to legally end Beckett's membership of the Resistance; in the letter, Beckett confirms that Déchevaux-Dumesnil took the same risks as he did during their time in the Resistance, and that she assisted him in his work (JEK A/3/77/13). It is, I think, important to have this more explicitly on record.

Despite his close relationship with Péron, who was fairly senior in the cell, it is clear that Beckett was not privy to detailed aspects of Gloria SMH's management, as confirmed in the report generated by W. H. Astor following Beckett's interrogation by the War Office in London on 16 April 1945 (KV 2/1313.114a). It is also apparent that Beckett's perception of Gloria was of a large, disorganized cell in which 'everybody used to know everybody else' (Knowlson and Knowlson 2007: 80). In most Resistance cells, members had limited knowledge of other cells, or even their own. Gloria's origins and the interconnectedness of its members in part lay in the earlier Musée de l'Homme group and Péron's first cell Étoile; it also had various relationships with cells such as Prosper and the Polish exile group Interallié (Bair 1980: 263, 573). This left the cell rather cumbersome in its operations, though it had a large network from which to draw resources and expertise.

Identifying Beckett's motivations for joining the Resistance is a complicated issue. As Beckett told Knowlson, Alfred Péron introduced Beckett and Déchevaux-Dumesnil to the cell Gloria SMH, though the couple's exact trigger for joining the Resistance, if there was one, is not documented. Synthesizing comments by Beckett to Alec Reid, Knowlson explains Beckett's Resistance membership via his virulent rejection of Vichy and Nazi antisemitism; Beckett's membership of the Resistance was made official just eleven days after the arrest of Paul Léon, Joyce's secretary, on 21 August (*DF*: 304).[16] Whether this context translates into cause is not definite, though. What can be said for certain is that Péron was responsible for Beckett joining Gloria SMH during a period of savage antisemitism in occupied France. Later in life, Beckett treated his Resistance membership with either scepticism – 'it was the boy scouts!', he once declared (qtd. in Cronin 1999: 341) – or with a certain distance that indicates his wariness of discussions that brought his life and his writing into proximity. His response to Richard Stern's question about his politics in 1977 is intriguing on this count: 'No [I wasn't political]. But I did join the Resistance' (qtd. in *PI*: 13). Terry Eagleton sees Beckett's turn to the Resistance in overtly political terms: 'In September 1941, one of the twentieth century's most apparently non-political artists secretly took up arms against fascism' (2006: 67). Such claims need to be 'examined closely', as Morin puts it (*PI*: 149). First, Eagleton notes that Beckett joined the Resistance 'secretly'. This is somewhat of a given since joining the Resistance required secrecy for the Resistance to maintain its ability to function covertly. Second, that Beckett's decision was 'against fascism' presumes a more specific political motivation than the evidence suggests. Eagleton's proposition relies on the suggestion of a unified Resistance or resistive consciousness in France, and his use of 'fascism' is a generic shorthand for the wide array of ideologies that dominated wartime France, from the occupying Nazis to the Vichy regime and other collaborationist groups, many of which would not come under the conventional definitions of fascism.[17] To read Beckett's membership of the Resistance as being 'against fascism' also implies a Leftist Beckett committed to the ideals that supposedly unified the Resistance. So, we risk assuming Beckett's political know-how and claiming Beckett's activities during the war as politically motivated rather than political by dint of what they involved. Echoing Knowlson above all, I think it is appropriate to see Beckett's motivation for his Resistance work as deriving from his encounters with both the oppressive regimes which occupied France and the terrible conditions of everyday life under war. That said, Beckett's own answer as to why he joined the Resistance –

---

[16] Emilie Morin suggests that Léon and Beckett's relationship was complex, and that Beckett disapproved of Léon's continued work in Paris despite his awareness of the peril he was in (*PI*: 157–9).

[17] Paxton (2004) has done much work to describe Vichy's particular strain of fascist thinking, identifying both similarities with and differences from Nazism.

'I was fighting against the Germans, who were making life hell for my friends, and not for the French nation' (qtd. in Bair 1980: 262) – speaks to the terms in which Beckett understood the war. While Bair reads this as Beckett remaining 'consistent in his apolitical behaviour' (Bair 1980: 262), there is an indication that Beckett saw his work in the Resistance as combative (*against* the Germans) as well as in defence of his friends, and that he was aware of the highly charged implications of fighting 'for the French nation' as it was understood both by Vichy during the war and Gaullism after the war. We can reconstruct Beckett's choice to join the Resistance through the narrative he created in later interviews, but to seek a clear and consistent politics in his Resistance membership is a fraught prospect. What is apparent, though, is that Beckett's involvement with the Resistance entailed a rejection of the conditions that war created and a desire to see the hellish aspects of the war diminish.

Beckett's Resistance work has often been cited as the impetus for the calculations and wordplay which recur in the *Watt* notebooks and the published text; so dense are the notebooks that the War Office confiscated them as part of Beckett's interrogation in London in 1944, believing them to be code (*PI*: 132).[18] Laura Salisbury, following Marjorie Perloff, has noted the resemblance of sections of the *Watt* notebooks to Resistance codes, arguing that the novel, even in its final form, captures 'what the reality of the war rendered compellingly explicit, to Beckett and many others, . . . the impossibility of ever producing conditions of perfect transmission' (2014: 156). Coded names are another aspect of the Resistance which at times appear to mark Beckett's work. Proving or confirming a name, both actual and code, governed much during the war, and the note in the *Watt* 'Addenda' to 'change all the names' has a striking resonance in this context (*W*: 222). A number of the names in the novel are also notable on this front. Among the staff of Mr Knott's house, Erskine is reported by Arsene to have replaced a man named Walter, the same codename used by one of Gabrielle Picabia's main contacts, William Ugeux, chief of the Belgian Resistance service and director of the Belgian SOE branch Service de renseignement Zéro (KV 2/1313/83xb; 87a). 'Arsene' also throws up several entries in War Office records. These include John Lodwick (KEW AIR 40/2559), John Goldsmith

---

[18] Direct references to the Resistance are difficult to find in the text, if they are there at all. Conceptually, 'resistance' has been used to read Beckett's work in a number of ways. Most famously, perhaps, Alain Badiou treats Beckett's work as 'resistant' in relation to his notion of 'rigorous negativity' in the face of 'what is' (2003: 58). For a discussion of Badiou's vocabulary in his analysis of Beckett's writing, see Barbara Will's 'The Resistance Syndrome: Alain Badiou on Samuel Beckett' (2014). Jackie Blackman sees Badiou's position as inflected by the sense in which 'Beckett's resistance' was to 'the prevailing culture of complacency and indifference [of] wartime and after' (2008: 71).

(KEW HS9/597/5) and Sgt John W. Ellis (KEW AIR 27/2142). In one of the many coincidences of Beckett's war, John Lodwick, the first 'Arsene' of the three, was an SOE agent with whom Beckett almost certainly crossed paths in Dublin during the 1920s and 1930s, given that Lodwick counted Francis Stuart and Georges Pelorson as close friends before and after the war (Elliott 2017: 51–8). Other works see code or nicknames deployed routinely. In *Waiting for Godot*, both Vladimir and Estragon go by multiple names: 'Gogo' for Estragon, 'Didi' and 'Mr Albert' for Vladimir. 'Didi' bears striking resemblance to the codename of André 'Dédé' Jarrot, one of the garage-owners who would help the Picabias across the occupation line (*DF*: 308). In *Pochade radiophonique* (*Rough for Radio II*), written in the early 1960s, a character who goes by Alfred Péron's codename and nickname, 'Dick', helps two others, 'Animator' and 'Stenographer', torture the silent 'Fox' into speech. Fox is unyielding, and, like both a prisoner of war and a weary wartime interrogator, Animator concludes the play by lamenting that 'Tomorrow, who knows, we may be free' (*CDW*: 284). As I argue further in Chapter 2, Beckett's post-war writing contains distinct traces of the everyday aspects of the war which prompted many to join the Resistance, marked as his texts often are by a sense of looming violence, restrictions over movement and bodily need.

The Resistance myth

In *Samuel Beckett's Political Imagination*, Emilie Morin raises the broader issue of certain narratives of the French Resistance which endure in many accounts of Beckett's membership:

> Beckett's decision to join Gloria SMH is commonly perceived as his clearest, most powerful and enduring political act. . . . [However,] such critical consensus does not account for the political make-up of Resistance movements, which encompassed the whole spectrum of political allegiances from the Far Right to the Far Left, and reflected a wide range of positions on French national sovereignty, republicanism and German occupation. . . . The idea of a unified Resistance that provides an explicit or implicit background to many accounts of Beckett's decision to serve in Gloria SMH should be approached with caution, for it is one of many Gaullist myths forged in the context of emerging Cold War tensions, when de Gaulle became increasingly keen to counter the ideological advances of the French Communist Party (*PI*: 149–50)

This 'Gaullist myth', or what Henry Rousso termed '*Résistancialisme*' (1991), demanded that France be conceived on a macroscopic scale, a nation unified in the defeat of Vichy and the occupiers, all the while ignoring the microscopic, everyday degrees of resistance and collaboration.

The Gaullist myth of the Resistance needs contextualizing here for both its content and its purpose. 'To deal with the trauma of defeat, occupation and virtual civil war, the French developed a central myth of the French Resistance', Robert Gildea writes,

> [f]irst, that there was a continuous thread of resistance, beginning on 18 June 1940, when an isolated de Gaulle in London issued his order to resist via the BBC airwaves, and reaching its climax on 26 August 1944 when he marched down the Champs-Élysées, acclaimed by the French people. Second, that while a 'handful of wretches' had collaborated with the enemy, a minority of active resisters had been supported in their endeavours by the vast majority of the French people. A third element was that, although the French was indebted to the Allies and some foreign resisters for their military assistance, the French had liberated themselves and restored national honour, confidence and unity. (Gildea 2015: 2)

Despite the medals awarded after the war, Beckett was, as a foreigner, excluded from the official Gaullist vision of the Resistance.

'Resistance' itself remains a disputed term among historians of the war. The most generative definition is that offered by Olivier Wieviorka, who describes 'resistance' in terms of 'a few criteria that illuminate the general contours of the internal French resistance': action, intent and transgression. Wieviorka argues that we can usefully distinguish between a 'Resistance organization', comprising a small minority, and a 'resistance movement', constituting a 'much vaster social phenomenon' (2016: 3). With this in mind, what Gildea calls the myth of a 'continuous thread' of the French Resistance is best seen as phases of anti-occupation and anti-Vichy activity. Much resistance activity between 1940 and 1941 involved the dissemination of anti-Nazi and anti-Vichy literature, most notably by cells such as the Musée de l'Homme, Étoile and the various groups which contributed to the clandestine publication *Combat*, later edited by Albert Camus and read by Beckett during the war and after (*PI*: 15; 25). Small acts of sabotage were common, such as cutting phone wires, damaging bridges and vandalizing German tires (Ousby 2000: 218). More idiosyncratic forms of resistance also took place. Refusing to change French clocks to German time was, according to Humbert, a 'symbolic gesture of resistance' (18 August

1940; 2009: 14). With the intensification of occupation and Vichy control later in the war, Resistance activity became centred around the movement and concealment of Allied prisoners and stranded soldiers, information gathering, and increasingly violent acts of disruption. From his flat, Beckett witnessed a 'spectacular raid' of the Renault factory in Boulogne-Billancourt on 3 March 1942 which left 500 dead and over 500 wounded (*PI*: 151); Alfred Péron had been part of the organizing team for the bombing (JEK A/3/77). Twenty hostages held by the Nazis were executed in reprisal (4 March 1942, *DDY*: 148). Over the following days, Vichy propaganda broadcasts reported the bombings with varying degrees of accuracy, stating on one occasion that the death toll was in fact 2,000, only to revise this again a day later. Guéhenno described Vichy's inflation of the numbers as 'chopp[ing] the dead to pieces to add to the horror' (6 March 1932, *DDY*: 148).

The myth of unified public support for the Resistance through the war is another exceptionally complicated element of France's wartime experiences. There was a demonstrable resistance movement (distinct from the minority of people involved in *Résistance* organizations) that functioned around a general preference for France not to be occupied and governed by Nazism (Wieviorka 2016: 3). However, the increasing violence in 1941, particularly from Communist cells following the Nazi invasion of the Soviet Union on 22 June, was not welcomed by the French public once a pattern of violence and reprisal became the norm. After a German naval cadet was killed on the Paris metro in August 1941, Hitler ordered fifty hostages to be shot for every German killed in France, and soon the warning came that 'male relatives, brothers-in-law and cousins of the agitators above the age of eighteen years will be shot' (Riding 2011: 131). The French public were critical of all sides during this period (Riding 2011: 132), and diarists such as Guéhenno recorded the general distaste for such violence: 'New armed attacks by the Resistance. We're sick of this atmosphere of murder' (5 December 1941, *DDY*: 133). Anti-Communist violence represented a particular threat to Déchevaux-Dumesnil's social circle as her Communist friends helped her and Beckett on several occasions with safe-houses and identity papers. The Resistance was comprised of vast numbers of Communist members or Communist-backed cells, and when combined with Beckett's intellectual sensibilities and foreign status, there was every risk that he and Déchevaux-Dumesnil could have fallen prey to anti-Communist legislation and reprisals in the occupier's battle against the Resistance.

The idea that Resistance cells operated with de Gaulle as a saviour figure speaking from the airwaves is also largely a post-war myth. In her occupation memoir, Agnès Humbert makes it clear that the Musée de l'Homme group were essentially unaware of de Gaulle or what he looked like (2009: 20–1).[19] Though de Gaulle gradually gained a reputation through his BBC broadcasts from London, it is apparent that many Resistance cells acted without a firm affinity to de Gaulle or his rhetoric. Much of the Resistance's allegiance to de Gaulle was cultivated retrospectively after the war. The British government did not formally recognize de Gaulle as the leader of France, not just the Free French Forces, until 1944 (Vinen 2007: 51).

More important to the Resistance was the networks of fellow agents and trusted individuals who could provide aid or information. As a result, however, daily life for those of Beckett's position in the Resistance came with the ever-possible threat of betrayal, be it from a collaborationist neighbour or a captured *résistant* giving information under interrogation and torture. If Beckett were revealed by a fellow cell member to be working for the Resistance, his stance as a neutral Irish citizen would have been a somewhat flimsy alibi in the eyes of Nazi officials and French police.

In the event, Beckett escaped arrest, but only just. The story of the collapse and betrayal of Gloria SMH is well known. The sometimes bloated and often uncoordinated cell was brought down by a double agent, Robert Alesch. Masquerading as a priest who could offer words of comfort to cell members alongside his own Resistance work, Alesch would secretly report to Nazi officers in exchange for vast sums of money (*DF*: 311–12). The first arrests took place on the 13 August 1942 when Germaine Tillion and Gilbert Thomason were captured by Nazi police; Beckett knew both Tillion and Thomason well (KV 2/1313/114a). Twelve members of Gloria SMH were executed, and 'a further ninety were deported to Ravensbrück, Mauthausen and Buchenwald' (*PI*: 147). The War Office papers at the National Archives reveal that other cell members were accused of betraying the group before Alesch was arrested.[20] Tillion and Jeannine Picabia were among the SOE's prime suspects. Tillion was one of the few to have escaped the earlier collapse of the Musée de l'Homme Resistance group, contributing to British suspicions about the fall of

---

[19] De Gaulle's public profile before the war was relatively low, though he had a reasonable reputation among France's military leaders. He had worked his way through the French army and had spent time as a ghost writer for Pétain (Vinen 2007: 58). By the invasion of France, de Gaulle was an armoured tank division commander. After the armistice, he fled to London where he managed the Free French military organization and slowly established himself as the leader of the Free French. For a discussion of de Gaulle and his impact on modern France since the end of the war, see Sudhir Hazareesingh's *In the Shadow of the General* (2012).

[20] At the time of writing, Laura Salisbury is the only scholar to have brought this to attention with a compelling account of Picabia's own interviews with the War Office (2013).

Gloria. Picabia, sometimes under the alias Marie Monnet, had been involved in the Resistance cells codenamed Walenty and Lucas (KV 2/1313/105a), both of which were compromised by German espionage, though in the event it was revealed to be the betrayal of Mathilde Lucie 'Victoire' Carré who had been turned by the Germans in 1941 (KV 2/928). By the end of 1944, Jeannine Picabia had been cleared by the British War Office of any role in Gloria SMH's betrayal (KV 2/1313/113a; Salisbury 2013), while her mother was deemed above suspicion in an internal memo in July 1943 (KV 2/1313/83y). Tillion was also cleared and went on to become a significant figure in French politics, particularly in opposition to the Algerian War, but the suspicion she and others were under following the betrayal of Gloria demonstrate the atmosphere of disinformation and fear which permeated Resistance work.

Beckett and Déchevaux-Dumesnil were alerted by a message from Alfred Péron's wife Mania warning them of Alfred's arrest; according to Nathalie Sarraute, Beckett had a notebook on him at the time containing eighty Resistance agents' names (Knowlson and Knowlson 2007: 81). The telegram came at 11.00 am on 15 August 1942, the Feast of Assumption, an important day in the Catholic calendar on which the Virgin Mary's rise to heaven is celebrated. It is a day Beckett wrote into Malone's grim portent of his own death:

> I shall soon be quite dead at last in spite of all. Perhaps next month. Then it will be the month of April or of May. For the year is still young, a thousand little signs tell me so. Perhaps I am wrong, perhaps I shall survive Saint John the Baptist's Day and even the Fourteenth of July, festival of freedom. Indeed I would not put it past me to pant on to the Transfiguration, not to speak of the Assumption. But I do not think so, I do not think I am wrong in saying that these rejoicings will take place in my absence, this year. (*MD*: 3)

This catalogue of holy and secular days which may or may not be witnessed collides the traditions of Catholicism (the Assumption), broad Christian faith (Saint John the Baptist's Day; the Transfiguration) and the French Revolution (Bastille Day), a key event in the history of modern France which Vichy sought to overshadow by naming its own national initiative the *Révolution nationale*. In many ways, Malone's remarks reconstitute as stages of decline and death the contradictions which remained at work in Vichy: the desire for revolution against the conservative distrust of the same, and the need for religious orthodoxy while allying with the fervently anti-religious National Socialists. There is too, perhaps, a dark joke in surviving the Assumption which recalls Beckett's own experience on 15 August 1942.

Soon after they received Mania Péron's warning of Gloria SMH's collapse – 'within the hour', Beckett recalled (Knowlson and Knowlson 2007: 8)[21] – Beckett and Déchevaux-Dumesnil left their flat. They spent a night with Mary Reynolds and the next few days in and around Paris in locations secured by Déchevaux-Dumesnil's Communist friends, adopting fake names and securing false papers (*DF*: 315–17; Knowlson and Knowlson 2007: 80). Beckett and Déchevaux-Dumesnil spent some time split up during this period and Beckett later told John Kobler that it was during this period that he witnessed the suicide by defenestration of another member of Gloria while he hid in a hotel (Bair 1980: 270). Croker's position standing on the window ledge in *Rough for Theatre II* as two figures review information about his life has a trace of this memory.

With Mania Péron's help, the couple reunited and travelled to Vanves on or around 4 September – Beckett recorded the date and place in the third *Watt* notebook (NB 3: 39r). They then secured ten days respite in Janvry with Nathalie Sarraute, the Russian-born French writer who housed Jewish refugees and

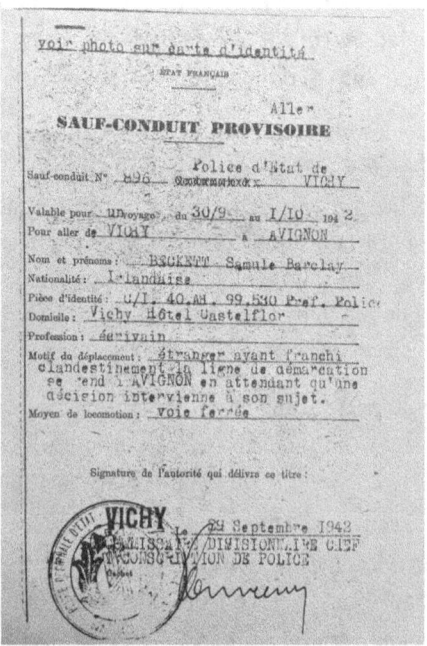

Figure 2 Beckett's *sauf-conduit provisoire* (provisional safe-conduct pass), 1942. ('Reasons for travelling: Foreigner having crossed the border illegally to go to Avignon while waiting for a decision to be made about him.')

---

[21] Bair gives 3.00 pm as their departure time, citing 'Marie [sic] Péron' (1980: 270).

other Resistance members during the period (*DF*: 316). The couple then decided to make for Roussillon in the Vaucluse after Déchevaux-Dumesnil recalled her friends Marcel and Yvonne Lob living there (Knowlson and Knowlson 2007: 85).

Beckett and Déchevaux-Dumesnil were smuggled over the occupation line by contacts of the aforementioned Dédé, going by way of countryside roads and hidden paths in the forests and streams of central France (*DF*: 321). They once again reached Vichy on 29 September 1942. Beckett had no French identification and, left unaided by the Irish Legation despite his inquiries, the couple were forced to admit to the Vichy police that they had been smuggled across the line. Beckett was fined 400 francs for the offence (*LSB II*: xviii), but he was granted a 'provisional safe-conduct pass' (Figure 2) to travel to Avignon. They then made their way to Roussillon. Travel and free movement, like food or even physical safety, had officially 'become provisional' in the 'universe' of occupation (*CSP*: 278).

'Down there everything is red': Beckett in Roussillon

Nestled on a hill in the Vaucluse, Roussillon offered Beckett and Déchevaux-Dumesnil sanctuary in October 1942. The physical landscape itself is distinctive. Surrounded by ochre cliffs, the ground is tinted hot red. It was so striking that Beckett could not help but include it in *Waiting for Godot*: 'down there everything is red!' (*CDW*: 57). The caves that surround the village – many of which were used for hiding arms caches, refugees and *maquis* members – perhaps also inform the cave the narrator inhabits in 'The End' with the night-time visitations of the owner bringing provisions and the 'light shone into the cave at regular intervals' (*CSP*: 89).[22]

While Roussillon was not itself formally taken over when the Nazis invaded southern France (in retaliation against Allied military landings in Africa on 8 November 1942), the surrounding region was fully occupied. Though little patrolled due to its awkward hilltop position, Roussillon was no stranger to either the propaganda of Vichy or visits from Nazi officials and the local *milice*. Even before the occupation of the south, 'safety' was a relative term in fleeing to the 'so-called unoccupied zone' of France in 1942. The south may have offered Beckett and Déchevaux-Dumesnil immediate safety, but the Vichy regime had by the end of August 1942 become entirely complicit in deportations to Nazi camps. It helped the Nazis transport thousands of Jewish people via Drancy transit camp in the north between 23 and 26 August and, by the end of the month, Vichy itself had deported 10,000 detainees from the unoccupied zone (Fontaine 2007).

---

[22] This sentence is missing from page 47 of the Faber 2009 edition of the text.

It is in this context that we can read Beckett's letters to the Irish Legation in Vichy. He attempted repeatedly to acquire papers that confirmed his Irish citizenship. While Beckett's letters are frustrated, even flippant, they are careful not to give any prying official any indication of his Resistance membership or liberal Parisian affiliations, and vocally deny the Jewish heritage he was so often thought to have. Beckett wrote of his encounters with Vichy officials to Cornelius Cremin, First Secretary of the Irish Legation, on 11 October 1942:

> Have had prolonged interviews with the local Gendarmes, in their barracks 6 miles from here. My history almost day by day from my first setting foot in France. They can't believe that I can be called Samuel and am not a Jew. Yesterday they took away my identity card I suppose to see if it had not been tampered with. My movements are restricted in the extreme, radius of ten kilometres about. (*LSB II*: xvii)

There is every sense that Beckett wished to work within the convoluted system of identification imposed on France during the war, aware as he would have been that his Resistance activity and his apparent 'Jewishness' could lead to problems. The process also revealed to him the irony of the term 'free France', as he expressed in a letter to Cremin on 27 October:

> in what exactly do the advantages of Irish nationality consist? Might I not as well be a Pole? This view as put forward by me having met with no success up to the present, I think perhaps it is time for the Legation to put it forward for me, with particular enquiry as to why I cannot move about freely in 'free France'. (qtd. in *LSB II*: xviii)

In a letter a year later in 1943 to Seán Murphy, another Irish minister to France in Vichy, Beckett lamented the 'constant prying into my identity, my past movements, my present movements, my means of existence, my mode of existence, why I am called Samuel, etc., etc., when all my papers are perfectly in order, when since arriving in the "free zone" I have neglected none of the formalities of declaration, registration, etc., imposed on foreigners in this country' (qtd. in *LSB II*: xviii). On 17 July 1943, Beckett confirmed to Murphy that the interference of the gendarmes had come to an end, though not without further inspections of his papers and identity card (*LSB II*: xix).

Alongside a growing German presence in the Vaucluse at the end of 1942, the area around Roussillon was increasingly populated by concentration camps. Many included those built to hold Spanish refugees, mentioned earlier:

> Detention of unwelcome persons [in France] did not start with Vichy. Thousands of people had been interned in prewar France. Most, about 465,000, were

Spanish republicans, who had fled their country after Franco won the civil war in February 1939, and members of the international Brigades who had fought in Spain. Camps for the interned, sometimes euphemistically called *centres d'accueil* [reception centres] or *centres d'hébergement* [shelter centres], were located in the area of Roussillon, such as Argèles or Saint-Cyprien in Poitiers. The camp at Poitiers, like others, was run by a small number of French gendarmes when it held Spanish refugees and gypsies. When in 1941 Jews were housed there, the local prefect refused to employ any more gendarmes and recruited extra civilians to join the existing police to guard the camp. (Curtis 2002: 156)

These camps were designed not as places of extermination but as intermediary centres run by French civilians and officials from which detainees were sent on to Nazi-controlled concentration camps. Vichy complicity, however, is not to be underestimated.

Anthony Cronin argues that Roussillon remained safe in part because of a fine line between right- and left-wing politics in the town (1999: 331). The village's mayor was appointed by Vichy, but the village had little chance of Nazi occupation due to its inaccessibility for heavy vehicles (*DF*: 319). Collaboration was not overt, but neither was there much Resistance activity in the village. However, the danger in which Beckett found himself in the south has been underestimated. Like most of France, Roussillon was under the constant threat of sweeps by Nazi offices looking to arrest refugees or resistors. The proximity of the camps in the area, coupled with Vichy propaganda and the risk of being identified as Resistance members, would have left Roussillon a place of uncertain safety for Beckett and Déchevaux-Dumesnil during the period. On at least one occasion, Beckett witnessed again the trauma of denunciation when Marcel Lob was arrested after a florist in the market town Apt informed the German authorities of his Jewish heritage. Acting quickly, Yvonne Lob, Beckett and Déchevaux-Dumesnil were able to coordinate and deliver a certificate of baptism to 'prove' Marcel was married to an Aryan (*DF*: 336). Marcel's fate was altered by the filing and manipulation of the correct papers, a stark example for Beckett of the violent intentions officialized in Nazi and Vichy documentation policies.

By mid-1942, alongside the aforementioned antisemitic policies, the Vichy government had developed a 'daily concern to tabulate, count, and verify all foreigners in the south' and, following an 18 November telegram instruction from Vichy to the Regional Prefects, 'all foreigners of subversive potential' were to be arrested. The dictate was broad, and officials were to 'let the camps and labour centres act as sorting stations later on' (Kedward 1993: 6). Foreigners were to be watched, documented and confronted by the authorities where possible. Beckett was faced with this situation throughout the war, and surveillance and its implied power dynamics are notable tropes in his post-war writing. Molloy stalks the figures he sees at the beginning of the novel, later facing authorities who themselves demand he identify himself. Most markedly, in 'The End', the narrator receives a visit from a policeman in his basement dwelling: 'He said I had to be watched, without explaining why. Suspicious, that was it, he told me I was suspicious' (*ECEF*: 43). The constant possibility of being watched, of not just institutional but community surveillance, mars the prospect of the basement ever being entirely secure. Like Big Brother in George Orwell's *Nineteen Eighty-Four*, the threat of surveillance is designed to instil in the narrator a self-corrective behaviour – it implies that the policeman will punish him if the authorities do not like what they see, and reminds the narrator that his safety and well-being are only ever provisional while he remains under suspicion.

Beckett's arrival in the south of France in 1942 also coincided with the *Relève*, legislation created by Vichy's head of government, Pierre Laval. The *Relève* traded French prisoners of war held in German labour camps for skilled French workers who were sent to German factories. Though Laval announced the law in June 1942, on 4 September it 'was given a conscriptive character' when all French men between eighteen and fifty and single women between twenty-one and thirty-five were made 'eligible for labour at the state's discretion' (Kedward 1993: 2). On 16 February 1943, the *Relève* became the *Service du travail obligatoire*, legislation which required all young men born between 1920 and 1922 to put themselves forward for labour in German factories. Proof of Beckett's Irish citizenship and his relationship with Déchevaux-Dumesnil became all the more pressing in this context. While Roussillon was not an appealing location for military occupation, both the Nazis and the gendarmes frequently searched the area to establish who should be sent to work under the *Relève*.[23] In Apt, only 11 kilometres from Roussillon, the Prefect of the Vaucluse headed a 'massive hunt' for those avoiding the *Relève* (Kedward 1993: 51).

In the village, Beckett and Déchevaux-Dumesnil stayed first in a run-down hotel which included a café frequented daily by villagers, members of the *maquis* and any locals who did not have access to a radio. With the help of

---

[23] Déchevaux-Dumesnil also had to be wary given her Communist associations, as the *Relève* was principally represented in propaganda and legislation as part of France's efforts to combat Bolshevism. 'They give their blood. Give your work to save Europe from Bolshevism' proclaimed a poster of the period which featured the image of a French POW standing over workers in blue and grey heading towards German factories.

the Lobs, Déchevaux-Dumesnil arranged for she and Beckett to rent a house in which they remained for the rest of the war. Though it was shelter, it was cold in the winter and symbolized life in Roussillon at the time, 'a village which in 1942 lived more or less as in the nineteenth century, without running water and hot baths, and in which someone called Samuel must be Jewish' (Rabaté 2013: 60). Beckett found work with local farmers, primarily the Audes and the Bonnellys. Both offered food in exchange for labour, likely with enthusiasm if they had lost farm labourers to the *Service du travail obligatoire* which, by the end of 1942, no longer included exemptions for agricultural workers (Kedward 1993: 19). As Knowlson observes, the knowledge Beckett gained of country life clearly informs much of the detail which appears in *Malone meurt/Malone Dies* (*DF*: 325), and Beckett and Déchevaux-Dumesnil's time among the farmers and the red soil of Roussillon are directly remembered in the French dialogue of *En attendant Godot*. Compared to the secrecy demanded by the conditions of the war, Beckett freely documents his hiding spot in the post-war drama, the details of which feature in the text from its earliest drafts to the final text (BDMP *Godot* module).

> VLADIMIR. Mais bien sûr ! Tu ne reconnais pas ?
> ESTRAGON. (*soudain furieux*). Reconnais ! Qu'est-ce qu'il y a à reconnaître ? J'ai tiré ma roulure de vie au milieu des sables ! Et tu veux que j'y voie des nuances ! (*Regard circulaire.*) Regarde-moi cette saloperie ! Je n'en ai jamais bougé !
> VLADIMIR. Du calme, du calme.
> ESTRAGON. Alors fous-moi la paix avec tes paysages ! Parle-moi du sous-sol !
> VLADIMIR. Tout de même, tu ne vas pas me dire que ça (*geste*) ressemble au Vaucluse ! Il y a quand même une grosse différence.
> ESTRAGON. Le Vaucluse ! Qui te parle du Vaucluse ?
> VLADIMIR. Mais tu as bien été dans le Vaucluse ?
> ESTRAGON. Mais non, je n'ai jamais été dans le Vaucluse ! J'ai coulé toute ma chaude-pisse d'existence ici, je te dis ! Ici ! Dans la Merdecluse !
> VLADIMIR. Pourtant nous avons été ensemble dans le Vaucluse, j'en mettrais ma main au feu. Nous avons fait les vendanges, tiens, chez un nommé Bonnelly, à Roussillon.
> ESTRAGON. (*plus calme*) C'est possible. Je n'ai rien remarqué.
> VLADIMIR. Mais là-bas tout est rouge !
>
> (1952: 85–6)

In the English version, Bonnelly and Roussillon become names which Vladimir fails to recall, while the Vaucluse moves north to the 'Macon country', and Estragon's 'Merdecluse' joke becomes 'Cackon' (*CDW*: 57).[24]

According to Cronin, Beckett participated in local *maquis* activity in the early months of 1943 (1999: 333). This period is the least documented of Beckett's war years, but we can surmise that Beckett purchased or had access to a typewriter during this period since he typed up sections of *Watt* which had been written in Vanves as well as new material written in Roussillon (*Watt* TS 228r–302r). If Beckett were involved with the *maquis* at this time, such activity would likely have involved moving goods from parachute drops, hiding arms and rations (Cronin 1999: 333–4), or simply taking note of local information using the acquired typewriter and the skills he put to use with Gloria SMH. A number of Beckett's friends had very different experiences that year. March 1943 saw Georges Pelorson become head of 'Les amis de Maréchal'; six months later, in September 1943, the same month Henri and Josette Hayden arrived in Roussillon, Péron was sent to Mauthausen (*BC*: 91).

In May 1944, Beckett formally joined the local *maquis* (Figure 3). The Vaucluse was a key region for Resistance activity, particularly the forests which provided shelter and camouflage. By 1943, the *maquis* had become the symbol of resistance in France. After the collapse of the military in 1940, it was not the image of the uniformed soldier that encapsulated France's fighting spirit; it was of fighters embedded in the countryside launching ambushes as though the landscape of France itself were attacking Vichy and the occupiers.[25]

Beckett's official membership of the *maquis* in May 1944 has several implications. In 1943, Michel Brault, 'co-ordinator and national leader' of the Service national du Maquis, set out a series of ideals for the *maquis* and established its relationship to France's military (Kedward 1993: 34). In a circular distributed across France, Brault wrote that 'any man [sic] who seeks entry into a *maquis* [is] a volunteer *franc-tireur* and an auxiliary of the Armée secrète of the forces françaises combattantes, commanded by General de Gaulle and the Comité national français' (qtd. and trans. in Kedward 1993: 34–5). This is why Beckett had to nominate Déchevaux-Dumesnil to formally end his membership of the Resistance while he was away from Paris in Saint-Lô in October 1945 (JEK A/3/77/13): officially, Beckett was a member of de Gaulle's armed forces. Brault's

---

[24] The joke recalls the economy of excrement used in Ballyba in *Molloy* and its manuscripts which Beckett worked on with Mania Péron (BDMP *Molloy* module).
[25] For a discussion of war and the French landscape under Vichy, see Pearson (2008).

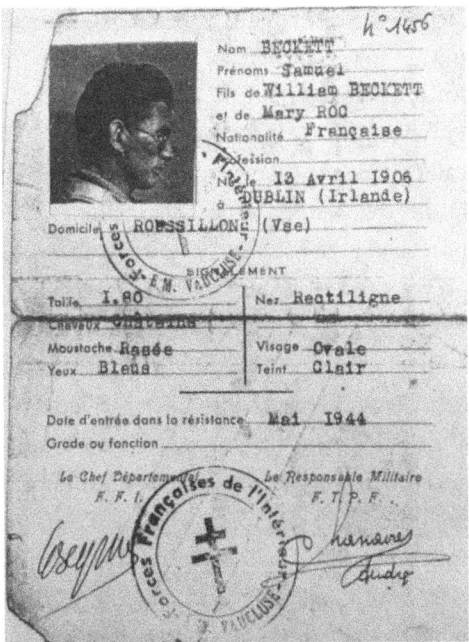

Figure 3 Samuel Beckett's *maquis* identity card, 1944. Reproduced with the kind permission of Edward Beckett, James Knowlson and University of Reading Special Collections. © University of Reading, Special Collections. Knowlson Collection, JEK A/3/77/13.

circular also contained his 'model construct' of the *maquis*, including ideals and tenets to which each member of the *maquis* was to adhere:

> to obey all orders from his appointed leader; to renounce all links with family and friends until the end of the war; to expect no regular wage or certainty of arms; to respect the private property and life of the population, not least because 'the men of the *maquis* are the élite of the country' who must set an example; to prepare for '*opérations de pillage*' directed against Vichy's police supplies; to respect opinions and beliefs of his comrades, whether Catholic, Protestant, Muslim, Jew, atheist, royalist, radical, socialist, or communist, and to surrender all egoism and individualism for the common cause. 'All men of the *maquis*', specified the final instruction, 'are the enemy of Marshal Pétain and the traitors who obey him.' (qtd. in Kedward 1993: 35)

The *maquis* were romantically conceived as the noble resistors ready to act at a moment's notice for a version of France violently opposed to Pétain and Vichy's image of the nation. Whether or not Beckett saw his activity in Brault's terms, we cannot say. That he would have been made aware of them, at least in May

1944 when he formally joined the *maquis*, is almost certain. By this point, the myth of the *maquis* was well established, particularly in the transformation from 'hunted' to 'hunters' during 'the struggle for control of rural areas' (Kedward 1993: 50). The opening pages of *Molloy* recall the *maquis'* methods of stalking their targets through forests and along mountain sides as the titular character observes C head to the 'treacherous hills' while he hides, 'perched higher than the road's highest point and flattened what is more against a rock the same colour as myself, that is grey' (*M*: 5–7). Being 'crouched like Belacqua' (*M*: 7) against the mountain face provides the perfect vantage point for Molloy to follow his subject.

By the end of 1943, with the *maquis* established as France's guerrilla fighting force and the cult-of-Pétain propaganda continuing at pace, Vichy's relationship to the French populace was one of 'total alienation' (Jackson 2001: 528). All of France was occupied by Nazi Germany and Vichy had no formal governing power. Vichy's propaganda still emphasized the tenets of renewal – labour, family, fatherland – and the official line was still to encourage the French to collaborate. However, in the second half of the war, the *Révolution nationale* frequently provoked laughter among the populace (Kedward 1993: 7). This does not mean that life became easier at the beginning of 1944, nor that France was no longer under the thumb of the racial dogma or authoritarian nationalism of Vichy. Rather, any lingering sense that Vichy presented a coherent ideology had all but dissipated in the last phase of the war.

Aside from his work with the *maquis*, Beckett's life in Roussillon was relatively quiet: long walks, farm labour, work on *Watt*, meals with the Haydens and one Mrs Beamish and her partner, and keeping a low profile. Alongside low-key activities with the *maquis*, Knowlson also details Beckett going out on patrol on a few occasions, and he received basic training with the gun he was issued in preparation for an ambush on German troops which did not, in the end, take place (*DF*: 338).

In the first months of 1944, the Allies were preparing for the liberation of France. BBC broadcasts to France assured those listening that American arrival in Europe was imminent. In April, large-scale bombing raids on Paris took place as part of the preparations for the D-Day landings in Normandy on 6 June 1944. While this represented a change in France's fortunes, it precipitated a wave of brutal reprisals, including the horrific massacre at Oradour-sur-Glane on 10 June when 642 civilians were murdered by the Waffen SS. The liberation of France also included successive bombing raids on various towns in northern France including Saint-Lô, a strategic target for both the Allies and the Nazis.

First, American bombers and artillery attacked Saint-Lô on the night of D-Day itself. On 17 July, it was the Germans' turn to bomb the city. By the end of the second assault, though 'liberated', most of the town was rubble.

American troops entered Roussillon in August 1944. Beckett and Déchevaux-Dumesnil celebrated quietly with the Haydens (*DF*: 339). As Saint-Lô had discovered, liberation and peace are very different things, but the end of the war was in sight. Paris was liberated on 24 August 1944 after rail workers and Parisian police went on strike in defiance of the remaining occupiers, most of whom were gone by 17 August. Borrowing money from the Audes, the couple returned to Paris in October 1944, though they found their flat had been ransacked during the occupation. They likely stayed in the Hôtel Lutetia (*BC*: 93), a hotel favoured by Beckett throughout his life which during the war served as a German military intelligence headquarters and became a repatriation centre for camp survivors after the war (Rousso 1991: 26; *PI*: 166–7). In January 1945, Beckett sent a letter home with the rue des Favorites address to his brother Frank via the Irish Legation: 'Sorry to hear you are without news. Write you regularly. All well here. Love. Sam' (*LSB II*: 9). Beckett suggests he had written to his family throughout the war. Some letters were sent through the Irish Legation (*LSB II*: xix). However, how many letters were lost due to the instabilities of wartime communications, not to mention censorship, is unknown. The interception of letters was inevitable during a war that relied as much on information as it did military strength. Britain alone had hired nearly 10,000 employees to monitor civilian post, some of which was destined for Ireland. While Ireland, by comparison, had only between 150 and 200 postal censors, all correspondences from the continent were subject to scrutiny where possible (Ó Drisceoil 1996: 62).

Paris was, unsurprisingly, a difficult place to live at the end of 1944 and in the early months of 1945. Food shortages persisted and the ghostly silences of the still under-populated streets meant the city was a shell of its former self. On 30 March, Beckett received the Croix de Guerre and later the Médaille de la Reconnaissance Française for his services in the war. His contribution to the French war effort was recognized alongside that of other foreigners who had participated in the Resistance, though the majority of liberation rhetoric remained focused on the French themselves.

On 8 April, Beckett left Paris for Ireland via London. He visited the Routledge publishing office to offer *Watt*, and was interrogated in the London War Office on 16 April 1945 by the aforementioned W. H. Astor. Alongside his identity papers, he had his manuscript notebooks confiscated as part of Astor's assessment of the collapse of the Gloria cell. Astor took note of Beckett's account of Gloria SMH and concluded that he neither posed a security risk nor could shine much light on what had happened during the cell's betrayal. What the report demonstrates, though, is that Beckett followed procedures with precision and awareness on the day of the collapse, removing all incriminating material and leaving the flat promptly; that he kept the book of eighty member's names rather than burn it was perhaps unwise, however. The report also reveals Beckett was 'anxious' both to get to Ireland to see his ill mother and to return to France, which he 'regard[ed] as his real home' (KV 2/1313.114a; qtd. in Salisbury 2014: 155). On the same day as his interrogation, Beckett met Jeannine Picabia in London, a remarkable coincidence among the blitzed streets of England's capital (*BC*: 93).

As Beckett travelled to Ireland in the spring of 1945, the war drew to a close. On 30 April, Hitler committed suicide amid the collapse of the German military as the Allies pressed in on all sides. A day later, Alfred Péron died in Mauthausen, though, as Pilling notes, Beckett did not find out until June (*BC*: 93). Berlin fell on 2 May. War in Europe came to an end, officially at least, six days later.

The end of the war brought a new phase in Beckett's life. With *Watt* finished – though it would not be published until the mid-1950s – Beckett began a fresh stage of writing, including short critical pieces, prose, drama, poetry and his first and only piece of journalism, which was never broadcast. He also settled back in Paris, though life in the recovering city was anything but settled. Before we focus on Beckett and the aftermath of the war, Chapters 2 and 3 examine more closely the various elements of Beckett's wartime experiences which shaped or resonate with some of his most evocative writing. The everyday elements of the war, in particular, are the focus of Chapter 2, illuminating the quotidian aspects of what has been traced here. This is followed by an analysis of Beckett's work in relation to Vichy propaganda. Together, these three chapters demonstrate the ways in which Beckett's imagination was informed by the war; the chapters in the second half of the book develop this analysis by thinking about the longer processes of liberation and recovery, including further discussion of the period between the liberation of Paris and the declaration of peace.

2

Beckett, War and the Everyday

One of the many problems faced by France after the war was the belief – most notably in Britain and the United States – that the French enjoyed a relatively 'easy' invasion and occupation. 'Many Englishman and Americans, on arriving in Paris, were surprised to find us less thin than they expected. . . . Perhaps they thought like the *Daily Express* that, compared to the English, the French did not have such a bad time during those four years,' wrote Jean-Paul Sartre in the postscript to the 1945 volume *French Writing on English Soil* (122), a collection of essays designed to, as the blurb puts it, 'throw some light on France and the French in the great crisis through which the country and its people have been and still are passing'. Compared to the popular imagination of Britain generated by press and public rhetoric where the resilient, back-against-the-wall notion of 'Blitz Spirit' – a 'wartime culture' generated by 'big propaganda machines [which] fabricated communal feelings' (Piette 1995: 2) – gave succour to the waning prospect of imperial dominance,[1] France suffered the problem of appearing to have been all too ready to surrender, such was the rapidity of the invasion and fall of Paris, and the ascent of the collaborationist Vichy regime under Pétain. France also had the 'image' problem of a capital city largely unscathed. When British newspapers and magazines did report on the French experience of the war, they often took the reader 'into a new peep-show or Chamber of Horrors, where the chief exhibit is France'; many articles were 'neither attempts at historical analysis or synthesis, nor criticism, nor political tracts' but instead only sought to 'show France through its sewers' (Labarthe 1945: 19).

---

[1] Marina MacKay notes that Britain's 'newly minor status' after the war required the 'nostalgia magnets' to be not imperial conquest or military triumph but the 'vulnerabilities' of 'the Blitz' and 'Dunkirk', which 'commemorate nothing more than the pathos of passive defence and a horrifically outnumbered retreat' (2007: 2).

Wartime propaganda in Britain quickly adopted a rhetoric of resilience and cohesion, weathering the effects of bombings, rationing and the possibility of invasion through the 'Blitz Spirit'. By contrast, the war in France seemed to defy explication during the 1940s in part because it was a changing, amorphous thing in which everyday life was shaped by both the conditions of occupation and a civil war between various factions of collaborationist, nationalist and Resistance forces. Accounting for such conditions and the language used to describe them is crucial when thinking through the impacts of the war on Beckett's writing, particularly the recurring tensions of the quotidian in the work of the 1940s and 1950s.

'The abstract, ambient horror': Absence in wartime and post-war France

In France, once the threat of physical destruction had passed and the invading forces became occupying forces, a chilling form of the everyday returned to the nation, what Debbie Lackerstein calls the 'unreality' of wartime France (2012: 242). When theatres, museums, operas and galleries began to reopen in 1940, many catering to Nazi tastes, it signified an official assimilation of the German forces into French life. Signs in German appeared everywhere. German rather than French police patrolled the streets. Life in Paris gained an atmosphere of silent peril, quite distinct from the picture imagined by the international community of 'Germans striding, revolvers in their hands, through streets of cowed and terrified civilians' (Kedward 1993: 1). As Sartre recounted, France's war at the level of the everyday was one of gradual terror, of the realization that absence was becoming the norm in French life, first in the absence of food and supplies, then of freedom, finally of people:

> [T]here was an enemy, of the most hateful kind, but his face was never seen. Or rather, those who saw it rarely came back to tell the tale. He could be compared, I think, to an octopus, which surreptitiously seized our best men and spirited them away. All around us, people seemed to be quietly swallowed up. One day you might ring up a friend and the telephone bell would throb for a long time in an empty flat. You would go round and ring at the door, but no-one would open. When the porter finally forced the lock, there would be two chairs standing close together in the hall, and between them a few fag-ends of German cigarettes. If the wife or mother of the vanished man had been present at his arrest, she would tell you that he had been taken away by

very polite Germans, like those who asked the way in the street. And when she went to ask for news of her husband at the offices in the Avenue Foch or the Rue des Saussaies she would be very graciously received and might be given comforting reassurances. And yet all day and late into the night screams of pain and terror could be heard coming from the buildings in the Avenue Foch and the Rue des Saussaies. Everyone in Paris had at least one relation or friend who had been arrested, deported or shot. It was [as] if there were hidden leaks in the city and its life were gradually draining away through them. Paris was suffering from a mysterious internal haemorrhage. It was spoken about very little. . . . That was, perhaps, the most painful feature; the abstract, ambient horror, inspired by an invisible enemy. It was certainly the first effect of the occupation. (1945: 124–5)

Following the invasion, over a million and a half French soldiers had been taken to Germany as prisoners of war (Kedward 1993: 1). Throughout the war, 'the fact, threat, or fear of enforced absence extended to increasing numbers of individuals, groups, and localities as the German presence intensified' (Kedward 1993: 1). Approximately two million POWs, deportees and labourers returned to France in 1945; the dead and dying were left behind (Quinn 2007). Beckett experienced this absence in various forms. Joyce's secretary, Paul Léon was taken as he walked the streets of Paris, and after the war, Beckett could only speculate at the fate of his friend (*LSB II*: 19), a sense of mortality inextricably tied to confirmation and knowledge, one which is detectable in various forms in Beckett's post-war writing: 'I don't know when I died,' the narrator of 'The Calmative' observes, seemingly speaking beyond the facticity of death (*ECEF*: 19). In a 'widely distributed poster' designed by Raymond Gid, the post-war returnees were imagined as ghostly, hollow-eyed spectres with the tricolour of France burning in their chests (Kelly 2004: 77).

Such patriotic notions as the tricolour-hearted returnees were used to aid in the reunification of France after the war. The absent were crucial to the idea of French sacrifice and martyrdom, ideas important to Gaullism and Pétainism alike. As Emilie Morin notes, Beckett's original title for *Malone meurt* was *L'Absent*, a title which intimates how the climate of absence percolated through his writing. The language of absence changed over the war, but it was always political. *Les absents* for Vichy were those soldiers who died in 1939 and 1940 and the POWs sent to the Reich; it was a term for military loss. For the provisional and Fourth Republic governments, *les absents* were the prisoners, deportees and refugees who returned after the war; they were recognized through an official

'Day of the Absents' on 8 October 1944 (*PI*: 143), which did not differentiate between different kinds of returnee.²

Though Beckett rejected *L'Absent* as the title of the second of his novel 'trilogy', its format and tone precedes the title of the third text, *L'Innommable* (*The Unnamable*). Beckett moves from 'absence' to 'unnamable', a transition of sorts from what Daniel Katz describes as 'ontology, matter, and presence, to naming, law, and signification', 'a shift from a binary oppositional structure of presence and absence into a differential, or supplemental schema [in which] a subject, ... if never present, is equally never absent' (1999: 96). Present absence haunted wartime France, a form of control through fear and disinformation. Traces of the oppressive presence of the occupiers and their attempts to normalize the increasing absences of daily life are perceptible in *The Unnamable* as the narrator recalls attempting to say 'I' while outside forces try to ram 'down [his] gullet' ways of being and ways of thinking, the violence of which serves to conceal or make normal the absence at their core. 'I am the absentee again,' murmurs the novel's narrator (*U*: 132). Stating one's absence: I am there and not there. In the novel, the absentee condition is connected to the concept of home and family, themselves rendered absentees too: 'Yonder is the nest you should never have left, there your dear absent ones are awaiting your return, patiently, and you too must be patient' (*U*: 29). That felt absence, that rupture of the 'nest' of community and nation, was replete through wartime and post-war France and was reasserted on the return of 'absent ones' – soldiers, refugees, deportees and camp survivors – many of whom had travelled hundreds of miles from where they had been sent, losing companions along the way (as with Alfred Péron). Some returned with little more than the ragged 'puttees' of *The Unnamable*'s narrator (15), many to places quite changed by the years of the war. Citizens were particularly shocked by the physical conditions of the camp survivors. They had 'expected to find the returnees in roughly the same condition as the prisoners of war' rather than the emaciated and injured figures who came back to France (Rousso 1991: 25). Attempts to treat all the returnees as one group with the same set of needs led to tensions among those tasked with caring for the camp survivors. Emmanuel Mounier, a staff member at the Hôtel Lutetia (where Beckett stayed after the liberation), remarked in September 1945 that 'victims are still a nuisance. . . . Some of them are even disfigured. Their complaints are tiresome for those who

---

² The *Journée du souvenir des victimes de la déportation* (Day to commemorate the deportation) was not established until 1954, and, as discussed in detail in Chapter 6, military commemoration for the war most often involved adding the war dead to memorials and events commemorating those killed in the First World War.

only wish is to return as quickly as possible to peace and quiet' (qtd. in Rousso 1991: 16). Many deportees found themselves met with 'rejection and repression' (Rousso 1991: 16) as their existence disrupted the official narrative of French recovery, a process Beckett was intensely scathing about in a letter from December 1946 to Arland Ussher. France was 'flourishing', he wrote acidly, 'particularly the military representatives' who were 'happily engaged in reorganising the salvation of the country'. 'They are prepared', he wrote, 'to forget and forgive – the so rude interruption' (11 December 1946, *LSB II*: 47). Beckett's inversion of the typical 'forgive and forget' phrasing emphasizes the priorities of the governing 'representatives' when it came to addressing matters like Vichy collaboration and the returning deportees. The idea of the war as an 'interruption', a part of Gaullism's attempt to situate Vichy as a digression from 'true' France's correct historical course, clearly rattled Beckett too. Gaullism's intention to pick up where the Third Republic left off was mirrored in the return of pre-war habits among the populace and the demand for 'peace and quiet'. However, as Kristin Ross observes, the war marked those habits and made the possibility of a return to old ways impossible. After the liberation, 'for a brief time', Ross writes, 'life was lived differently. . . . But the promise of social transformation gave way to a gradual submersion in old, daily patterns and routines. As the trappings of the everyday re-emerged . . . old routines were suddenly all the more palpable and visible – and thus all the more difficult to bear' (2008: 43).

Morin notes that all deportees experienced roughly the same treatment at the Lutetia, a process of 'disinfection with DDT powder, medical examination and interrogation', after which they 'were given papers ascertaining their identity, some clothing and a small sum of money' (*PI*: 167). As Morin observes, these 'concerns bear heavily upon the narrative of return developed in "Suite"', the early version of 'La Fin' published in *Les Tempes modernes* in 1946 (*PI*: 168), particularly the narrator's descriptions of the wounds on his head later excised from the final text. Elsewhere, in 'L'Expulsé' ('The Expelled') the narrator recovers from his fall down the stairs by watching the 'thorough cleansing' of his former room which is 'in full swing'. After 'a few hours', he remarks, 'they would close the window, draw the curtains and spray the whole place with disinfectant' (*ECEF*: 5–6). The texts reflect the normalization in post-war France of medicalized administrative procedures for dealing with those made vulnerable by the war, be they returnees, veterans or the homeless.

Dislocation is another, consistent thematic echo of this time in Beckett's post-war writing. War is disorientating in many ways, and language is often deployed in propaganda and official discourse to this effect. In occupied France, German became an official language. From the onset of occupation, German replaced or joined French on street signs, in advertisements, on restaurant menus and many other items. Those who returned before the liberation, and even after, were met with the German language, the language of occupation. Vichy also asserted itself through street names, reconceptualizing geographical spaces to fit its political agenda. Jean Guéhenno recorded at the end of December 1940 that places were being renamed after the head of Vichy:

> Something new to offend us every day. Last night they announced that Place Jean Jaurès in Toulouse will be called Place Philippe Pétain from now on. This morning Tours, Algiers, etc. have already applied the same decree. The new prefects certify and guarantee the spontaneity of the decisions. All this is more stupid and tragic . . . this revolution in street names. (*DDY*: 50)

Recalling this 'revolution', the narrator of 'The End' finds himself entirely turned around after he is ejected from his lodgings:

> In the street I was lost. I had not set foot in this part of the city for a long time and it seemed greatly changed. Whole buildings had disappeared, the palings had changed position, and on all sides I saw, in great letters, the names of tradesmen I had never seen before and would have been at a loss to pronounce. There were streets where I remembered none, some I did remember had vanished and others had completely changed their names. The general impression was the same as before. It is true I did not know the city very well. Perhaps it was quite a different one. I did not know where I was supposed to be going. (*ECEF*: 40)

Beckett's novella evinces a lostness unique to someone who encounters a city greatly changed, and the war can be felt throughout, from the 'whole buildings' apparently 'disappeared' as though destroyed to the signs in a language he is 'at a loss to pronounce'.[3]

The feeling of disorientation on return is also recalled in *The Unnamable* with the stories of Mahood. The text describes a return home to a scene frighteningly reminiscent of the gas chambers which would be uncovered at the end of the war, 'a kind of vast yard or campus, surrounded by high walls, its surface an amalgam of dirt and ashes' which, the narrator observes, 'seemed sweet to me after the vast and heaving wastes I had traversed, if

---

[3] Beckett was sensitive to place names, including streets. Some of the pages of the 'German Diaries' are entirely devoted to street names (McNaughton 2018: 71). Seán Kennedy (2010) also locates in the discombobulation of 'The End' the upheavals of Irish urban reconfiguration. Beckett's historical dislocation sustains the two, and it is productive to see both at work in the text.

my information was correct' (*U*: 29).⁴ The text makes use of the disturbing combination of the absentee–returnee narrative and the emotive description of 'dirt and ash', referencing the recent history of the extermination camps without direct representation to create an atmosphere of suspended horror. The narrator describes the relief of the 'campus' sweet with decay, a kind of dark satire of the celebratory nature of narratives of return couched in patriotism or humanistic harmony. Such narratives dominated de Gaulle's declarations of a unified France as absentees returned to find a broken nation on the brink of civil war between resistors and collaborators, and between resistors and resistors. *Les absents* returned to find themselves homogenized into the category of *les déporté* (the deported) in government legislation. The narrative of a unified France in resistance to a small cabal of traitors required clear definitions of heroes and villains. It also required deportees to be defined collectively as martyrs and survivors. As James Quinn writes, '[t]he repatriation plan that the ministry developed and enacted consciously treated all returnees in essentially the same manner and orchestrated a public information campaign encouraging the public to see them as a homogeneous group' (2007). Though all were survivors who made it back, the experiences among the returnees were quite distinct. Different treatment had awaited different prisoners in the camps. Approximately 97 per cent of Jewish deportees were murdered, while less than 2 per cent of prisoners of war and workers died or were executed (Quinn 2007). On their return, camp survivors first wore their striped pyjamas in the liberation parades, visible to all the spectators. However, 'these were soon banished from official commemorations' as 'the return of victims from the Nazi concentration camps' became the event 'most quickly effaced from memory' (Rousso 1991: 25). The symbols of the camps were efficiently erased to sustain Gaullism's representation of the war.

Alongside Mahood informing the narrator that his family died of food poisoning, he also reports that his physical condition, reminiscent of a war injury, did not 'affect' his family greatly – 'My missing leg didn't seem to affect them, perhaps it was already missing when I left' (*U*: 30). A scene of idyllic domesticity follows: 'In the evening, after supper, while my wife kept her eye on me, gaffer and gammer related my life history, to the sleepy children. Bedtime story atmosphere. That's one of Mahood's favourite tricks, to produce ostensibly

---

⁴ McNaughton traces the wartime evocations of this passage to the accounts of Alfred Péron in Georges Loustaunau-Lacau's book *"Chiens maudits": Souvenirs d'un rescapé des bagnes hitlériens*, which Mania Péron owned, identifying in the traces of details such as the 'campus' and the piles of corpses an 'ethical core' preserved in a 'version of survivor guilt', one articulated too in the utter failure of the narrative voice to provide coherent testimony (McNaughton 2018: 106).

independent testimony in support of my historical existence' (*U*: 30). Existence is dependent on testimony, the text tells us. *The Unnamable* viciously, harshly even, satirizes the very necessity of testimonial confirmation, the 'trick' to support 'historical existence'. The text is one of 'survivor guilt' (McNaughton 2018: 106), but it also takes to task the process of glorifying the returning absentee, the same methods by which the narratives of deportees could be co-opted for official liberation propaganda, which erased the unique subjectivity of the deportees, demanding their 'historical existence' be subsumed into the rhetoric of national resistance and sacrifice.

'This frightful silence': War's ineffability

Absence defined the physical emptiness of Paris and other French towns during the war. Buildings were destroyed. People fled, were killed or simply went missing. An absence of language also prevailed in the 'unreality' of wartime France. The need for silence among resistors and their networks was paramount. Militarized German silenced the French in the streets. The dead no longer spoke. Many who experienced the war also identified the more intangible effect of the war on language itself. As noted in Chapter 1, Beckett marked the onset of the war with ellipsis. At the point of invasion, he couldn't find the words: 'But now . . .' (*LSB I*: 680). In 1945, as the war came to a close, Sartre emphasized how language had been rendered incapable of communicating the true nature of life in occupied France:

> How can the people of the free countries be made to realize what life was like under the occupation? There is a gulf between us which words are powerless to bridge. When Frenchmen speak amongst themselves about the Germans, the Gestapo, the Resistance Movement and the Black Market, they understand each other quite easily, because they have lived through the same events and are full of the same memories. But the English and the French have no longer a single memory in common; a past which fills London with pride was, for Paris, marked with shame and despair. We must learn to talk about ourselves without passion, and you [the English] must learn to understand us, and above all to grasp, behind the words used, what can only be suggested or signified by a gesture or by silence. (122)

For Sartre and many others, to speak of the occupation after the war was to risk diminishing the truth of the experience. During the war, speaking, the failure to hold one's tongue, risked betraying one's intentions, risked an accusation of collaboration and risked the accidental denunciation of another. But silence was also a mode of communication, acknowledgement and reciprocation. In many ways, Beckett's greatest literary challenge was to speak of, within and from silence: 'it was silence adequate to our condition he tried to attain,' as Anne Atik remarked (2006: 456). How to attain an expression of the ineffable? This is an aesthetic problem, certainly, but speaking through silence was an imperative in wartime. In their preoccupations with the ineffable, Beckett's works reveal that, as Gill Plain puts it, 'if war is a subject that evades direct expression, it is nonetheless an event that indelibly imprints itself upon language, reorienting and distorting expressive possibility' (2019: 334). Despite the sometimes radical alienation of Beckett's characters, their relationship to language and silence is uniquely prescient to those whose 'condition' was war and its aftermath, a historical moment that demanded the rationalization of language yet defied explication: 'we may reason on to our heart's content', the narrator of 'The Expelled' observes, 'the fog won't lift' (*ECEF*: 7).

In France, silence imprinted itself on the language of the occupation. 'The silence is deathly,' recorded Agnès Humbert on 8 June 1940 (2009: 2). 'I am going to bury myself in silence,' remarked Jean Guéhenno in one of the early entries of his occupation diary (25 June 1940, *DDY*: 3). As occupation set in, Guéhenno recorded the unsettling quiet of life in occupied France: 'Cold and hunger for many people. Dire poverty. And this frightful silence' (23 December 1940, *DDY*: 44). Writing both against and within the silence plagued Guéhenno. 'How to write a diary of emptiness?', he worried as he made note of Pétain's broadcasts to Paris on 23 December 1940 (*DDY*: 44). The clash of the 'frightful silence' of the occupation with Vichy's bombastic propaganda and incessant radio broadcasts was another part of the war's 'unreality'. The 23 December broadcast was an example of the disorganization that plagued Vichy. Pétain blamed the regime's instability on Pierre Laval, who had recently been removed from the cabinet, and assured the population that collaboration was the right course of action. In the same speech, Pétain celebrated the return of the ashes of the duke of Reichstadt, Napoleon's son, from Schönbrunn to Paris, calling it a '"magnanimous" gesture of the Führer' (*DDY*: 43). Pétain's attempt to distract the French populace from the regime's ineptitude was not lost on Guéhenno.

Amid the din of nationwide propaganda and the appropriation of French culture and history in the authoritarian vision of Vichy, silence could also mean violence, be it the covert activities of resistors or the interrogation-torture-deportation routines of the occupiers. 'For some time now', Guéhenno wrote on

10 July 1942, 'our guests have been committing their crimes in silence. They have been executing people every day in the prisons, but no notice was published' (*DDY*: 163). The methods of interrogation and deportation altered how language and silence functioned. They could bring violence, pain and control, what the thirteenth of Beckett's *Texts for Nothing* calls the 'silencing of silence', the violent possibility in 'every mute micromillisyllable' and 'the screaming silence of no's knife in yes's wound' (*TFN*: 53). Under interrogation, 'no' and 'yes' can both wound, even kill.

At times, though, silence was also resistance during the war: 'silence had its eloquence, by signifying refusal,' as one Resistance member put it (Jacques Debû-Bridel, qtd. in *DDY*: xxi). Even the narrator of *The Unnamable* sees the affirmative potential of silence. 'To feel myself silent, one with all this quiet air shattered unceasingly' by his 'voice alone', the narrator posits, would mean that he might not 'die a stranger in the midst of strangers, a stranger in my own midst, surrounded by invaders' (*U*: 115). In this instance, silence is defiant, a repelling force. It was the resistive potential of silence which marked the launch in 1942 of Beckett's long-time publisher Les Éditions de Minuit with the release of Jean Bruller's *Le Silence de la mer*. In the novella, a father and daughter resist the Nazi occupation by remaining obstinately silent in the presence of the German officer living in their home. The text was a watershed moment for long-form Resistance literature, and the negotiations of silence in Beckett's post-war works are part of this lineage in the Minuit canon.[5] Completed by November 1941, Bruller approached the Parisian printer Ernest Aulard to make copies of the text. Soon after, they began discussing a clandestine publishing house which could confirm 'that French intellectual life survived under the Nazi heel' and document that 'France, amid misfortune and violence, was able to keep faith with her highest purpose: her claim to think straight' (Bruller 1991: 1). Though Aulard and Bruller saw eye to eye 'on the Red Army's Resistance, on Britain's tenacity', the scale of the project was too much for Aulard to take on. Instead, Bruller was directed to the operation of Georges Oudeville who produced 'wedding and funeral cards, in premises across from a German military hospital' (1991: 2). The operation was dangerous from the start, not least for Yvonne Paraf and her volunteers who gathered in Paraf's apartment to make the physical, hand-stitched books 'that were then hidden in closets and cupboards to await distribution' (1991: 3). Codenames were adopted. Bruller took 'Vercors' for writing, the name derived from 'the

---

[5] See Morin (*PI*: 215–38) for a discussion of the later context of Minuit's stance on the Algerian war for Beckett's writing.

imposing massif near Grenoble' (1991: 3) where he had demobilized during the 1940 defeat, and 'Drieu' for publishing, a name intended to slight Pierre Drieu La Rochelle, collaborationist editor of *La Nouvelle Revue Française* (1991: 3). For Bruller, Paraf and the network that contributed to the founding of Les Éditions de Minuit, publishing creative and intellectual books from within wartime Paris was to resist both the oppression of the occupiers and the perception of French intellectual stagnation by the outside world. Bruller was compelled to write by what he saw as the rapid accommodation of occupation conditions by the French populace. This was not always active collaboration per se but might involve, for example, adapting to German tastes in cafes and shops in the hope that officers and soldiers would spend money. However, Bruller saw such changes as part of a sinister process of occupation and thought control at work across France. It also included the cultural collaboration of magazines like *La Nouvelle Revue Française*, the censorship and burning of books, the emergence of journals like *Au Pilori*, a French antisemitic publication with Nazi support, and even 'the need to obtain gas coupons and an identification card (the ubiquitous *Ausweis*)' (1991: 8). It was against these measures of oppression that clandestine publishers such as Minuit operated.

Silence retained its political import in France following the war. To remain silent on the subject of naming and identifying collaborators was to risk complicity. To fail to condemn those who had collaborated was to do likewise. Many who returned from deportation fell into terrible bouts of depression, unable to express or fully articulate their experiences (Beevor and Cooper 2007: 149). Beckett's turn to silence as a central aesthetic motif is indelibly imbedded in this wartime and post-war moment, the 'obligation to express' despite the lack of a proper means to do so, where 'the same silence' is both despairing and resistive, the 'murmurs' still murmuring when all is 'silent and empty and dark' (*TFN*: 52–3).

War, the everyday and the politics of material conditions

So much of war and occupation can and must be understood through day-to-day conditions. Food and fuel supplies were essential in France during the Second World War, particularly given a series of harsh winters and the brutal compensation orders enforced by the Nazis. New forms of state and individual power formed around legal and black-market access to supplies and the documentation of travel. In the circumstances of a continent at war, particularly under occupation, the everyday – routines of labour, finding food, waiting – gained a fraught sense of fragility and danger. Yet war also makes this fragility and danger quotidian. When scarcity and restriction are a part of daily routine, they are tempered by boredom, disconnection and dislocation. This form of the everyday is evident throughout Beckett's post-war writings as his narrators and characters try to survive in their half-realized surroundings, reflecting what Kristin Ross, following Henri Lefebvre, calls the 'inherent ambiguity of the quotidian'. While 'the everyday' consists 'of that which is taken for granted: the sequence of regular, unvarying repetition', the war cast sharp relief on the fact that 'in that very triviality and baseness' lay the 'seriousness' of the everyday: 'in the poverty and tedium of the routine lay the potential for creative energy' (2008: 43–4). This 'energy' of the everyday – that exchange between 'baseness' and 'seriousness' – is a generative source for creativity in *Watt* and many of Beckett's writings from the post-war years, most notably the novellas of the 1940s, *Molloy* and *Waiting for Godot*.

One of the most common experiences of life in wartime and recovering France involved encounters with legislation, documentation and administration, be it for securing food or proving one's identity. The absurd degree of documentation that war necessitated, of providing 'your papers!', is reconstructed in Molloy's encounter with the police in which we learn that Molloy has no 'occupation, nor any domicile' and that his surname 'escaped' him (*M*: 19), all details that, in wartime, could have left him excluded or arrested. Indeed, Molloy's inability to prove affiliation or occupation effectively leaves him the status akin to a foreigner in wartime: suspicious and to be monitored, even detained, deported and, potentially, subject to harm because his 'sense of identity was wrapped in a namelessness hard to penetrate' (*M*: 29). The degree to which authority derives from the control over documentation is, for Molloy, little more than an opaque logical conundrum: 'If it is unlawful to be without papers, why did they not insist on my getting them. Because that costs money and I had none? But in that case could they not have appropriated my bicycle? Probably not, without a court order. All that is incomprehensible' (*M*: 21). If the need for papers was 'incomprehensible', though, it would never have been far from Beckett's concerns as a foreigner, then as a Resistance member and, later still, as a hungry refugee.

Beckett's texts also recall the restrictions on movement imposed by conditions of conflict, reproducing memories of travel documentation that Beckett himself used. When seeking out finances, the narrator of 'The End' makes sense of his situation via the sudden memory of a safe-conduct pass (see Figure 2 in Chapter 1):

> A man came in and made a sign to me to follow him. In the hall he gave me a paper to sign. What's this, I said, a safe-conduct? It's a receipt, he said, for the clothes and money you have received. What money? I said. It was then I received the money. (*ECEF*: 38)

The scene implies that the safe-conduct is either a present necessity or was required at some point in the past. That the narrator leaps to the conclusion over the receipt so quickly suggests the safe-conduct is fresh in the memory. The scene is comic in tone, but the humour makes light of, and so sheds light on, the way conditions under occupation shape habits, routine and expectations. The narrator presumes that an encounter with paperwork and officialdom is concerned with free movement. Such documents were emphatically provisional, though, denoting safety only up to the point of expiry, between one location and another.

Food was also governed by paperwork and systems of limitation during the war. Rationing came into effect early in France, and large portions of native produce were sent to Germany. The hunger of the nation, the cities in particular, was exacerbated by limitations on transportation and travel, and the system of rationing required documents which not all citizens could access. This link between documentation and food is remembered by the narrator of 'The Expelled' when he learns that people are looking for him. Since 'you can hardly have a home address under these circumstances,' he remarks of his homelessness, it was 'with a certain delay that I learnt they were looking for me, for an affair concerning me. I forget through what channel. I did not read the newspapers, nor do I remember having spoken with anyone during these years, except perhaps three or four times, on the subject of food' (*ECEF*: 10). For wealthier and more well-connected citizens, food packages could be solicited from connections in the countryside. 'Life in Paris is growing very difficult,' Guéhenno wrote on 3 January 1941, 'we have ration tickets, but we can't buy anything with them anymore. The shops are empty. At home, we live exclusively on parcels sent by friends and cousins in Brittany for the past two weeks' (*DDY*: 51). By February 1941, food access revealed the stark class distinctions present in French society: 'One feels rather ashamed to eat. The poor people in the neighborhood have no more bread. As of now, they have used up all their February ration tickets. If we're still eating in our house, it's because we're members of the bourgeoise and can send for packages from Brittany at great expense' (21 February 1941, *DDY*: 60). Under the occupation, if you did not have the right papers, you risked going days, even weeks, without access to proper food. Food is an obsession in many accounts of the occupation. For the poor who left Guéhenno ashamed, the obsession is magnified. As the narrator of 'The Expelled' confirms, when food is absent and hunger becomes routine, there is little else to think about.

Food also occupies a significant space in *Watt*, particularly the topic of Mr Knott's meal. Under the directions that have passed from one servant to another, Watt turns a decadent list of ingredients into a soupy grey mass of indistinguishable slop. Served cold, twice a day, Mr Knott's pot is prepared in bulk in the kitchen so as to provide him with a dose of food containing 'the maximum of pleasure compatible with the protraction of his health' (*W*: 73). The leftovers, which appear to be frequent, are given to a starving dog. Dwelling on the abundance of the Irish Big House, the description of the dish relishes the plenty it imagines, a plenty set in terms of both 'pleasure' and 'health', both of which are in short supply when food access is limited. The scene evokes both the history and politics of food central to Ireland's colonial history – particularly the control of food by the landlord classes – and the war itself, in which rationing signified not only the plunge into conflict throughout Europe but also the realities of day-to-day survival:

> This dish contained foods of various kinds, such as soup of various kinds, fish, eggs, game, poultry, meat, cheese, fruit, all of various kinds, and of course bread and butter, and it contained also the more usual beverages, such as absinthe, mineral water, tea, coffee, milk, stout, beer, whiskey, brandy, wine and water, and it contained also many things to take for the good of the health, such as insulin, digitalin, calomel, iodine, laudanum, mercury, coal, iron, camomile and worm-powder, and of course salt and mustard, pepper and sugar, and of course a little salicylic acid, to delay fermentation.
>
> All these things, and many others too numerous to mention, were well mixed together in the famous pot and boiled for four hours, until the consistence of a mess, or poss, was obtained, and all the good things to eat, and all the good things to drink, and all the good things to take for the good of the health were inextricably mingled and transformed into a single good thing that was neither food, nor drink, nor physic, but quite a new good thing, and of which the tiniest spoonful at once opened the appetite and closed it, excited and stilled the thirst, compromised and stimulated the body's vital functions, and went pleasantly to the head. (*W*: 72–3)

A send-up of medicinal consumption, the 'new good thing' concocted each time both enlivens and kills the consumer, their 'vital functions' at once 'compromised and stimulated'. Not only is the excess itself parodied but the fantasies of infinite supply – such as a hungry wartime citizen might entertain – are themselves satirized with the notion of eating oneself to death as the meal both compromises and stimulates the body. In wartime, eating oneself to death was possible not because of excess but because of a lack of nutrients in available food, notably fat and protein.[6]

The scene survives from the Quin-stage of the manuscript: its first iteration is from the period of writing in Roussillon, as we saw in Chapter 1. In its earlier incarnations, the dish is given a full recipe format with measurements and calculations for producing the dish on a weekly basis. The earliest version of the sequence contains more specific details for some of the ingredients. Alongside the whiskey, originally 'tailor Canadian rye whiskey', mentioned in Chapter 1, the soup in the published text was initially '1 large tin of Heinz's asparagus soup' and the stout was originally '1 bottle Beamish's 4X stout' (HRC, *Watt* MS, NB3: 71r). The letter draft thanking the unknown recipient for the Canadian rye, also mentioned in Chapter 1, indicates that the list in part at least derives from the availability of foods in the war, a creative confrontation with the 'day-to-day political effects of shortages in France' and how 'food became a personal *and* a political issue during the Second World War' (Fogg 2009: 2; emphasis in original). Though the names and their amounts are excised from the published text, the production of this all-in-one meal survives into *Watt*, wryly described as 'a great saving of labour' (*W*: 74).

A politics of food access emerged in wartime France as shortages 'dramatically changed traditional social structures and inverted concepts of privilege as peasants, with their direct access to meat, vegetables, milk, and eggs, claimed a greater standing in society' (Fogg 2009: 3). Such social structures were invariably vexed by the presence of 'outsiders' who were often portrayed as the saboteurs of food production. Beckett's status as an 'outsider', one which he regulated through claims to Irish neutrality, would have affected his relationship to food during the war:

> Even more than socioeconomic status, one's position as a foreigner, 'undesirable', or stranger in a community could affect access to food despite the equality implied by rationing and the state's elaborate system of tickets, cards, and registration. . . . People on the margins of society such as evacuees, refugees, Jews, and Gypsies had fewer connections and thus fewer opportunities for extra-legal access to food and other supplies. (*DF*: 299)

---

[6] 'In France', Kenneth Mouré writes, 'the physical impact of malnutrition was clear in the increased incidence of TB and diphtheria, increased mortality rates for infants and the aged, anaemia and vitamin deficiencies, weight loss and stunted growth for children and adolescents. In hard-hit regions, mortality rates increased by as much as 50 per cent in the period 1941–43; infant mortality increased significantly, from 63 per thousand in 1939 to 91 per thousand in 1940 and 109 per thousand in 1945' (2010: 263).

Alongside the history of famine and class-based food control in Ireland, the systems of food in the Knott household – elaborately detailed in the manuscripts – reflects the politicized structures of wartime provisioning and the reconfiguration of plenty and scarcity that defined everyday life during wartime. Mr Knott has available to him all he could require for nourishment, a plenty possible only while the surrounding tenants and animals starve. Rationing, inflated prices and the cruel winters of the 1940s produced starvation across France while Beckett wrote the novel. Hunger persisted throughout the war, right up to the liberation and beyond it. 'We are not living well. We are getting thinner. A kilo of butter costs a thousand francs. A kilo of peas, forty francs. And then, you have to find them,' recorded Jean Guéhenno in August 1944 (*DDY*: 266).

Rationing continued until October 1945, when the French government abolished it (just in time for elections) only to find resources still lacking. Rationing returned in December 1945; rioting ensued. The scheme finally came to an end in 1949. Beckett had returned to Ireland in 1945 'looking emaciated' (*DF*: 344) and food remained an issue in France as damaged supply chains slowly recovered. Beckett's work captures these conditions in minute yet sometimes seemingly ephemeral detail. In his theatre writing in particular, such details presented visceral images unavoidably reminiscent of the war to the imagined audiences of the plays. His first complete drama, *Eleutheria*, ends with the silent, famished body of Victor '*turning his emaciated back on humanity*' (1996: 170). In *Waiting for Godot*, Beckett's tramps wait by a roadside, running low on supplies, and begging for bones from passing travellers. Elsewhere, in *Molloy*, Moran notes that he'll 'soon be dead of inanition' if he does not 'succeed in renewing' his 'provisions', a situation in which the 'question of calories and vitamins' and the creation of 'menus' recedes at the prospect of imminent starvation (*M*: 156).

Food changes in status under the limitations of war and occupation. Hunger becomes quotidian, satiety and good health extraordinary, and the transformative effects of war mean that the lengths to which people go to acquire food can become commonplace, even banal. The politics of food has become increasingly significant in the study of wartime France, and scholarly descriptions are sometimes starkly reminiscent of *Waiting for Godot* and the prose from the 1940s:

> The hunt for food could become a full-time occupation. Searchers often had no destination in mind upon setting out from their homes. All they knew was that the chance of finding something to eat was better when one went directly to the source as rationing and restrictions tightened. The process was by no means easy. Due to shortages of gas, most expeditions took place on foot or by bicycle. Unpaved roads, out-of-the-way farmhouses, and patrols of law enforcement officers checking for purchases of rationed or excessive amounts of goods made

the task even more difficult. Furthermore, there was no guarantee of returning home with any more than one left with. (Fogg 2009: 26)

Food shortages existed in France from the moment war was declared. First, food was redirected to the fighting French troops. Then, after the fall of France, Germany demanded occupation costs 'at the rate of twenty million Reichsmarks per day' and, by the end of the war, this included '2.4 million metric tons of wheat, 891,000 metric tons of meat, and 1.4 million hectolitres of milk' transferred from France to Germany (Fogg 2009: 4). The black market represented a direct assault on occupation and Vichy governance, but it also influenced the very survival of the nation's citizens. The average calorie intake available to a Parisian in 1942 was approximately 1,725 calories from rations, 200 from food packages sent by connections in the countryside and 200 from the black market (Vinen 2007: 233). Begging and homelessness like that of Beckett's narrators in the 1940s, particularly in the short stories, were common. Access to food also reflected the priorities of Vichy: by 1941,

> [a]dults between the ages of 21 and 70 (Category A) received a standard ration. . . . Workers who performed heavy labour and fell within the adult age range (Category T) received tickets for supplemental amounts of bread, meats, fats, and wine – this included physical education teachers, in line with Vichy's emphasis on athleticism and a healthy body. Agricultural labourers (Category C) and rural residents were expected to provide for themselves from their land and therefore received a reduced ration. (Fogg 2009: 5)[7]

Vichy's vision of a nation self-sufficient through a largely agrarian workforce devoted to labour and physical prowess can be easily identified in the ration system in place throughout the war. Indeed, such a vision could be managed through the control of supplies that rationing entails.

Aside perhaps from the 'emaciated' figure of Victor in *Eleutheria*, Beckett's most vivid depiction of hunger and survival comes in *Waiting for Godot*. This is a text which, in its dramatic asceticism of plot and staging, evokes the war both in image and in feel as Vladimir and Estragon attempt to pass the time, waiting for something a little better, or at least a little less the same. The conceit of waiting is undeniably of the wartime moment, as the wartime diaries of people like Guéhenno demonstrate. So too is the play's attention to the activities in which a couple or group may engage when forced together for extended periods of time. It captures the boredom that war can entail, a boredom which sets in despite the

---

[7] Category T received 350 grams a day of bread compared to the Category A 200 grams (*DDY*: 80).

possibility that the tramps might starve to death at the roadside or be beaten while they sleep.

'Waiting' took many forms in the France of the 1940s: waiting for the end of war, for liberation, for food, for aid. Waiting could be life-threatening. Waiting too long in one place could give the authorities a reason to suspect a person of being a Resistance agent (Crowdy 2007: 23). Andrew Gibson has identified the stance of *attentisme* (wait and see) as central to French consciousness across the country during the war, especially in relation to the Vichy regime's aggressively nationalist *Révolution nationale* propaganda programme.

> *Attentisme* was the attitude of those who did not believe that 'the Pétain experiment' would succeed, but argued that there was no possibility of an immediate return to the battlefield. It was necessary to defer any final decision until the situation 'clarified itself'. France should wait for the right moment 'to jump back into war'. . . . *Attentisme* involved a particular kind of ambiguity, and a particular disposition towards it. [Robert] Paxton suggests that it was probably the philosophy of the majority of Frenchmen and women under Vichy. To intellectuals, radicals and anti-Fascists, it was the least objectionable position outside the Resistance. The Vichy government hated it.
>
> One reason for this was that *attentisme* flouted if it did not actively oppose Vichy ideology. It took revenge on Pétainism on behalf of the obstinately unreconstructed and resiliently commonplace strata of Vichy society. For Vichy called for the moral renewal of France. (2010a: 103–4)

Such a condition of waiting imbues Beckett's *Waiting for Godot* with notably historical, even political, edge. As a mark in French cultural history, too, it is resonant in this regard. One of the most popular French songs of the war was 'J'attendrai' (I will wait), first released by Rina Ketty in 1938 and rerecorded in 1939 by Tino Rossi and Jean Sablon (Jackson 2001: 156). In many ways, 'J'attendrai' and Beckett's *Godot* bookend the war in France, the transformation of one form of waiting into another, the former a song of hope during the build-up to conflict, the latter an acknowledgement, and hyperbolic realization, of what waiting actually involved during the war.[8] The buoyant cheer of 'J'attendrai' elides the reality of waiting during the war, but so too does the assumption that *attentisme* was actively political. By this, I mean that many of those in France who took to 'fence sitting' during the war were doing so not in active defiance of Vichy but for the simple necessities of food and fuel, politicized though they

---

[8] The tune of 'J'attendrai' also formed the basis for Yiddish songs sung in Auschwitz (Kaczerginski 1948: 407).

were; going too far one way from the fence would draw the eye of the occupier, the other the Resistance, the latter's presence sooner or later leading to the arrival of the former.

Waiting for Godot arises from and transmutes the anxieties of the war and their lingering effects in the post-war years. It is a play not about the war but of the war. The play captures what Jean Guéhenno recorded as the interminable banality of occupation that carried with it pervasive hunger and want, all of which prompted the kind of grand, metaphysical questions which disintegrate into the desire for food: 'Wait. Nothing to do but wait. But wait for what? Oh, how tempting it would be to decide that the follies of this phantasmagoric world do not concern us . . . but it is harder and harder to fulfill our material needs; potatoes are becoming rare' (23 December 1940, *DDY*: 44). Given that the tramps and Lucky are presented as derelict figures apparently on the margins of society, attending to the policies of treatment for such figures in the context of wartime hardships reveals much about the play's historical resonances. Hunger and marginalization are always modified by socioeconomic conditions, but the exclusionary politics of Vichy and the Nazis exacerbated this severely. As Fogg observes, 'the French State used access to food as one means to tighten its control over society and separate "true" French from the undesirables' (2009: 14), including stamping ration cards with 'JUIF' or 'JUIVE'. In the early drafts of *Waiting for Godot*, Beckett used the name 'Lévy' before 'Estragon' (Rabaté 2016: 187), suggesting Jewish origin for at least one of the central characters. The use of 'Lévy' in early drafts is politically potent in itself, and it is all the more charged when contextualized by the intertwined politics of food and identity from the war.

Waiting for Godot: Staging hunger

There is no shortage of readings of *Godot* which place it within a wartime and post-war context. However, the play has only recently been read in the context of Vichy and its political structures. Resisting readings that interpret the play as a humanistic response to universal suffering, for example, Hannah Simpson has shown (2020a, 2020b) that the play's staging of debilitated bodies has specific historical resonance with the fetish of the athletic body common in mid-century fascist thinking. But it remains the case that the turn to the everyday in studies of the war years has yet to be fully applied to the play. To do so, we can look again to Kay Boyle's comment from her 1957 talk 'The Tradition of Loneliness' on the war's effect on Beckett, that 'Beckett's casual remark that he stayed in Paris until 1942 covers more peril, more pain, and more actual hunger than many of us have ever known' (*LSB III*: 56). Beckett remarked that Boyle's were 'the most sensitive, imaginative, inseeing, painstaking comments I've read' (*LSB III*: 55), and noted that Boyle's 'Occupation interp. is perhaps a little tiré par le 2-Millimeterschnitt, but formidably ingenious (Pozzo-Bozzo gem) and after all for the likes of some of us it's that way always and no Nono zone inside or out' (*LSB III*: 56). Beckett's commendation discloses the idea that he had no notion of the 'Pozzo-Bozzo gem', that 'Prussians invariably pronounce "B" as "P" and "P" as "B"', as Boyle noted (qtd. in *LSB III*: 57). Yet his reply suggests that though he could not condone the 'Occupation interp.', he did see himself in a milieu or grouping for whom 'it's that way always'. Beckett's elliptical phrasing suggests the war was unavoidable. There was no 'nono zone', no unoccupied zone, 'inside or out' when writing. The war occupied everything, inside and out, the little world and the big.

Under occupation, the encounters and exchanges between Vladimir, Estragon, Pozzo and Lucky could be construed as illicit, even illegal activities that risk the very 'peril' to which Boyle draws attention. Information is swapped and food is offered to the hungry tramps. The master–slave reading of Pozzo and Lucky is all too familiar in the context of wartime Nazism, but Pozzo is also evocative of the well-to-do rural landowners who, through Vichy's attempted agricultural reforms, were most likely to keep themselves well fed and in profit. Poor and rich in the countryside alike received lower rations based on the theory that Vichy's agrarian focus would increase food production, which inevitably harmed the impoverished and left the rich fairly unscathed (Fogg 2009: 5). The harsh winters and demands of reparations to Germany left any promise of a farming revolution untenable, and many starved. While the rich could survive more prosperously during times of hardship, though, they still relied on their workers. Pozzo is not ignorant of the power his access to food commands, nor is he unaware that his access to food is reliant on his labourers and staff. He knows well the routine of giving the bones of his meal to his long-suffering servant.

The appearance of food in the play is also the appearance of hunger in its most terrible form, bringing out anger or desperation in Estragon as he asks Vladimir for food:

ESTRAGON. [*Violently.*] I'm hungry.

VLADIMIR. Do you want a carrot?

ESTRAGON. Is that all there is?

> VLADIMIR. I might have some turnips.
>
> ESTRAGON. Give me a carrot. [*VLADIMIR. rummages in his pockets, takes out a turnip and gives it to ESTRAGON who takes a bite out of it. Angrily.*] It's a turnip!
>
> VLADIMIR. Oh pardon! I could have sworn it was a carrot. [*He rummages again in his pockets, finds nothing but turnips.*] All that; turnips. [*He rummages.*] You must have eaten the last. [*He rummages*]. Wait, I have it. [*He brings out a carrot and gives it to ESTRAGON.*] There, dear fellow. [*ESTRAGON wipes the carrot on his sleeve and begins to eat it.*] Give me the turnip. [*ESTRAGON gives back the turnip which VLADIMIR puts in his pocket.*] Make it last, that's the end of them.
>
> (CDW: 21)

In act 2, Estragon recalls a time when he could act on preference, rather than necessity. No excess can be catered for in Vladimir's fastidious inventory-keeping:

> VLADIMIR. Would you like a radish?
>
> ESTRAGON. Is that all there is?
>
> VLADIMIR. There are radishes and turnips.
>
> ESTRAGON. Are there no carrots?
>
> VLADIMIR. No. Anyway you overdo it with your carrots.
>
> ESTRAGON. Then give me a radish. [*VLADIMIR fumbles in his pockets, finds nothing but turnips, finally brings out a radish and hands it to ESTRAGON, who examines it, sniffs it.*] It's black!
>
> VLADIMIR. It's a radish.
>
> ESTRAGON. I only like the pink ones, you know that!
>
> VLADIMIR. Then you don't want it?
>
> ESTRAGON. I only like the pink ones!
>
> VLADIMIR. Then give it back to me.
>
> [*ESTRAGON gives it back.*]
>
> (CDW: 63-4)

We learn too that carrots have, it would seem, run out: 'I'll go and get a carrot,' says Estragon, but '*he does not move*' (CDW: 64).

The pathetic vegetables produced by Vladimir indicate their supplies are low. That Estragon would later risk a kicking from Lucky, and eat food off the ground, says something of the real hunger and desperation that the pair must be facing. Yet these exchanges also come under the daily routines of grey- and black-market transactions which took place in wartime France (Fogg 2009: 6). The farm-owning 'Mr Godot', who we know at least keeps goats and has a barn with a hay loft where the boys sleep (*CDW*: 50), will, our tramps believe, offer respite, even salvation, perhaps in exchange for work, as appears to be the case for 'the boys'. That the pair is to meet him on an unremarkable piece of road in the countryside suggests an arrangement which is clandestine in its ambiguity, if nothing else. Indeed, as Jean-Michel Gouvard observes, details about Godot suggest the *passeur* (smugglers) who brought people from the occupied zone and into the 'free' south as long as their 'family', 'friends', 'agents', 'correspondents', 'books' and 'bank account' made it apparent that it was safe and, more often than not, worth their while financially (2019: 8). Such a process often required the use of false monikers or codenames which, as we saw in Chapter 1, could well include the various names the tramps go by, and even 'Godot'. Even if Vladimir and Estragon mean to meet 'Mr Godot' on semi-legal terms – the exchange of food for labour – they are engaged throughout the play (with each other, with Pozzo, even with the Boy) in 'making do', what was called during the war 'Système D', *système débrouillard* (Fogg 2009: 6). In the everyday lives of those under Vichy and the occupation, 'Système D' existed in the same realm as the grey and black markets. Fogg notes that 'such activities could include gardening, raising rabbits and chickens, purchasing goods on the black market, bartering, or making trips to the countryside' (2009: 6). Pozzo's trip to the market is as mysterious as Vladimir and Estragon's arrangement's with Mr Godot, both of which appear to take place out of the sight of any greater authority or official structures. The play evokes the power dynamics of food in the war. The need to secure food involved a constant confrontation with the state, both Vichy and occupier; as Fogg writes, '[t]hese survival tactics', those trips to the countryside, the engagement with the black market, 'often included technically illegal exchanges and challenged the government's authority on a daily basis' (2009: 6). In this sense, Beckett stages in his play a challenge to the kinds of authority and controls which persisted until the liberation.

The particular images of hunger in *Waiting for Godot* offer striking evocations of wartime shortages and food access, as has been well acknowledged in biographies and Beckett scholarship generally. Yet, while James Knowlson notes the frequency with which items like turnips became a staple of hungry French dinner plates, the choice of a turnip in *Godot* is not just a passing nod to the war's conditions and the hunger Beckett and Déchevaux-Dumesnil experienced. It is an evocation of the very desperation that the turnip represented. As Fogg notes, many records from hungry citizens in the war return to parents battling to get their children to eat turnips (Fogg 2009: 2); as such the politics of hunger (one that would have been particularly palpable to early French audiences) becomes a fundamental vein that runs through Beckett's most famous piece of theatre. If we understand the importance of hunger for everyday life during the war, the fact that 'sometimes a turnip is simply a turnip', as Mark Nixon suggests (2019: 3), transmutes into the inclusion of a foodstuff that contains within it the weight of hunger and daily survival in the war. We 'see' the war's reality through the food itself, a reality of hunger, of scavenging, of begging, of the difference between surviving another day and dying of starvation. The play is all about the everyday, its fraught tensions, its unifying potential, its unremarkable remarkability, the entrapment the everyday can become, an imaginative iteration of what Beckett noted in his 'German Diaries' as 'the fragile habit of getting up, dressing, moving, eating, undressing, going to bed' (7 March 1937, *GD*: 57). Such a focus on the everyday is a manifestation of what Thomas S. Davis identifies as the 'late Modernist' urge to 'render legible their moment of systematic disorder by attending to the particulars of everyday life' (2016: 15). 'Never neglect the little things,' as Vladimir puts it (*CDW*: 12).

The play's visual imagery is also evocative of food-related propaganda of the war, specifically the work of Philippe Noyer for Equipe Alain Fournier, a collaborationist poster production house (Figure 4). The black market represented one of the most important avenues of food access for many French citizens during the war. Noyer's poster shows, though, that it was also a phenomenon that allowed Vichy to lay the blame for its hungry populace at the feet of those engaged in illicit activities, rather than acknowledge that its various concessions to German control included the divergence of staggering volumes of food and the deportation of French labourers to German work stations. Effectively, Vichy could re-inscribe its narrative of 'saving France' through imposed authoritarianism onto food itself: to resist engaging with the black market was to help shield France from further oppression (at least from outside forces); to engage with the black market was to shatter French 'community' and risk the hanging of the nation by its own hand. That it was harsh winters and German occupation costs which caused most of the food shortages mattered little. The black market was, according to Vichy, a product of French weakness and Resistance conspiracy. In reality, to deal through the black market was to resist, but it was also to survive. The noose in the poster as much suggests death will come for those who do not do all they can to get food as it

Figure 4 'Marche Noir', 1943, Phillippe Noyer, Equipe Alain Fournier, copyright holder not located.

does imply that the gallows await those who trade bread and money behind the government's backs.

The poster is remarkably, frustratingly reminiscent of Beckett's two tramps before a lone tree, debating whether to hang themselves (*CDW*: 18). It is frustrating because, of course, we cannot say that Beckett saw such a poster; remarkable because we can only again wonder, given that most French public buildings were plastered with such images (Jackson 2001: 253), at the true resonance for early audiences of the sight of two hungry bowler-hatted vagrants considering a tree for hanging as they pass food between one another waiting for a man they have seemingly seldom or never met. The pair choose not to use, or at least reason their way out of using, the option of the noose, erring on the side of collaborating with and accommodating Godot's request for them to wait, a pragmatic solution given that the path of defiance, of resistance to Godot's order to wait, is death. Yet the image of the noose – explicit in the poster, imagined in the play – is inescapable once it is introduced. The torment and joy alike that Vladimir and Estragon go through is suddenly imbued with the question which so many of Beckett's existentialist contemporaries saw as unavoidable: Why don't they kill themselves? Is it better to live there, at the side of the road? The spectre of death looms over the needs that the poster depicts and the needs that the tramps experience: the need for food, for interaction, for companionship, for *communauté*, for what Pozzo calls 'society' in the English but 'compagnie' in the French (1952: 37). These all became, under Vichy and the occupation, encoded with issues of legality, administration and, at their worst, isolation, deportation and the risk of death.

Administration and food merge together in the centrality of rations during wartime: by September of 1940, it could already take five hours of queuing to receive ration cards (Guéhenno 16 September 1940, *DDY*: 20) and, by January 1941, shops were empty more often than not (3 January 1941, *DDY*: 51). It is no surprise, then, that Beckett's works of hunger predominantly fall during the period between 1946 and 1949 when rationing remained in place in France. In 1947, Beckett put such conditions in the same tones as Guéhenno had in 1941: 'Life even for margin people like me is increasingly difficult' (SB to MacGreevy, 24 November 1947, *LSB II*: 65; cf *DDY*: 51). Rationing lingered, a wartime restriction that was used throughout the late 1940s to control France's recovery, confirming that the 'end' of the war does not so neatly map onto the announcement of liberation, that the 'end' to hunger and want does not come with the cessation of official hostilities.

Across this book, Beckett's notion of the 'provisional' reveals itself to be inherent to his and many others' experiences of the war and its aftermath, and it is a key aspect of the form of war writing his texts take. We might also see Becket's recurring tropes of the wartime everyday – hunger and impeded travel, primarily, but also the silences and absences that shadow the texts – as symptomatic of the different forms war took in the 1940s. Molloy's encounter with figures of apparent authority seeking identity papers is inescapably evocative of the multitude of checkpoints, random searches and administrative webs that descended on occupied France, likewise in the multiple occasions where Beckett's narrators in his short prose of the 1940s must establish their identity or make a case for their being in a particular location. Meanwhile, the wartime conditions of suspicion, the black market, illicit transactions, the lack of food and the desire to wait and see if someone is coming to help all undergird *Waiting for Godot*. It is these repeated motifs that allow us to locate Beckett's work within the genre of war writing while also preserving its allusive nature, a war writing specifically derived from the multitude of everyday forces which pressed themselves onto Beckett throughout the conflict in France.

3

Revolution and Revulsion
Beckett and Vichy France

During the Second World War, the collaborationist Vichy regime oversaw the collapse of the French economy, the accommodation of Nazism and the renunciation of democracy. Its public face was Marshal Phillippe Pétain. While Pétain's grip on Vichy governance itself remained unstable through the war, he was the undisputed figurehead of the regime. In this chapter, we will explore the various ways in which Beckett's works can be read in relation to Vichy discourse and the prolific propaganda campaign which persisted throughout, and even beyond, the war in France.

After the liberation of France, Pétain was put on trial alongside many of the Vichy elite and other collaborators. Pétain was charged with 'abhorring the Republic' and accused of planning with Charles Maurras the return of the French monarchy, of entering into a 'degrading collaboration' with the Nazis, and copying 'German legislation regarding Jews, Freemasons, and Communists' ('Pétain trial opens today', 1945). The defence for Pétain and Pierre Laval, one of the most active collaborationists of the Vichy government across the war, claimed that they gave up foreign Jews and other 'undesirable' peoples in order to protect the native French population, a defence used by many members of the regime who argued that Vichy guarded France against German dominance. For figures like Laval, this was untenable, known as he was to many French citizens as 'the Germans' man' (Chambrun 1984: 50). 'I hope for a German victory,' he had declared numerous times in radio broadcasts during the war (Marrus and Paxton 1995: 231). Pétain and others also claimed that they had not been aware that it was death that awaited those sent to Nazi camps.[1]

---

[1] For a discussion of the various ways in which these claims are disputed, see Michael R. Marrus and Robert O. Paxton's *Vichy France and the Jews*, 346–56. Paxton's work on Vichy's politics and history, most notably *Vichy France: Old Guard and New Order, 1940–1944* (1972), has been central to more focused work on the regime. Specific criticism devoted to the *Révolution nationale* has been a more

In a letter of 19 August 1945 sent from Saint-Lô, Beckett wrote to Thomas MacGreevy of the mood around the French trials:

> Apart from the castle crowd, full of the poor old misled man and hero of Verdun, the verdict seems to be universally oppressed. Laval, we read, has a bullet 2mm. from his heart, cancer of the stomach and a boil on his neck. (*LSB II*: 19)

Beckett was immersed in a French community keeping a close eye on the post-war events. He was also clearly aware of the propaganda discourse that surrounded Pétain, founded as it was on his status as a hero of the First World War, and the conflicting sentiments of sympathy and disgust which Pétain elicited in the years after the liberation.

Four days earlier, on 15 August, Pétain had been found guilty of treason by the High Court. He was sentenced to death, though Charles de Gaulle lowered the sentence to life imprisonment due to Pétain's age and services during the First World War. Pétain was sent to Île d'Yeu where he remained for the rest of his life, exiled just as Napoléon Bonaparte was to Saint Helena, a war hero in disgrace. He died in 1951 at the age of ninety-five. Despite this undistinguished end, Pétain's reputation as a hero of the First World War remained intact. The trials and de Gaulle's intervention confirmed this, but the trials also confirmed that Pétain had come to believe in the character of *le Maréchal* which Vichy had constructed. He appeared throughout the court proceedings in full military uniform and medals. It was a sign of how naive Pétain's leadership of Vichy had been and a recognition of the extent to which Pétain himself had come to believe the cult-like propaganda that had underpinned the regime. Beckett's sarcastic sentiment of the 'poor old misled man and hero of Verdun' is a clear rejection of Vichy's idealization of Pétain and the bankrupt notion of the term 'hero' he represented, be it in the context of collaboration or the abhorrent death tolls of the two world wars in which Pétain played leading roles. The Pétainist rhetoric of heroism (and its politically inverted doppelganger in Gaullism, as explored in Chapter 5) is as removed as possible from what Beckett in his 'German Diaries' termed 'Das notwendige Bleiben' (the necessary staying-put) and the 'acceptance

---

recent occurrence in Anglophone writing, with Julian Jackson (2001) incorporating the programme fully into his extended study of France's war years. Debbie Lackerstein's (2012) work has brought to light the particular continuities that existed between French right-wing politics in the 1930s and that of Vichy, notably in terms of political rhetoric focused on decadence and decline. French criticism began earlier, representative of which are Robert Aron (1954) and Eberhard Jäckel (1968). The publication of Pétain's speeches (1989) enabled a new generation of French critics to examine the regime.

of which is the *fundamental unheroic*' (18 January 1937, 'German Diaries'; qtd. in *GD*: 73; my emphasis). The post-war period seemed to all but confirm Beckett's suspicion of the language of heroism as Vichy's elite proclaimed their innocence in the courts.

However, five years earlier, on the brink of invasion, Pétain's appeal had not been confined to the extreme political right with which Vichy is usually associated. Many from both left and right supported Pétain during the sudden, shocking collapse of France's military in 1940. For some, any French control, superficial or otherwise, was better than the humiliation of full-scale occupation. For others, circumstances simply necessitated certain concessions. Take the case of Gertrude Stein. Stein's project between 1941 and 1943 while living in occupied France was to translate and introduce Pétain's speeches to an American public: 'I want to present to my compatriots, the words that Maréchal Pétain has spoken directly to the French people, Maréchal Pétain who in the last war saved France by a great victory, and in this war has saved them throughout their great defeat' (1996: 93). Wanda Van Dusen (1996) suggests that Stein was sincere in the support of Pétain, despite her otherwise iconoclastic habits. However, Barbara Will (2004) argues for further nuance to this conclusion, suggesting that Stein's translations and her status as a Jewish foreigner in wartime France indicate a high possibility that the project was done under duress or to publicly distract from her Jewish heritage.

Despite massive wartime support generated by a continuous propaganda campaign, the logic by which Pétain led Vichy was always somewhat paradoxical:

> The hero who symbolized resistance to Germany in the First World War called for collaboration with the hereditary enemy. . . . The proponent of National Revolution saw traditionalists and nationalists lose power to technocrats and pragmatists. The saviour of his people saw the loss of Alsace and Lorraine, 30,000 shot, 60,000 deported and 76,000 Jews sent to their death. . . . The man who heralded the family as the most important social unit and emphasised the cult of youth was a philanderer who kept trunks full of love letters, did not marry until sixty-four and had no children. The person educated by Jesuits and Dominicans who relied on Catholics for political support was essentially secular. The unideological individual of the political non-extreme right became the proponent of elaborate social and political change. The aloof private person became the centre of adulation and a cult object. . . . The embodiment of power implied at the end that discriminatory acts of the regime were performed by others. The honoured general of the First World War never understood the ideological dimensions of the Second World War, the world conflict or the true nature of the Nazi regime. (Curtis 2002: 72)

Throughout the war, the Vichy government was plagued by political squabbling, contradictory policymaking and instability. The public image of Pétain held it together, and he was supported by a prolific, nationwide propaganda campaign: the *Révolution nationale*.

Vichy's brief political power and longer-standing cultural and social influence emerged from a handful of key areas: ruralism and a turn to folklore; religious and familial reforms; the cult of the leader; and perfectionist narratives of the body, specifically the male body. Vichy constructed a history and vision of French identity that promoted the family over the individual, land over cosmopolitanism and service over freedom. Though Vichy shared the racial logic deployed by the Nazis through falsified biology and racist anthropology, the *Révolution nationale* was a uniquely French cultural and religious revolution that positioned Pétain as a model of heroic duty, spiritual salvation and the bodily incarnation of France. Vichy was to be a 'strong, hierarchical and authoritarian system' and 'the head of state was to be the key legal figure and in theory an absolute monarch'; by 1941, 'all high officials and dignitaries of the state' had to 'take an oath to the chief of state, "swear allegiance to his person" and be personally responsible to him' (Curtis 2002: 71). The nation state was defined in terms of what Pétain was supposed to represent in Vichy propaganda: a military leader with religious backing whose interest lay in restoring the dignity of the French family, French physical labour and French traditions. The cult of Pétain emphasized his spirit and body as representative of a lost tradition of nobility in France and used the military nostalgia he symbolized to plot a course of historical progress towards authoritarian liberation and away from the 'decadent' democracy of the Republic.

Révolution nationale

On 22 June 1940, Pétain saw through the signing of the armistice with the Nazis, ushering in the collaborationist government and the German occupation of France. This was also the beginning of the *Révolution nationale*, a propaganda programme which sought to overturn what Pétain and his followers saw as the weaknesses of France and its people, and to return France to a predominantly rural, agricultural and hierarchical society. Debbie Lackerstein identifies five catchwords that describe the basis of Vichy's project and what it desired to abolish or achieve: 'Decadence', 'Order', 'Action', 'Realism' and 'New Man' (2012: 8). Though this overlays a far more structured framework on to Vichy's ideas than the reality of their execution, these terms are useful for identifying the basis of the regeneration project. One of the most succinct, symbolic pieces of propaganda related to these catchwords was the rapid replacement of the Third Republic's slogan of *Liberté, Égalité, Fraternité* with Vichy's own: *Travail, Famille, Patrie* (Figure 5).

The *Révolution nationale* was based on three principal claims: it would revive the French race and nation, restore the prestige and order 'lost' in the French Revolution and expunge the 'excesses' and 'decadence' of the Third Republic and its accommodation of internationalism and 'undesirables'. According to Vichy's narrative of the war, the defeat of France in 1940 was a result of the physical, moral and spiritual weaknesses of the French race under the Third Republic.

Once Pétain's government took power, the *Révolution nationale* came into immediate effect. In a flurry of propaganda, Vichy announced a suite of social, economic and political reforms designed to bring France out from the shadow of defeat by focusing the nation on physical work, family and traditional national culture. In doing so, Vichy revealed a nationalist and authoritarian agenda akin to Nazi Germany, though differences are worth noting. Vichy was, like Nazi Germany, virulently antisemitic, and was compelled by what the proto-fascist commentator Charles Maurras described as a fight for France against the 'four

Figure 5 *Révolution nationale*, R. Vachet. n.d., c. 1940. Public domain https://commons.wikimedia.org/wiki/File:Revolution_Nationale_propaganda_poster.jpg.

confederate states of Protestants, Jews, Freemasons and foreigners' (qtd in Junyk 2013: 16). Yet, while state collaboration with Nazi Germany represented a participation in and sanctioning of extermination practices, the *Révolution nationale* itself was a public-facing campaign that pursued racial reimagining primarily through attempts to reform the values that underpinned the French nation and populace. Vichy made particular effort in its propaganda to assert the importance of communal and familial life dedicated to working the land. Lackerstein writes:

> As in some warped reflection of socialism and Communism, 'fascist man' and 'Vichy man' became the new *frères ennemis* of the Occupation. However, within these two visions there was in fact a great deal of disagreement. The French fascist man was a slave to many masters. Vichy, as in all its policies, sheltered different ideals, and ambiguities and contradictions obscured its vision. . . . [However,] even the most imitative of fascists was obliged in some degree to identify a specific Frenchness in his ideal man in the Nazi New Order. The new man had to have an ancestry rooted in French soil. (2012: 164)

Although such contradictions hampered Vichy's ambitions for a full national revolution, the rhetoric of 'French soil', rural labour and moral fortitude that comprised the most common aspects of day-to-day propaganda continued unhindered throughout the war.

The 'new man' and 'new' France were to be achieved through the positive encouragement of economic, social and cultural measures such as youth groups, labour reforms and veterans' associations, and the negative characterization of 'undesirable' bodies in France and their effects on national well-being. For the governing circles of Vichy, French racial stock was diminished because the Third Republic had celebrated the intellect rather than physical work and had 'indulged' in the trappings and comforts of modernity. This discourse of degeneration in turn gave currency to eugenic thinking that had existed in France, and Europe more broadly, since the nineteenth century. While extermination was not a central tenet of Vichy racism, institutions such as Alexis Carrel's Fondation française pour l'étude des problèmes humains (Foundation for the Study of Human Problems), established in 1941, are indicative of the more extreme eugenic views that gained legitimacy (and state funding) during the war. However, as Julian Jackson observes, '[t]he real significance of the *Fondation Carrel* was to provide a quasi-scientific legitimization of the traditionalist agenda of the National Revolution' (2001: 329). Vichy only officially promoted one 'eugenicist measure', designed to address France's low birth rate: alcohol restrictions and medical check-ups for newlywed couples to guard against venereal disease (Jackson 2001: 329). Rather than eradication, Vichy's public rhetoric declared that it would change France by 'restoring' traditional values and political structures in order to wrestle control into the hands of 'true' French citizens. Distinguishing Vichy's authoritarianism from the fascism of Nazi Germany is not to absolve Vichy of its collaboration with deportation policies that were death sentences in all but name, but to emphasize the particular nuances of the publicly authoritarian, traditionalist vision of France and the French people that the *Révolution nationale* represented.

The speed with which Vichy disseminated its propaganda following the 1940 defeat would have made the *Révolution nationale* an unavoidable presence for Beckett in both Paris and the unoccupied zone: 'the regime's propaganda was on a scale unprecedented in France', with posters blanketing city walls and village noticeboards alike (Jackson 2001: 253). Vichy took over press outlets – including Harvas, the national independent press agency – and remodelled them as dispensers of *notes d'orientation* that detailed the ambitions of the revolution and the failures of the Third Republic. Propaganda documents were distributed throughout France, not just the Vichy-controlled south. By 1942, the Nazis agreed to a Vichy-run, single company 'with exclusive rights to edit and distribute all newsreels in France' (Jackson 2001: 254–5), meaning that promotion of the *Révolution nationale* continued despite Nazi occupation of the south in the second half of the war (Jackson 2001: 255).

The ideals of Vichy were deeply entrenched in the long history of traditionalist French conservatism, the modern incarnation of which was Charles Maurras's concept of the 'real nation', an idea developed in the pages of *Action Française* and gathered in his 1941 study *La Seule France*. This was a text which attempted to defy German influence by promoting an extreme French nationalism steeped in conservative values and racial hierarchies. As Lackerstein suggests, the ideology that Maurras represented had 'exerted a broad political and strong educational influence since the end of the nineteenth century', particularly in the support of antisemitic policies (2012: 135). Maurrassian ideas sat at the heart of Vichy's project of revolution and regeneration.

Maurras was also a vocal supporter of the return to a society made up of a few elite and a large peasant population. For Maurras and Vichy more broadly, the 'real nation' was

> incarnate in the peasant, blood and soil of France and also in its pre-Revolutionary institutions, social hierarchy and classical traditions. It stood in opposition to the 'legal nation' – the 'artificial laws' and 'vague' idealism of the

Republic. Those who thought liberalism and romanticism alien and a source of national weaknesses, readily found in them the explanation for defeat in 1940. Such ideas meshed with broader conservative beliefs in core values that anchored individuals in their family, community and region and bound the people together in a strong, stable, and purposeful nation.... Though France had lost touch with its true and unique identity [Maurras and Vichy claimed], the underlying message of the National Revolution's promise of regeneration was that it would restore the real France. (Lackerstein 2012: 135–6)

Andrew Gibson has demonstrated Beckett's awareness of the French extreme conservative tradition of figures like Maurras and Maurice Barrès through his Trinity tutor Thomas Brown Rudmose-Brown. Barrès was a particularly powerful voice in the 'cult of the soil' movement, and Rudmose-Brown was a fan of his writing (Gibson 2015: 288).[2] Beckett's early-formed distrust of nationalist sentiments of all kinds, and his specific dislike of Maurras, Barrès and other figures before the war, would have left him with little tolerance for Vichy's revolution campaign.

Figure 6 'Image d'Épinal', artist unknown, n.d., *c.* 1941. Public domain https://commons.wikimedia.org/wiki/File:Imagerie_de_la_R%C3%A9volution_nationale.jpg.

---

[2] Beckett dismisses Barrès in a July 1930 letter to MacGreevy (*LSB I*: 32). MacGreevy's work on T. S. Eliot would also have meant that Beckett was familiar with Eliot's enthusiasm for Maurras's monarchism (Asher 1998).

Vichy's support of rural work and domesticity resulted in the creation of labour unions such as the Corporation paysanne (Peasant Corporation) in Paris in 1941. Like much of Vichy's governance, it was dogged by contradiction and inadequate management. The principle of the Corporation was to create a corporate-style system whereby the farming communities across France would govern all the stages of production, from tenants to landowners to workers. Vichy believed an agrarian society was physically healthier, morally superior and, ultimately, more 'French' than the France of the Republic. As widely circulated posters from the period show (Figure 6), Vichy dogma presented a rural and bucolic vision of France powered by farm labour and factory work with the elite at the top and the peasantry at the bottom. For Vichy, this was how France would recover from defeat and become ready for a Nazified Europe. The poster also shows the inscription of normative gender roles in Vichy's national vision: males working the land or in industry, and females producing many, healthy offspring.

Watt, ruralism and Vichy: 'The knotty problem'

It is likely that Vichy's vision of France would have recalled to Beckett the social and cultural politics of Ireland from the preceding decades. Seán Kennedy acknowledges as much, writing that 'certain aspects of life under Vichy would have seemed like uncanny repetitions of events in Ireland' (2010: 103). Particularly evocative would have been Vichy's emphasis on a predominantly Catholic nation steeped in tradition and folklore, as well as the attempt to reconceive France as a largely agricultural and rural economic state. In Ireland, the Irish Literary Revival of the late nineteenth and early twentieth century had seen Irish folklore and mythological histories return to the centre of national culture, a culture which was intertwined with the idealization of domesticity and the rural under the Irish Free State.[3] Like the Free State, Vichy also favoured historical figures who they could incorporate into their discourse of moral reform. Joan of Arc was a frequent example in this regard:

> The cult of Joan of Arc [saw] Joan above all as a model for moral rearmament and the enemy of the rottenness that had brought France to its knees in 1940.

---

[3] Texts like W. B. Yeats's *Fairy and Folk Tales of the Irish Peasantry* (1888) and *The Celtic Twilight* (1893) are two of the most famous examples of the folklore gathered during the Irish Revival. Beckett was staunchly critical of such practices, particularly in the 1934 essay 'Recent Irish Poetry' (*Dis*).

This was the style of official commemorations of Joan of Arc in the unoccupied zone on 10 May 1942. The key slogans imparted to 2,000 young people drawn up on the Place Bellecour at Lyon were 'restoration', 'redemption' and 'resurrection', in the sense of moral purification, not a call to arms. (Gildea 2015: 163)

Gibson argues that similarities between the Irish Free State and the Vichy regime would have been more apparent to Beckett than Kennedy suggests: 'It is worth asking whether Beckett's works of the 40s does not partly address a system of representation within which Vichy France and de Valera's Ireland seem to be, not only allegories and mirror-images of each other, but alike caught up in the development and consolidation of a new, Catholic conservatism of the 30s and 40s' (2015: 292–3). Gibson identifies this through the post-war writings, particularly the short stories of the 1940s, but Beckett's wartime novel *Watt* also contains a striking parody in which Vichy can be located.

Much of Beckett's creative production during the war, what would eventually become *Watt*, revolves around ironically reimagining the strands of modern Ireland with which he was intimately familiar, particularly the decline of Protestant rule and the cultural idealization of the rural and the folkloric. It is to this mode of identity construction that Beckett's wartime writing attends, and I suggest that *Watt* allows us to explore much of the peasant-nation ideology that preoccupied the Vichy regime. It is worth noting that Kennedy in particular has attempted in recent work to more firmly contextualize Beckett's writing of *Watt* in relation to modern Ireland, suggesting that Beckett is emphatically *not* responding to Vichy in the wartime novel, particularly with reference to the descriptions of the impoverished Lynch family, the peasant tenants which surround Mr Knott's house: 'If we cite the Lynch family in *Watt* as evidence of sectarian eugenicism, we have to situate them against the utter impotence of Mr Knott in the same work: where Catholics are too wretched to endure, Protestants are too impotent to matter. In the manuscripts, the degeneracy of all concerned is asserted relentlessly. And this is not about Vichy' (2019: 109). Despite Kennedy's careful historical recreation – particularly his negotiation of the complexities of Beckett's multi-directional parody – we might be wary of such definitive claims. Undoubtedly, the historical referents are the specific conditions of Ireland which Beckett evokes. Yet Kennedy elsewhere has made much of Beckett's ability to 'condense' historical references, to draw out or reveal parallels between historical situations which disclose the deeper structural elements of political control (2020). In this instance, Beckett's Lynch family as they appear in the *Watt* manuscripts are defined by (and satirized through) an obsession with ruralism and folklore – two tenets fundamental to both the Irish

Free State's vision of modern Ireland and to Vichy's image of the 'new' France. While the specific references are Irish, the text's satirical focus on the rural fantasies common to the Irish Free State and Vichy represents a substantial engagement with a 'once-potent political iconography' (McNaughton 2018: 20) shared by so many mid-century authoritarian ideologies.[4] *Watt* and its manuscripts may not be 'about' Vichy, but the wartime context is relevant to understanding the full force of the text's political potential and the kind of power structures it lampoons, both generically and specifically, as well as providing further context for the material Beckett produced in the specific circumstances of the war.[5]

Early in the first of the *Watt* notebooks, Beckett wrote a statement of purpose for the text he envisioned, derived from the categories of being with which he began his notes, discussed previously:

> To endeavour to formulate a modest demand as to of whom it is in question. And as to of what. To essay a tentative outline or rough-sketch of mind of same. And of body of same. To hazard a manner of enquiry or search after possible relations with other persons. And with other things. To throw out a cautious feeler with regard to the situation in time. And with respect to the situation in space. To propose with gentlemanly diffidence: the vexed question of the possession; the knotty problem of the act; the well-known tease of the suffering. (*Watt* NB1: 17r)

Remaining 'tentative[ly]' connected to the categories with which Beckett began writing (who? when? etc.), this passage anticipates some of the central themes found in *Watt* and the 'vexed question' of *what* it is actually about. The passage also intimates that 'relation' was an important starting point for Beckett's creative energies. This is figured both in terms of a subject in relation to others – 'a manner of enquiry or search after possible relations with other persons' – and a narrative attention to temporal and spatial structures through a 'cautious feeler with regard to the situation in time' followed by 'respect to the situation in space'. Surrounded by the calamity and dislocation of war, Beckett began his wartime writing by thinking about how exactly, and by what method, one person relates to another and to the world around them.

---

[4] Nazism was also obsessed with the peasant figure, most notably with reference to the *Lebensraum* policies. Italian fascism under Mussolini also celebrated the idea of the 'good peasant', a collective identity propagated by the regime as part of its attempts to move away from liberal and democratic governance (Dagnino 2016).

[5] To this extent, I am in agreement with Kennedy's earlier analysis of *Watt* and the Irish Big House (2014). Kennedy suggests that Beckett turned to an Irish setting in order to mediate his response to the politics that surrounded him during the war.

At this early stage of writing, Beckett displays a desire to abandon conventional and linear narrative progression. Likewise, he does not detail much in the way of a setting in which his 'endeavour' will take place. However, these tentative statements of intent – 'to hazard a manner of enquiry . . . to throw out a cautious feeler' – coupled with the triptych prospect of a text investigating 'possession . . . act . . . suffering' are important indications of where *Watt* will later formulate its more absurd explosions of rational progression and narrative order. The problem of Mr Knott for Watt is foreshadowed in the penultimate phrase of these notes ('the knotty problem'). Before writing of Watt and Mr Knott, though, Beckett spent much of the first manuscript notebook and accompanying typescripts exploring the life of a big house landlord named James Quin, a man beset by a 'feeling of nothingness', born 'in [him] with the first beat of his heart' (*Watt* TS: 55r).

As Julian Moynahan (1995) and Seán Kennedy have argued (2014), the *ur-Watt* offers both a record and critique of the declining but still politically active Anglo-Irish Ascendency class in the Irish Free State, particularly as formulated by W. B. Yeats and Elizabeth Bowen, as well as a more ambivalent negotiation of the persistence of the Big House literary tradition in Irish cultural consciousness. Set in modern Ireland, the early drafts work through various details of Quin's personal and family history. Much of the content was deleted or refashioned as Beckett worked on the novel, yet substantial sections inform the final version of *Watt* and appear as fragments in the 'Addenda' chapter. The second entry in the 'Addenda' on 'Art Conn O'Connery' (*W*: 215), for example, is plucked from the description of the artist who painted the portraits of Quin's father in a long section devoted to the deaths and illnesses in his family (*Watt* TS: 91r). The 'Addenda' is a record of the text's previous incarnation as a more direct sociopolitical satire of Anglo-Irish lineages and big house power.

One of the most extensive sections rewritten between the manuscripts and the final novel is devoted to the Lynch family. Living in hovels and huts, the Lynch family are among the tenants who reside in the lands around Quin's big house. The family are introduced in the published novel by way of the problem of the dog's dinner and the apparent paradox of its consumption. The published novel recounts what is required for this to occur:

> it was necessary that a dog from outside should call at the house at least once every day, on the off chance of its being given part, or all, of Knott's lunch, or dinner, or both, to eat. (*W*: 76)

Given 'the large numbers of hungry and even starving dogs with which the neighbourhood abounded, and doubtless had always abounded, for miles around, in every direction' (*W*: 76), this should not prove a problem. However, due to Mr Knott's inconsistent habits of rising and retiring, the routine of the leftovers cannot be predicted to Watt's satisfaction: 'the days on which [Mr Knott] neither rose nor retired, and so left both his lunch and his dinner untouched, were of course wonderful days, for the dog. But they were very rare' (*W*: 77). In his attempt to uncover 'by what means then were the dog and the food to be brought together' (*W*: 77), Watt accommodates the routine of the household into which he has entered and tries to encircle the process with 'solutions' and 'objections' (*W*: 81). C. J. Ackerley describes the sequence as a kind of battle for Watt: 'Watt does not ask why the scraps are given to a dog, but instead must find the right combination of meaning and words to construct a web so exhaustive that he can be sure to have imprisoned the solution to his question within it' (2004: 109). Watt's insistence on finding 'the right combination' and the novel's exhausting lists of permeations whenever Watt tries to come to any solution leaves one reeling. The addition of each detail, each permeation, also conceals the truth of the matter: the goal is not for Watt to find every possibility in some abstract application of reason, but to prevent a dog from starving. Beckett recorded his distaste with Nazism's rationalizing impulses in his 'German Diaries', and the potential for reason to be barbaric is reproduced in Watt's ignorance of the dog's anguish as he favours calculation and computation, that 'well-known tease of the suffering' foreshadowed in the early draft notes.

In the event, a solution to the food problem presents itself to Watt in the form of a local person who could bring a starving dog to the door. This figure is described, somewhat caustically, as 'an unmistakeable specimen of local indigent proliferation' who is drawn from the 'immense impoverished families [who] abounded for miles around in every conceivable direction' (*W*: 84). Of these families, it is the Lynches who, after establishing that they are the owners of the dog, are listed and detailed like 'specimen[s]' from births to deaths: 'Five generations, twenty-eight souls, nine hundred and eight years, such was the proud record of the Lynch family, when Watt entered Knott's service' (*W*: 84). The Lynches are 'wretched' in their numbers, Quin/Knott 'impotent' in his lack, to use Kennedy's terms.

In the novel, the Lynches are introduced as part of the solution to Watt's issue with the famished dog. In the manuscripts, the section devoted to the food, the dog and the Lynches is far longer, including a complex description of the Lynches' tradition of betting on a mass orgy of dogs which has the apparent aim of producing the ideal animal to eat Quin's food:

> The best breed of dog for this purpose was found, after various breeds of dog had been tried and found wanting, to be a cross between an Irish Setter and the Palestinian Retriever.... Then the work of crossing began[.] (*Watt* TS: 275r–7r)

It is soon established that the Lynches turn such 'erotic data' into a monetized 'spectacle':

> a spectacle whose naked grandeur, in order to be believed, required to be seen [the cost of which was] sixpence, reduced to fourpence in the case of the clergy of the Western Churches and members of the police force.... Sometimes on a fine evening as much as ten pounds changed hands this way. (*Watt* TS: 277r)

Representatives from both institutional religion and the state authorities are not only involved but given special treatment. The language of the scene also recalls the celebration of native 'grandeur' pursued by the artists and writers involved in the Irish Revival, a gathering of national folklore and traditions which often involved ignoring the social reality of the peasantry in favour of a mythologized wisdom and moral purity (Kelly 2008: 9–12). Similarly under Vichy, 'regionalism was synonymous with traditional values' and so 'folklore studies flourished', supporting 'ethnological work on peasants and local cultures' while 'folklorists reciprocated by creating a National Committee for Propaganda through Folklore, which published a journal, *L'Echo des provinces*, which extolled the National Revolution and the role of folklore in it'. The state 'also supported regional folklore museums' and 'mobilized artists to paint idealized pictures of daily life among peasants and artisans' (Christofferson and Christofferson 2006: 48).

Written mostly while Beckett was hiding in Roussillon, the dog copulation scene involves detailed descriptions of the systems of betting and dog breeding, as well as speculation on the origins of the 'spectacle':

> What mind, whose mind, first meditating on these things, these habits of love, thus first assembled them, for the delectation of generations to come? Quin's? A Lynch's? The same that solved the problem of how Quin's food should be prepared? The same that solved the problem of how Quin's food should be given to the dog? Or another, in contact with the world of Quin's food, of Quin's dogs, of Quin's servants? Or another, not of Quin's world, but of another, or of another age perhaps, or of another country, or any two, or all three, in a word, an outsider? (*Watt* TS: 293r)

The enquiry takes a decidedly historical turn that attempts to pin the origins of the tradition on the arrival of Quin and the subsequent 'rise of the Lynch family':

> Local tradition dated this spectacle from the coming of Quin to the neighbourhood and the rise of the Lynch family. Before the coming of Quin to the neighbourhood, and the rise of the Lynch family, which dated from the coming of Quin to the neighbourhood, no such spectacle had ever been held in the neighbourhood, according to local tradition. (*Watt* TS: 294r–5r)

Quin and the Lynches are intertwined, the elite and the tenant peasants each depending upon one another. The narrator then notes the historical details of the 'spectacle':

> In the annals, or archives, open at certain hours of the morning and the afternoon to inspection by the public, of the places in question no reference to the Quin or Lynch spectacle has ever been found, nor was there any allusion, in the local tradition dealing with the Quin or Lynch spectacle, to any spectacle of a similar kind existing elsewhere. (*Watt* TS: 295r)

The passage expands on larger and larger spheres of possibility for records of the 'spectacle', widening the search for a trace of the tradition's origin, emphasizing that nowhere else participated in these rituals 'any longer':

> In no part of the British Islands did anything remotely resembling the spectacle in question any longer exist, though in certain areas of that gallant expanse, and notably in the Hardy country, traces of its having done so in comparatively recent times survived. But from these scanty and unreliable memorials, of whi[c]h some were written, some oral and not a few anal, but little information was to be obtained. Their tone, in every case, was that tone of impatience, disgust and even anger so often employed by British Islanders when writing, speaking or otherwise emitting their opinion of such alien entertainment as flea-racing, bullfighting and belly-dancing. (*Watt* TS: 295r)

The text parodies the fetishization of the practices of the rural class, and roundly mocks 'anal' histories (a pun suggesting both fastidious detail and non-generative historical accounts) that arose from passionate sentiments of 'disgust' and 'anger' at classes or peoples deemed 'alien'.

In similar detail, 'European mainland', 'Africa, Asia, Australia, America and the islands great and small', 'and the Poles' are all reported to retain 'no trace' of the spectacle (*Watt* TS, 295r–6r). In a parody of the Irish Literary Revival's penchant for using myth in the construction of Irish history – the legends of Cuchulain, for example – the text also cites the mythological lands of 'Pelasgia', the supposed origin of the first humans in a number of Greek myths, 'Atlantis' and 'Hy-Brasil', a mythical island of Irish folklore that Beckett first alludes to in *Dream of Fair to Middling Women* and which gives its name to Jack B. Yeats's 1937 painting *A Race in Hy Brasil* (Ackerley and Gontarski 2006: 267). Collected in W. B. Yeats's *Folk and Fairy Tales of the Irish Peasantry*, a poem by Gerald Griffin entitled 'Hy Brasail – The Isle of the Blest' tells the tale of a man who sets sail from 'Ara', an ancient name for the area of County Tipperary, in search of the 'blest' 'Hy Brasail' that is said to be 'a region of sunshine and rest' (1888: 212). As in the tales of Atlantis, the isle does not materialize and the man 'died on the waters, away, far away'. Yeats references the island in his *Mythologies*, writing of the omens to be found in Drumcliff, which include the 'dread portent' of seeing Hy-Brasil on the horizon. A place where one may 'enjoy the conversation of Cuchulain and his heroes', it is nevertheless ill fortune to spy off the coast (1998: 92). By contrast, in *Dream*, Beckett parodies the utopian notion of the island: 'Beyond Cobh across the harbor fireflies are moving in Hy-Brasil's low hills, the priests are abroad there with bludgeons' (*Dream*: 140).

Throughout the dog sequence in the *Watt* manuscripts, Beckett produces a hyperbolic and perverse fiction that imagines an exaggerated reality of rural life which runs counter to any idealized vision of pastoral culture, one that indulges in a stylized formulation of the Irish peasantry which the Irish Revival and the Free State alike imagined at the base of their political foundations. Likewise, Vichy's bedrock was the image of local artisan-peasant workers labouring, rearing children and sharing tales and myths of the region with one another, and these were captured and preserved in images, museums and journals which became widespread across wartime France. If the sequence is difficult to square with the war years, so steeped as it is in parody of the Irish milieu it evokes, it nevertheless provides a stringent satire of the political mechanisms which attributed mystical value to the peasant classes. Instead of attending to the real economic and social needs that such classes required, the traditionalist, conservative nationalisms of Vichy and the Irish Free State conjured moral imperatives out of myth, fetishizing the peasantry so that they could be patronized and ignored. The 'spectacle' of social uplift made by heralding the folkloric concealed exploitation and, in the case of Vichy, a debasement in the value of labour as the majority of produce from French farming made its way to Germany as part of the Nazi occupation payments.

'Thy name be hallowed': The cult of Pétain

Vichy's prolific propaganda campaigns and the regime's mark on mid-century France can also be felt in Beckett's post-war writing. By the late 1940s, France had changed significantly for Beckett. 'All the wrong things, all the wrong way. It is hard sometimes to feel the France that one clung to, that I still cling to' (*LSB II*: 72), he wrote to Thomas MacGreevy on 4 January 1948, as he continued to grieve for the nation that had attracted him in the 1930s. In this section, I look to the prose of the 1940s and 1950s to examine Beckett's negotiation of the lingering presence of Vichy after the liberation. Though a handful of scholars have illuminated much of Beckett's life and works through a French wartime critical lens, the post-war prose's negotiations of the ideology of Vichy and its material propaganda remain an under-considered area.[6] In part, this might be due to the apparent historical disparity between Vichy's existence as an active regime and Beckett's writing of the post-war texts themselves: Why would Beckett's work continue to negotiate, mock, even resist political ideas that were no longer dominating the political landscape of France under the restored Republic? Why, in short, would Beckett continue to reference a regime that had been defeated? In the first instance, Beckett's creative imagination throughout his career makes use of all manner of sources combined in myriad ways. More directly, the end of the war, the moment in which Beckett began writing his post-war works, was a period of immense upheaval and tension. The occupiers and the Vichy regime were gone but not forgotten, and Beckett returned to a nation much transformed by the war: 'All the wrong things, all the wrong way' (*LSB II*: 72).

The nation had changed irreparably as a result of Vichy's governance. Though by 1942 the regime had become largely powerless due to further Nazi occupation, Vichy continued to confront the populace with racist and nationalist dogma until the end of the war. As H. R. Kedward argues, the rapid accommodation and eventual indifference towards Vichy's 'revolution' during the war represented a disquieting effect of the war on the French people at the time (1993: 5). Vichy's was a vision of France which Beckett would have detested for its authoritarian nationalism, reactionary traditionalism and overt collaboration. It was also a version of France in which he could be actively persecuted for his politics, social connections and avant-garde cultural sensibilities. This is not an atmosphere that simply dissipates.

Vichy was a manifestation of the pre-war conservative French political classes' hostility to the liberal, progressive, intellectual culture of the Third Republic, but it also arose out the desire for stability brought about by the nation's collapse in 1940. The allure of the authoritarian focus on order makes it ideal for a crisis like the defeat in 1940, and Vichy propaganda presented its authoritarian nationalism as a source of peace. Beckett was all too aware of that allure and

---

[6] See work by Lois Gordon (1998), Marjorie Perloff (2005), Laura Salisbury (2014), Andrew Gibson (2010a, 2010b, 2013, 2014, 2015) and Emilie Morin (2017). As with Perloff, Salisbury and Gibson, I focus on the prose here. Despite the wealth of work done on Beckett's theatre, there is much scope for an extended, close examination of the early drama in the context of wartime and post-war France. Hannah Simpson's work (2020a, 2020b) is particularly significant in this regard.

its expression in propaganda, of the Nazi 'litany' (*GD*: 86) he heard recited by citizens in Germany in the late 1930s, of the appeal such narratives could have in times of chaos and how they could influence thought and values.

Beckett's works present an often-ironic confrontation with the 'litany' that underpinned the cult of Pétain that propped up the regime. With its unabashed deification of a military leader, the religiosity of this cult was particularly suitable for Beckettian mockery. In many ways, Pétain's leadership was heralded as the return of an empowered monarch sanctioned by the French Catholic Church. For the regime's supporters, a modern incarnation of the divine right of kings was a solid foundation on which the 'new' France could be built. As Erna Paris writes,

> Up to and including the Nazi occupation and the creation of Vichy France, the French Catholic Church was a bedrock of nationalist ideology: as an institution, it was delighted with Philippe Pétain, since the stated values of the new regime [*Travail, Famille, Patrie*] complemented its teachings. 'These three words are our own,' applauded Cardinal Gerlier the day of Pétain's first visit to Lyons. 'France is Pétain, Pétain is France.' (2002: 91)

Pétain was the figurehead of Vichy's revolution, presented as the divine saviour in France's hour of need. Praise for the marshal appeared daily in press and on the radio, repeated like a mantra with an emphasis on his health, strength and paternal image – 'He is a fine old man, strong and straight as a Druid's tree. He is Marshal Pétain, our Marshal, Father of all the children of France' (qtd. in Sowerwine 2001: 179). France became the fatherland, Pétain its father. Busts appeared in every town hall, and he was 'the first political figure since Napoleon III to have his portrait on postage stamps and coins' (Sowerwine 2001: 179). Life in France involved handling Pétain's visage on a daily basis, probably one source for Beckett's doodle of Pétain in profile in the *Watt* notebooks. Napoleon III was the last emperor of France, whose defeat in 1870 ushered in the Third Republic; wartime propaganda implied Pétain would pick up where the emperor left off. Beckett was familiar with the Napoleonic lineage in which Vichy placed Pétain, given that Beckett's work on *Dream* 'began with assiduous work on military history and the life of Napoleon Bonaparte' (*PI*: 29).

During the war, Pétain was celebrated with religious fervour. In June 1941, on the anniversary of Pétain's coming to power, a hymn called 'La Française: Hymne au Maréchal' was performed live in Paris and broadcast across the nation (Sowerwine 2001: 179). The Catholic Church made multiple declarations of support for Pétain. In his honour, Saint Philip's Day replaced Labour Day during the war. As Robert Paxton notes, the scale of this cult of personality was colossal:

> No other figure in recent French history has inspired the same hagiographic *imagerie d'Epinal*: the children's coloring books, the songs, the paraphrase of the Lord's Prayer – all the symbolism of a paternal and once-victorious savior in whom the French people tried to rediscover a lost greatness. (1966: 154)

Vichy's paternalistic and religious characterization of Pétain cemented his influence over France, presenting him as a strong and stable leader who could both guide France and collaborate with the occupying Nazi forces.

The 'paraphrase of the Lord's Prayer' is of particular interest. Unsurprisingly, Pétain readily approved of it (Sowerwine 2001: 179). The prayer was published in the national press and broadcast on the radio:

> Notre Père qui êtes / à notre tête, / Que votre nom soit glorifié / Que votre règne arrive / Que votre volonté soit faite / Sur la terre pour qu'on vive, / Demeurez sans retour / Notre pain de chaque jour. / Redonnez / l'existence / à la France, / Ne nous laissez pas retomber / Dans le vain songe / Et le mensonge / Et délivrez-nous du mal / O Maréchal ! (qtd. in Mathis 1988: 311)
>
> (Our Father who is / At our head / May your name be glorified, / May your reign come, / May your will be done / On this earth in order that we live, / Bring home to us / Our daily bread / Give back / existence / to France, / Don't let us fall back / On the vain dream / And the lie, / And deliver us from evil / Oh Marshall!)

The prayer is indicative of the larger culture of heroism devoted to the marshal that filtered through wartime Vichy discourse, one that firmly placed Pétain at the 'head' of the nation (recall Figure 6 in this chapter) and celebrated his position as the father of a glorious 'reign' that would do away with the 'vain dream' of the Third Republic.

Throughout Beckett's post-war writing, there is a stringent rejection of institutional religion and appeals to religious authority. *The Unnamable* includes religion in the 'lectures' to which the narrator has been subjected where the divine is positioned as part of a hierarchy of power dynamics: 'They also gave me the low-down on God. They told me I depended on him' (*U*: 8). We might look too to Moran's section of *Molloy* after he has begun his steady 'degeneration' in his pursuit of Molloy, soon becoming 'rapidly unrecognizable' (*M*: 178). This process accelerates as Moran reflects upon the 'journey home' which he undertook due to his devotion to the quasi-religious prospect of 'Youdi's command' (*M*: 174). A ghostly image of mass death briefly threatens the narrative as Moran 'pass[es] over in silence the fiends in human shape and the phantoms of the dead' that try to prevent him 'from getting home'. He then turns to the 'questions of a theological nature' which 'preoccupied' him (*M*: 174). These questions are a parody of theological seriousness, indicating the collapse of Moran's connection to his religious sensibilities, signified earlier in his concern over missing Mass (*M*: 98).

One example of Moran's spiritual transformation is found in his 'pretty quietist Pater':

> Our Father who art no more in heaven than on earth or in hell, I neither want nor desire that thy name be hallowed, thou knowest best what suits thee. Etc. The middle and the end are very pretty. (*M*: 175)

As Andy Wimbush has shown, 'Beckett lifted the prayer from a satirical text written in the seventeenth century, at the height of the Christian quietist controversy . . . by the essayist Jean de La Bruyère (1645–96)' in which the author 'attempt[s] to make the quietists look like confused and immoral heretics' (2015: 441). Wimbush links Beckett's use of the prayer with his affection for quietist ideas (largely via Arthur Schopenhauer's enthusiasm for the doctrine), an affection encapsulated in the humour of the satire, and he identifies a strong aesthetic component to Beckett's interest in quietism, one that centres on the decomposition of the self and the incoherence of being. In conjunction, however, there is in Moran's encroaching quietism a rejection of the kind of orthodoxy that Vichy called on in its vision of French revival, particularly in Moran's move away from the rituals and habits of holy observance. Sending up a mode of theological practice 'supersaturated with ideological investment' (McNaughton 2018: 14), Moran's spiritual decline scrutinizes the general structures of faith and doctrine, yet it is also charged with the specific historical resonances of Vichy's assimilation of religious practices and language in its deification of Pétain as the father-god, the *pater*, of France.[7]

The context of Vichy's bid for spiritual revolution through Pétain amplifies the satirical nature of Beckett's adoption of a quietist 'pater' in his writing. Drawing on the historical associations of heretical religious activity, the quietest satire rejects the kind of cod-spirituality adopted in Vichy's Pétainism. Moran's prayer certainly points to a clear affinity between Beckett's work and the unconventional Christianity of the quietist heresy – particularly around the disintegration of the self into God – yet it also produces a double sense of critique and satire. On the

---

[7] The French version of the prayer in *Molloy* begins 'Dieu' (God) in a direct address to the divine that forgoes the paternalistic metaphor. The conventional Lord's Prayer in French begins 'Notre Père', so there are grounds for reading Beckett's translation choice as another example of his manipulation of historical references when moving between languages (as we see, for example, in the Roussillon references in *Waiting for Godot*).

one hand, it is a parody of the Lord's Prayer itself, a critical part of the communal activity of Christian faith which returned to the centre of French culture in a particular conservative Catholic form under Vichy. On the other, it is a parody of the quietist tradition. As Wimbush writes, the prayer is from the fifth dialogue of La Bruyère's text: 'the penitent tells the director: "I made myself a version of the Lord's Prayer in our style. I would like to say it, adjusting it to our principles and our doctrine"' (2015: 442). (Incidentally, the 'fifth dialogue' quotation serves as a neat summary of the deification of Pétain and Vichy's religious propaganda, adjusting French Catholicism to its 'principles' and 'doctrines'.) As well as denoting the aesthetic and philosophical ideas that are clearly shared between quietist faith and Beckett's poetics, the appeal in *Molloy*, even in satirical form, to a *heretical* form of Christian doctrine enacts a rejection of religious orthodoxy. In historical terms, this becomes a rejection of the dominance of particular kinds of religious doctrine, such as the modes of state control employed by Vichy through its deification of Pétain.

Under Vichy and the occupation, state religion became another form of control:

> The people of France, citizens no longer, were subjects now, and it was with the rituals of *Action Française* and the Catholic Church, and using the words they used, that Pétain was welcomed to power. He told the French that they had lost 'their spirit of sacrifice', which had been replaced by a decadent 'spirit of pleasure'. It was now time for 'atonement for their sins'. (Callil 2007: 200)

Such atonement would come through the moral worth ascribed to physical labour, traditional domesticity and unquestioning patriotism. The Pétainist Lord's Prayer not only celebrated Pétain's celebrity, then, but also condensed political and religious authority into religious practices which were then made part of Pétain's cult. Like Youdi to Moran, the prayer is the handing down of a command which is to be obeyed and feared. While Pétain's *Pater Noster* deifies his name and being, Beckett's cribbed 'pretty . . . Pater' offers the simple, blasphemous rebuke to the 'Father' it addresses: 'I neither want nor desire that thy name be hallowed' (*M*: 175).

Strength and weakness: Vichy's oaks

The cult of Pétain emphasized the religious elements of Pétain's 'true' French spirit. It also attached to him images of strength and solidity which were rooted in the French past through symbols which drew on the natural landscape of the nation, particularly the forests.

Under Vichy, the woodland became 'a link between France's past and present' and contributed to the image of an 'illustrious and traditional' nation in which the population could live harmoniously without the trappings of modernity (Pearson 2008: 56). The forests were also used in the propaganda promotion of Pétain. Widely disseminated posters, press images and leaflets, as well as literature, particularly books for children, were circulated with images of Pétain visiting and enjoying France's forests. The oak tree was of particular importance to Pétainist propaganda as it represented longevity and strength. Oak leaves featured on *Etat française* currency minted during the war and can be seen encircling Pétain in posters like Figure 6. In the children's book *La Belle histoire d'un chêne* (1943), Yvonne Estienne 'compared France to a forest that had just been struck by a fierce storm: "all the forest is unhappy. It looks for help"' (qtd. in Pearson 2008: 59). Luckily, a 'tall, beautiful oak, already old but so valiant . . . stood strong to protect everybody. And this tall, beautiful oak was called Marshal Pétain' (qtd. in Pearson 2008: 59). At Tronçais, in a ceremony organized by Jacques Chevalier, Vichy's minister for public instruction, Pétain 'christened' a huge oak tree with a plaque with the inscription 'Chêne Maréchal Pétain' (Pearson 2008: 59).

Beckett subjects the overcharged symbology of the oak tree to an inversion via a French literary figure well loved by Vichy itself: the Huguenot writer-soldier Agrippa d'Aubigné. In 'The Calmative', written in December 1946, the ambling narrator finds himself in a 'grove':

> little by little I got myself out and started walking with short steps among the trees, oh look, trees! The paths of other days were rank with tangled growth. I leaned against the trunks to get my breath and pulled myself forward with the help of boughs. Of my last passage no trace remained. They were the perishing oaks immortalized by d'Aubigné. It was only a grove. The fringe was near, a light less green and kind of tattered told me so, in a whisper. Yes, no matter where you stood, in this little wood, and were it in the furthest recess of its poor secrecies, you saw on every hand the gleam of this pale light, promise of God knows what fatuous eternity. Die without too much pain, a little, that's worth your while. Under the blind sky close with your own hands the eyes soon sockets, then quick into carrion not to mislead the crows. (*ECEF*: 20)

In the French, the reference for the oaks is even clearer:

> petit à petit je sortis et me mis à marcher, à petits pas, au milieu des arbres, tiens, des arbres. Une végétation folle envahissait les sentiers d'autrefois. Je m'appuyais aux troncs, pour reprendre haleine, ou, saisissant une branche, me tirais en avant. De mon dernier passage il ne restait plus trace. C'étaient les chênes périssants

de d'Aubigné. Ce n'était qu'un bosquet. La lisière était proche, un jour moins vert et comme dégueuillé le disait, tout bas. Oui, où qu'on se tint, dans ce petit bois, et fût-ce au plus profond de ses pauvres secrets, de toutes parts on voyait luire ce jour plus pâle, gage de je ne sais quelle sotte éternité. Mourir sans trop de douleur, un peu, cela en vaut la peine, fermer soi-même devant le ciel aveugle ses yeux à caver, puis vite passer charogne, pour pas que les corbeaux se méprennent. (1958: 41–2)

Various Beckett scholars identify the 'chênes périssants de d'Aubigné' as the 'chênes superbes' in d'Aubigné's *Les Tragiques* (Gontarski and Ackerley 2006: 29–30; Perloff 2005: 19). However, the 'ugly and macabre' (Greene 2002: 31) countryside scene evoked in lines 81 to 104 of d'Aubigné's earlier *Printemps* likely lies behind Beckett's 'perishing oaks':

Tout cela qui sent l'homme à mourir me convie,
   En ce qui est hideux je cherche mon confort;
   Fuyez de moi, plaisirs, heurs, espérance et vie,
   Venez, maux et malheurs et désespoir et mort!

Je cherche les déserts, les roches égarées,
   Les forêts sans chemin, les chênes périssants,
   Mais je hais les forêts de leurs feuilles parées,
   Les séjours fréquentés, les Chemins blanchissants . . .

Heureux quand je rencontre une tête séchée,
   Un massacre de cerf, quand j'oy les cris des fans;
   Mais mon âme se meurt de dépit asséchée,
   Voyant la biche folle aux sauts de ses enfants.

(1972: 6)

(All that smells of man invites me to die,
   I seek for comfort in whatever is hideous.
   Flee from me, pleasures, good fortune, hope and life,
   Come, evils and mischances and despair and death!

I seek deserts, unfamiliar peaks,
   Pathless forests, perishing oaks
   But I despise forests whose leaves are adorned,
   Frequented retreats, whitened paths . . .

I am happy to come upon a dried skull,
   The massacre of a stag when I can hear the cries of fawns,
   But my soul perishes with embittered spite
   If I see the doe mad with pleasure at the gambols of her offspring.)

(trans. in Greene 2002: 31–2)

While Becket would certainly be attracted to the frenzied erotica of the verse with its echoes of Petrarch's nature poems and Sir Thomas Wyatt's sonnets, it is the association with a forest decaying, the 'chênes périssants', which underpins its reworking in 'The Calmative' into a scene of ethereal rot.

The dying forest also holds historical and political charge, as does the specificity of the perishing oaks of d'Aubigné in a Vichy and post-Vichy context. Kristen Stromberg Childers suggests that d'Aubigné enjoyed remarkable popularity under Vichy with his emphasis on family and lineage. He was paired with figures like Montaigne during school lessons to attest to the ideals of 'community and continuity': 'The association of great literary figures with the cause of the family enabled the Vichy regime to ground its own ideology in an illustrious and traditional past, free of the taint of present-day concerns' (2003: 96). Authors like d'Aubigné represented 'lessons from former centuries that could be profitably impressed on young minds in secondary school' (Stromberg Childers 2003: 96). Those 'young minds' and the literature and ideology they were fed were the remit of Beckett's friend Georges Pelorson during his tenure working on youth propaganda for Vichy. As Jacques Ellul writes, common to all forms of 'totalitarian attitude' is the belief that 'educational methods play an immense role in political indoctrination' and that 'one must utilize the education of the young to condition them to what comes later' (1973: 13).

For Vichy, the forest symbolized the vitality of 'true France'. In Beckett's adaptation of d'Aubigné, it is death, decay and the hiding place of an elderly narrator. Perloff astutely identifies this as Beckett's 'signature' method of 'embedding complex allusion' into his text (Perloff 2005: 19), a process which takes the past as a lens through which the present can be navigated and examined. 'Like d'Aubigné', Perloff writes,

> Beckett was a minority Protestant in a Catholic country (first Ireland, then France), and the 'perishing oaks' of sixteenth century France are once again the victims, this time of the Nazi terror, the irony being that although a 'religious' group, the Jews, is now being persecuted, in the current war, religion has been replaced by a relentlessly secular political ideology. (2005: 19)

Where Perloff reads the withering trees as symbolic of Nazi racial violence, I suggest that the specificity of the oak tree and the reference to d'Aubigné combine into a substantial riposte to the specific imagination used in Vichy's National Revolution. D'Aubigné's poem is focused not on the celebration of strength but on an indulgence in decay and an ecstatic anger at the joys of 'offspring'. Vichy celebrated the role of the family through figures like d'Aubigné, and Pétain above all was the strong oak tree supporting the regime. However, as we have seen, Vichy's ideology was comprised of a 'mixture of intentions and contradictions that characterized the National Revolution' (Munholland 1994: 806). Pétain's image was no exception, that supposedly strong oak who was privately in constant proximity to 'désespoir et mort'. The contradictions and ironies which accompanied Vichy's propaganda are preserved in Beckett's dying forest in 'The Calmative' as he deploys Vichy's cultural resources against its own aspirations. Beckett finds in d'Aubigné's own work the means to diminish the ideals which Vichy deployed: decay not strength, decline not continuity. Conscious or otherwise, Beckett's attribution of death to the 'perishing oaks' also captures the fate of Pétain's own christened oak tree. In 1943, 'a resistor reportedly scaled [the] oak, replacing the plaque bearing the Marshall's name with the following: Chêne Gabriel Peri / French Patriot / Shot by the Nazis. Consequently, Pétain's oak is now officially known as the "Oak of Resistance"' (Pearson 2008: 61–2). In *Mercier et Camier*, the specific practice of using a tree for political commemoration is evoked with a darkly humorous reversal when Mercier and Camier find themselves in a square with a 'sign rudely nailed to the bole' of a beech tree which commemorates 'a Field Marshal of France peacefully named Saint-Ruth' who was killed by a cannonball fired from his own troops (*MC*: 5).[8] In the course of their historical echoes, Beckett's works often recall the political doubling that the war in France produced: symbols could be adopted by both Vichy and the Resistance simultaneously or in succession. Joan of Arc is again a useful touchstone here, as are the writings of Charles Péguy, a 'common point of reference for resisters, Vichy conservatives, and Paris-based fascists alike' (Jackson 2001: 4). For some, the forests represented the ideals of strength and tradition championed by Vichy; for others, they were symbols of resistance, hiding the *maquis* who hunted collaborators and occupying forces.

In a certain sense, Beckett shared a historical perspective with Vichy, looking to the past to understand the present, and particularly to moments of comparable historical pressure in which multiple versions of national or religious identity underscored conflict. Where Vichy sought strength in the past, though, Beckett most often finds patterns of violence and logical absurdity brought to consciousness through referents which reveal decay and weakness, as seen in 'The Calmative', or the futility of reason and logic, as in the irrational core of the Quin/Knott household and Watt's attempts to bring order to his experiences.

---

[8] We return to Saint Ruth in Chapter 6. I use Beckett's translation here. The scene is preserved despite Beckett's radical streamlining of the text when working on the translation in the 1970s.

While Pétain and Vichy looked to the past for symbols, strength and stability, Beckett only finds the (often blackly humorous) contradictions which reveal the ironies and failings at the heart of traditionalist, nationalist, history-facing projects, including Vichy and its 'Druid tree', Pétain.

Vichy masculinity and Beckett's bodies

Images of oak-like strength were vital to Vichy, as they so often are for the authoritarian imagination. Throughout the *Révolution nationale* propaganda cycles, Pétain's government sought to regenerate the French nation through reforms that would inculcate its three principles of *Travail, Famille, Patrie* into the heart of French life. As I have observed, although the Vichy government became largely a puppet cabinet after 1942, the ideology and rhetoric of the revolution remained in place as Vichy prepared France for a Europe under Nazi rule. The French, and particularly French men, were to be strong not only in spirit and patriotism but also in physicality. Vichy cherished the ideal of a redefined French male body, one that was strong, healthy, reproductive and devoted to physical labour and patriotic duties. It was to be 'more national, more virile, more human', Pétain declared, and unhindered by the weaknesses of modernity that had, according to Vichy, caused the 1940 defeat (qtd. in Gerber 2018: 11).

Against this backdrop, there is something oddly defiant, even resistant, about Beckett's post-war depictions of physically debilitated and suffering bodies, both on stage and in his prose works. Many of Beckett's bodies are unsettling, upsetting even, in their lived suffering, and the disquiet caused by descriptions of figures like the limbless narrator of *The Unnamable* contrasts with how visible the strong, athletic body was in Vichy propaganda. Critical attention has revealed much about the importance of the body to Beckett's aesthetic, illuminating how the author's work reflects the extent to which 'the body has become central to numerous artistic, critical, ethical, scientific and medical discourses and practices' (McMullan 2010: 2).[9] Like the pained, limping or immobile figures in works such as *Waiting for Godot* and *Endgame*, the bodies in Beckett's prose trilogy of the 1950s are presented with an emphasis on physical limitation, weakness and absent body parts: physical forms which parallel the increasing

---

[9] McMullan's work joins Ulrika Maude's (2009) as touchstones in explorations of the affective possibilities of Beckett's use of the body. This specific aspect of Beckett's drama has been re-emphasized in Charlotta P. Einarsson's work (2017).

instability of linguistic expression in the texts.¹⁰ These bodies, according to Shane Weller, 'resist the very principle of identity that would govern every system, not least the totalitarian systems that came to dominate the century', (2009: 32). Such a resistance emerges because 'on closer inspection, the unruliness of the body also forms its dissident and individuating power' (Maude 2009: 112), a process in which Beckett's bodies exemplify what Rachel Russell identifies more broadly as the 'demands of rapidly changing cultural norms and values' (2000: 108) in the construction of the modern body against normative, traditional parameters. My concerns in this section are the historical conditions of Vichy as a factor in the 'unruliness' of the bodies in Beckett's post-war prose. The trilogy's extreme imaginings of physical decay offer a rejection of normative expectations of health and physical fitness which, when reinserted into the historical contexts of Vichy and its propaganda campaigns, translates into a potentially defiant politics of the body that disrupts the discourse of bodily health that Vichy articulated in nationalist and authoritarian terms.

Together, *Molloy*, *Malone Dies* and *The Unnamable* chart a degeneration of language and narrative which is mirrored in the steady decay of the narrators' physical forms as they reach towards a silence of mind, body and speech in order to 'finish dying', as Molloy puts it (*M*: 3). The still prevalent critical position on these texts is of a philosophical kind which suggests that they exemplify a 'writerly practice that makes a virtue of impasse, failure, and the aporetic method of discouraging reduction to the identical' (Moorjani 2015: 19). However, a historically conscious analysis yields its own productive insights when we configure Beckett's 'virtue of impasse' as a negotiation of political conditions, including the social and cultural narratives at the core of Vichy's propaganda.¹¹ Returning us to the idea of the equation of 'baseness' and 'seriousness' in the everyday, the impaired bodies of Beckett's post-war writing articulate a resistance to Vichy moralizing by producing what Andrew Gibson calls 'a kind of weird, ironical hymn to incapacity, to the "second-rate" or "defective" body, the base, sometimes outrageously or hilariously base body' (2015: 295). In presenting

---

[10] The nature of prose as a specific medium for Beckett's linguistic degeneration has invited a series of engagements, particularly in terms of the evocations of death and the dissolution of meaning that the texts enact. Christopher Ricks (1993) sees Beckett's syntactical experimentation as charting the question of personality's relationship to death. Kathryn White (2011) develops this idea, seeing decay as the primary element of the Beckettian aesthetic. Elsewhere, preceding Maude's incorporation of the question of technology, Yoshiki Tajiri (2007) examines the Beckettian body through a framework of physical and linguistic prosthesis which reads Beckett's rendering of organs and senses as integral aspects of the modernist understanding of the body as a site of conflict.

[11] Historically orientated studies of the novels include Patrick Bixby's (2009) analysis of the trilogy and the postcolonial novel genre, and James McNaughton's (2018) examination of *The Unnamable* as a formal response to the Holocaust and other mass-murder events.

various images of bodily 'incapacity', Beckett's texts confront the conflation of physical strength with moral and social value. The ideal French body under Vichy was one such image, and Beckett's rejection of such an archetype manifests in the decaying bodies of his trilogy. To demonstrate more fully the political and historical significance of the body in Beckett's post-war prose, this section considers the trilogy within the context of the pervasive propaganda of masculinity disseminated by the Vichy regime in its drive for national renewal, positioning the male bodies in Beckett's trilogy against the regime's images of the 'perfect' French physical form, an ideal which has its origins in French preoccupations with racial degeneration that emerged after the First World War. Read in the context of Vichy's renewal campaign, Beckett's move from the limping Molloy to the bed-bound Malone and finally to the physically limbless figure of *The Unnamable* offers a startling rejection of the pervasive image of the virile male body that circulated in wartime France.

'Health, courage, discipline': Vichy masculinity

According to Vichy, the Third Republic oversaw a radical debasement of French masculinity. As Joan Tumblety writes, the regime's 'observations of poor male physique routinely functioned not only as an explanation for military defeat but as a rationale for a certain model of national renewal' (2012: 205). This preoccupation with the male body was also at the centre of the Vichy campaign for improving the nation's birth rate and raising healthy offspring. As we have seen, children were to be the cornerstone of the nation's regeneration, taught to be active members of the state from birth. Boys were to be athletic and ready for physical work. Girls were to be trained in domestic labour and child-rearing. All would grow up with France as their 'fatherland', labour as their service to the nation and family as the drive for ethical and moral choices. Paul Baudoin, minister of foreign affairs under Vichy, declared that children were 'the hope of the new France, because adults are not ready to make a blank slate of their values. Children are the France of tomorrow. To remake France is above all else to remake French children' (qtd. in Gerber 2018: 9). Children were taught that physical exercise led to moral fortitude and encouraged to aspire to careers involving physical labour.

The regenerated version of French masculinity that would produce these new generations of French children was to be virile, muscular and active, a vision informed both by classical notions of the male form and by an emphasis on the heroic French bodies of the First World War. While French conservatism had long been obsessed with racial decline in the light of modern conveniences like the car and industrial automation, the view that the French male body had failed against Nazi strength spanned the political spectrum: 'the majority of the troop officers were young reserve men recruited among the bourgeoisie, who manifested the defects of their class', wrote Pierre Cot (1941: 439), air minister for the leftist Popular Front. 'The soldiers of 1939', Cot declared, 'were not worth those of 1914; they did not oppose the invader with that stubborn resistance which marked the defenders of Warsaw, the Greek and Yugoslavian troops, or which the Russian soldiers show' (1941: 446–7). In this regard, Vichy's proposed *homme nouveau* was not a solely conservative concern. However, it was under Vichy that this cruel summation of the suffering experienced by French soldiers on the battlefields in 1940 was used to articulate the need for a new France rooted in traditional national values. Once again, these values were supposedly symbolized most potently by the 'oak-like' figure of Pétain. Pétain's own radio broadcasts and speeches often returned to the 'problem' with modern French bodies: '[W]e are setting out to destroy the fateful prestige of a purely bookish pseudo-culture, guide to idleness, and generator of uselessness.... The development of a sporting youth will address part of this problem' and 'give back to the French race health, courage, discipline' (Pétain 1940, qtd. in Tumblety 2012: 210).

Pétain's focus on the importance of physical activity and a 'sporting youth' over intellectual pursuits was also not unique to the regime. It had its origins in the French physical culturists of the early twentieth century who emphasized bodily fitness as the path to proper social and moral hygiene. Many promoters of physical health came to prominence following the First World War in response to the wounds and trauma experienced by soldiers in the trenches. As Joan Tumblety suggests,

> the problem of postwar reconstruction was often fixed rhetorically and legislatively on the body itself. For a start, the physical impact of the First World War on French men was all too visible. Not only had 1.3 million died in battle, but a million more drew invalid pensions as late as 1930. The figure of the disabled war veteran was omnipresent – in the Armistice Day parades, in the popular press, and on the street corners of French towns. (2012: 3)

Spurred on by concerns over a low birth rate in France following the First World War, physical culture in France in the 1920s and 1930s was the combination of a capitalist expansion of the health industry, the pan-Western rise in eugenic thinking amid a fear of European racial degeneration, and the belief that national dignity could be restored by a return to classical forms of fitness and masculinity.[12] In France, this form was identifiably male, heterosexual and white, and it was this body that was perceived to be under threat by the Third Republic during the interwar period. Such anxieties were discernible across public discourse, particularly in popular physical culture magazines such as Edmond Desbonnet's *La Culture physique*, which promoted social and moral hygiene as the ultimate goal of physical well-being. These publications were outlets for prominent scientific figures who supported racial rejuvenation in the years before the war, especially Georges Hébert, the promoter of the nationally renowned 'natural method' of outdoor exercise. Dr Paul Carton was another popular figure of the interwar years, a prolific holiday and fitness camp organizer who proclaimed Hébert's fitness routine to be the perfect way to 'rebuild our race, . . . its physical vigour and its spiritual worth!' (qtd. in Tumblety 2012: 26) – one might recall here Vladimir and Estragon going over their 'exercises' in *Waiting for Godot* (*CDW*: 71). Advertisements for fitness regimes and home gym equipment in physical culturist magazines also contributed to ideals of physical well-being that Vichy later incorporated into its youth and athletics programmes. Many adverts conceptualized strength in terms that asserted both classical aspirations and a culture of gender division. An advertisement for an elastic exercise band in the 1937 editions of *La Culture physique* proudly offered versions of the product in ascending order of strength with the titles 'lady', 'adult', 'man', 'athlete', 'Hercules' and 'Super Hercules' (Tumblety 2012: 25). France was body- and gender-obsessed well before Pétain's declarations of revolution and renewal.

Under Vichy, however, this emphasis on the relationship between 'spiritual worth', physical fitness and masculinity translated into an authoritarian assertion of France as a nation of the land and the family. The apparent weakness of the military was even attributed to a pre-war decline in agricultural work: 'this scandal [of French masculinity] required a redemption – a virile song of men working on the fields' (qtd. in Jackson 2001, 329). The implicit idea that French soldiers – and French men more broadly – had been 'softened' by contemporary French culture was recurrent under Vichy, a notion bolstered by the repeated characterization of the Third Republic as feminine in contrast to the 'more national, more virile, more human' France of Vichy's imagination (Jackson 2001: 328).

---

[12] Kennedy (2015) has argued convincingly that the prevalence of 'degeneration theory', particularly the work of Max Nordau, could not have escaped Beckett's notice given its popularity not only in France but also in Nazi Germany and in the race discourse of figures like W. B. Yeats (195–9).

Figure 7 'Laissez-nous tranquilles!' (Leave us in peace!), G. Mazeyrie, Té, 1941. Copyright holder not located.

The idea of virility being attained by labour 'in the fields' was also one inherited from the physical culturists of the 1920s and 1930s. Hébert's 'natural method' focused on the natural movements of the body and was designed to reintroduce physical activity into French masculinity as a counter to the 'bookish' culture of the Third Republic. The theory went that pushing the male population towards an active, practical lifestyle would help pass on this revived masculinity to future offspring, instilling them with a moral fortitude that would be reflected in their athletic, muscular forms. By the time of Vichy, this practical activity had been enfolded into a form of masculinity that not only worked the land but also, in doing so, held at bay the forces deemed to be eroding and attacking French society (Figure 7).

Molloy and the male body

The persistent rhetoric of the male body in Vichy's propaganda offers a rich vein for thinking through Beckett's debilitated and impaired post-war bodies. In a stark inversion of Vichy's image of masculinity, Beckett's post-war male forms embrace decay, pursuing their own ideals of a male form stripped of its athletic and sexual potential. In the first novel of the trilogy, Molloy moves from abstaining from physical activity to a fantasy of degeneration and sexual debilitation through amputation. After running over Teddy, the dog, with his bicycle, Molloy joins the distraught Lousse in burying her pet with a spade. However, Molloy does not participate in this labour, due to what he claims to be the physical impediment of his leg:

> It was she dug the hole because I couldn't, though I was the gentleman, because of my leg. That is to say I could have dug with a trowel, but not with a spade. For when you dig a grave one leg supports the weight of the body while the other, flexing and unflexing, drives the spade into the earth. Now my sick leg, I forget which, it's immaterial here, was in a condition neither to dig, because it was rigid, nor alone to support me, because it would have collapsed. I had so to speak only one leg at my disposal. (*M*: 33)

Though unable to dig, Molloy can quite precisely describe the physical movements that would occur if he did. Because his leg is 'rigid' and unable to support his weight, Molloy cannot produce the natural movements expected when digging. As a result, the logic runs, Molloy cannot take up the role as the 'gentleman' who asserts himself through physical activity, as depicted in the poster image in Figure 7. Molloy's refusal to participate in this depiction of traditional masculinity both parodies and diminishes the very foundations on which this view of gender is predicated and, by extension, rejects the system of value by which Vichy conceived its ideal French man.

As the dog is buried, Molloy not only abstains from the normative masculine activity, letting Lousse dig the hole on her own, but also fantasies about his own amputation, first the removal of his 'rigid' leg, then his genitals:

> I was virtually one-legged, and I would have been happier, livelier, amputated at the groin. And if they had removed a few testicles into the bargain I wouldn't have objected. For from such testicles as mine, dangling at mid-thigh at the end of a meagre cord, there was nothing more to be squeezed, not a drop. . . . [W]orse still, they got in my way when I tried to walk, when I tried to sit down, as if my sick leg was not enough . . . the best thing for me would have been for them to go, and I would have seen to it myself, with a knife or secateurs, but for my terror of physical pain and festered wounds. (*M*: 33–4)

This fantasy of degeneration quickly centres on the possibilities of virility and male sexual prowess, unsettling the locus of social, moral and political power ascribed to masculinity and the male form, and disrupting the kind of body politics that Vichy made fundamental to its racial reimagining.

Testicles, bodily dysfunction and frailty again feature when Molloy describes his intercourse with the character named as both Ruth and Edith, another blackly humorous parody of conferring value on traits of virility and athleticism:

> She had a hole between her legs . . . and in this I put, or rather she put, my so-called virile member, not without difficulty, and I toiled and moiled until I discharged or gave up trying or was begged by her to stop. A mug's game in my opinion and tiring on top of that, in the long run. . . . Perhaps she too was a man, yet another of them. But in that case surely our testicles would have collided, while we writhed. Perhaps she held hers tight in her hand, on purpose to avoid it. (*M*: 56)

The possibility of reproduction is deferred through the combination of a language of sexual difficulty – the particular choice of 'toil' also evoking the fieldwork prized by Vichy's labour propaganda – and the introduction of a potential homosexual sex scene. Rather than healthy new offspring and the demonstration of a traditional, virile masculinity on Molloy's part, it is finally only bodily failure and tiring physical exertion that are imagined as the inevitable outcomes of what is ruefully declared the 'mug's game' of intercourse.

Malone, Pétain and the ageing male body

In *Malone Dies*, the possibilities of physical exertion are further reduced as the novel focuses on the daily routines of the aged Malone in the confines of an institutional bed:

> Not only am I here, but I am looked after! This is how it is done now. The door half opens, a hand puts a dish on the little table left there for that purpose, takes away the dish of the previous day, and the door closes again. This is done for me every day, at the same time probably. (*MD*: 9)

Malone does not know when he arrived in the space he occupies. Using his body and a minimal understanding of his own experiences, he estimates his age – 'I call myself an octogenarian, but I cannot prove it' (*MD*: 10) – and in so doing draws particular attention to the condition of the ageing male body. With Vichy in mind, the propaganda that surrounded the aged Pétain looms in the characterization. This is not to say that Malone directly represents Pétain; the text's vague historical setting resists such an association. Rather, the novel's descriptions reverse the ideals set out in the propaganda relating to Pétain's embodiment of a noble image of older French masculinity through Malone's stark description of the aged, apparently infirm body receiving care.

Pétain's significance for many of the French populace transcended political boundaries before the war, a seemingly ageless yet grandfatherly figure who was pivotal to the concept of French heroism. Crucially, Pétain had shepherded the nation through the horrors of the First World War's most vicious fighting. Following the defeat of 1940, Pétain made his body – in terms that defied any limits of age – the symbol of French patriotism. As Ralph Albanese writes,

> As an octogenarian, Pétain conjured the image of Corneille's *nobles vieillards* [noble old men] in the collective imagination. Declaring on June 17, 1940, 'I give to France the gift of my person, in order to alleviate her misfortune', Pétain justifies the armistice in light of the national drama of suffering and redemption. In effect, he indulges in self-sacrifice or, to use the Corneillian lexicon, he martyrs himself in the name of France. (2008: 75)

Martyrdom was a key part of Vichy vocabulary, the idea that individuals should sacrifice themselves for their nation. In his speeches, Pétain presented himself as the embodiment of this ideal. Beckett had disliked the 'Corneillian lexicon' of heroic old men since his studies at university, so much so that he participated in a 'politically orientated satire' (*PI*: 41) of Corneille's *Le Cid*, co-written with Georges Pelorson.

Pétain's reputation as a heroic, militaristic figure was replicated in Vichy's mobilization of older veterans through the Legion of Combatants, founded in 1940 by Xavier Vallat with the order that they 'must form groups down to the uttermost village in order to have the wise counsels of their leader of Verdun heeded and carried out' (qtd. in Paxton 1972: 190). Vichy encouraged the Legion, particularly its eldest members, to 'play the civic role' (Paxton 1972: 190) as a nationwide presence that emphasized the militaristic nature of Vichy, revived the martyrdom rhetoric of the First World War and facilitated a connection between the government and the public, particularly on matters of the *Révolution nationale*. With the physical presence of the Legion's members and a vast number of wartime publications devoted to the institution (Evleth 1999), the image of the First World War's 'war veteran . . . on the street corners of French towns' (Tumblety 2012: 3) was transformed into a symbol of the revolution itself. Ever-present in Vichy, and always accompanied by Pétain's rhetoric of nobility and national strength, such fetishizing of France's war veterans would not have escaped Beckett's notice. Indeed, his post-war texts suggest as much. In the 1946 novella 'The End', the elderly, homeless narrator laments his failure to secure lodgings despite begging with a 'method of doffing my hat at once courteous and discreet' (*ECEF*: 41). Though unsuccessful, the narrator notes his own 'wise counsel' about public charity in a clear allusion to the war veterans so commonly seen across Europe during the period: 'I subsequently solved this problem, always fundamental in time of adversity, by wearing a kepi and saluting in military fashion.'[13] The narrator then corrects himself ('no, that must be wrong, I don't know, I had my hat at the end') as an uncertainty akin to the fog of war memory and combat trauma clouds his account. Amid the confusion of remembrance, the narrator is nevertheless sure of one thing: 'I never made the mistake of wearing medals' (*ECEF*: 41). For Beckett's beggar, alms are to be gathered through the ritual of begging, not sympathy for the image of the venerable war veteran.

Despite the 'Corneillian lexicon' that surrounded Pétain, the physical aspects of ageing – so central to much of Beckett's post-1945 work – occupied an uncomfortable place in Vichy's depiction of its leader, and texts like 'The End' replicate this confusion in the narrator's various contradictions and memory issues. The regime often played down Pétain's age so as to contest notions of frailty or ill health, even going so far on occasion as to resist the 'Lion of Verdun' moniker so as not to draw attention to the length of his career. Instead, Pétain's blue eyes, upright posture and physical energy were routinely emphasized (Atkin 1998: 108–9). The central contradiction of the elderly Pétain revered both for his youthful vigour and for his long service to France clearly did not escape Beckett's notice; consider again his characterization of Pétain as 'the poor *old* misled man and *hero of Verdun*' (*LSB II*: 19; my emphasis).

The unheroic Malone is far from the upright, broad-shouldered Corneillian image of the marshal from Vichy propaganda:

> My body is what is called, unadvisedly perhaps, impotent. There is virtually nothing it can do. Sometimes I miss not being able to crawl around anymore. But I am not much given to nostalgia. . . . It is on my back, that is to say prostrate, no, supine, that I feel best, least bony. (*MD*: 10)

> I turn a little on my side, press my mouth against the pillow, and my nose, crush against the pillow my old hairs now no doubt as white as snow, pull the blankets over my head. I feel, deep down in my trunk, I cannot be more explicit, pains that seem new to me. (*MD*: 24)

While Vichy masculinity was to be dutiful and physically powerful in old age, Beckett's Malone meticulously recounts the small movements of his ageing body

---

[13] It is worth recalling again Beckett's doodle of Pétain wearing a kepi in the *Watt* manuscripts, as detailed in Chapter 1.

to emphasize debilitation, limitation and pain. Impotent and frail, the text rejects the very tradition of the noble old man on which Pétain himself capitalized, inverting that nobility and giving voice to a character who embodies a form of male ageing that, when it came to Pétain, Vichy sought to conceal from public view.

'Why should I have a sex?': *The Unnamable*

The disrupted male form finds its clearest expression in *The Unnamable*. In particular, it is with the imminent arrival of 'Mahood', the 'vice-exister' named with a near homonym of manhood, that we encounter the most striking image of the decayed male body: 'I feel my back straight . . . my neck stiff and free of twist and up on top of it the head, like the ball of the cup-and-ball in its cup at the end of the stick' (*U*: 15). The image begins to crystallize as an only vaguely or perhaps previously human form is conjured:

> No, no beard. No hair either. It is a great smooth ball I carry on my shoulders, featureless but for the eyes, of which only the sockets remain. And were it not for the distant testimony of my palms, my soles, which I have not yet been able to quash, I would gladly give myself the shape, if not the consistency, of an egg – with two holes no matter where to prevent it from bursting, for the consistency is more like that of mucilage. (*U*: 15)

Eventually, it is revealed that the narrator has achieved what Molloy desired, the removal of his genitals and so the signifier of biological sex: 'Why should I have a sex, who have no longer a nose? All those things have fallen, all the things that stick out, with my eyes, my hair – without leaving a trace' (*U*: 16). Rather than becoming the muscular, heroic male ideal imagined in Vichy propaganda, the male body in the trilogy degenerates into a being that would 'gladly give' itself the shape 'of an egg'. Stripped of recognizable physical form, this body is presented as the source of expression and narrative in the text. The narrator dismisses all identifiers of sex or biology, subsuming the traditional associations of the egg with reproduction and renewal into a grotesque visage of stasis and silence. Such a violent dissolving of the body and the narrator's 'sex' denotes a rejection of everything the physical body represents, disrupting the very basis of narratives of race and gender, of human perfectibility and bodily prowess.[14]

---

[14] For a discussion of the role of sex and sexuality in Beckett's aesthetic, see Stewart (2011).

The emphasis on the negation of gender is also resonant here with Vichy's drive to solidify normative gender roles. Again, this had its origins in an interwar rhetoric to which Vichy gave platform during the war. In his 1935 treatise on modernity and the human body, *L'Homme, cet inconnu* (*Man the Unknown*), Alexis Carrel wrote: 'The sexes have again to be clearly defined. Each individual must either be male or female, and never manifest the sexual tendencies, mental characteristics, and ambitions of the opposite sex' (trans. and qtd. in Jackson 2001: 32). Under Vichy, this emphasis on masculinity, virility and physical prowess also carried with it an implicit rejection of non-normative sexualities. The assertion of specific gender roles – designed to re-enforce family values and promote the production of offspring – meant that any sexuality that was not heterosexual was deemed a slight against the vision of France that the *Révolution nationale* promoted. Across Beckett's trilogy, sexuality and reproduction are treated with indifference or mockery. *The Unnamable*'s rejection of reproductive body parts brings to fruition Molloy's dream of testicular removal, and Molloy can hardly remember whether Ruth was female or male, nor seems much bothered by either prospect. Repeatedly, at times incessantly, the trilogy disrupts the Vichyite fantasies of separating the sexes, legislating on sexual habits and the production of numerous offspring.

The aesthetics of physical decline to which Beckett was drawn following the Second World War mark a sharp turn against both pre-war French physical culture and the pervasive image of masculinity through which Vichy hoped to restore the French race and nation. In most readings, Beckett's degenerating bodies are recognized as extreme depictions of suffering which speak to a central aspect of the human condition. For Kathryn White, for example, Beckett's trilogy offers an articulation of the inevitable facticity of physical human existence in a manner that is ultimately redemptive:

> Beckett magnifies the infirmities that affect us all; hence, this amplification of physical malaise enables us to relate to the characters, as we recognize that their pain is an illustrated intensification of our own suffering. Beckett's representation of the reality of the human condition... forces us to acknowledge the inadequacy of the physical body and recognize its inevitable failure. (2011: 9)

While some form of empathetic relation may be established between Beckettian character and Beckettian reader, it is important to recognize that White here sounds out a paradox within this humanistic notion that Beckett is representing 'the human condition' in all its feeble physicality. How might Beckett be a 'representation of the reality of the human condition' yet also offer an 'illustrated intensification of our own suffering'? The term 'intensification' is paramount here: Beckett intensifies, parodies and stylizes physical degeneration such that the 'relat[ability]', the 'our', is placed under strain. Beckett's depictions of illness, age and amputation generate forms of physical degeneration which dramatically clash with the fantasies of authoritarian body politics, Vichy's above all. The texts produce their own body fantasies, images of post- or non-human bodies whose distinguishing fleshy features have, in a text like *The Unnamable*, simply disappeared. Though the novels replace the fantasy of bodily prowess with bodily decay, they ultimately generate forms which are as little representative of the human as the idealized vision of physicality that Vichy constructed for the French people. The novels not only point to the universal fact that the human body can and does decay but also offer an unremitting counter to heroic notions of the physical and the normative attachment of value to athleticism, which dominated mid-century fascist and authoritarian narratives of race and nation. The novels chart the very degeneration that so many mid-century ideologies feared or diagnosed within European society, one which was perceived by Vichy to be the root of the defeat of France's fighting bodies. In *Molloy*, Moran even adopts the language of post-defeat 'regeneration' found throughout Vichy's propaganda: 'to be literally incapable of motion at last, that must be something! ... And to dread death like a regeneration' (*M*: 146). Dismissing the ideal of the body as a site of revival or restoration, Moran deploys but inverts the language of Vichy's revolution. He desires decline rather than revival, stillness rather than motion, death rather than life, upsetting the rhetorical and legislative power which regimes like Vichy gave to notions of physical and national health.

Set against Vichy's emphasis on the virile male body, Beckett's post-war writing produces a counter-history that gives voice to human forms rejected by mid-century ideologies, including those that Pétain and others characterized as products of a weak and decadent Republic. Such connections do not limit Beckett's degenerating bodily forms to a single historical situation, nor to a narrow conception of resistance that ultimately seeks a redemption in the bodies described. The bodies of the trilogy are, after all, suffering. They are also unsettling. We likely recoil, even for just a moment, from Molloy's amputation dream, Malone's pains and the oozing egg with endless tears that babbles in *The Unnamable*. In recoiling, we acknowledge the 'dissident and individuating' power of these bodies (Maude 2009: 112), a process with striking historical and political dimensions when read in the context of the healthy, distinctly male and infinitely perfectible muscular form that Vichy incorporated into its programme of national regeneration. Not only degrading but also fantasizing further impairment, Beckett's bodies mock, aggravate and challenge the idolization of a male form that is underpinned by the essentialisms that allowed Vichy to participate in, and sanction its own part in, the deportation and eradication of excluded bodies. By attending to the reality of Vichy's drive towards the ideal male body, we can detect in Beckett's prose a biopolitical counterpoint through which images of physical debilitation emerge as a rejection of the association between the body and hereditary, hierarchical, and political power, and a resistance to the conflation of bodily perfection with moral and social value.

The bodies rejected by Vichy haunted the liberation, both those of the soldiers killed or maimed in the 1940 defeat and those deported to Nazi gas chambers and labour compounds. While revelations of the camps continued in the post-war years, de Gaulle and the Fourth Republic attempted to reconceive the narrative of the war:

> In 1944, [de Gaulle's] government issued an ordinance declaring that all Vichy's legislation was null and void: history would resume where it had stopped in 1940. When de Gaulle was asked in liberated Paris to announce the restoration of the French Republic, he refused – on the grounds that it had never ceased to exist. This legal fiction became the foundation of a heroic reinterpretation of the Dark Years. (Jackson 2001: 1)

According to de Gaulle, Vichy was a betrayal of the Third Republic by a select group of corrupted elites swayed by Nazi imperialism. The political fragility of the post-war period was an unavoidable reality, one that would have been particularly keenly felt by a writer like Beckett who, from the mid-1940s, was increasingly sensitive to motifs of failure. Vichy had failed, but Gaullism failed too in reckoning with Vichy's role in France's wartime experiences. De Gaulle could legislate on political memory, attempting to pick up where the Third Republic left off, but the post-war government could not control the lingering presence of Vichy's failed revolution of mind and body as the country began to rebuild.

Vichy's ideals were sometimes mirrored in the rhetoric of Gaullism. The post-war period required its own structures of control and order, and de Gaulle's narrative of French heroism contained its own nationalism, its own idealism of a France 'liberated by itself . . . with the support and aid of France as a whole, of fighting France, of the only France, of the true France, of eternal France' (qtd. in Rousso 1991: 16). The very notion of a 'true' France was as necessary to Gaullism as it had been to Vichy, so much so that at times Gaullists appeared 'heirs of the regime they fought against' when it came to the topic of defining the nation state (Marc Ferro qtd. in Rousso 1991: 253).

Beckett retained a powerful scepticism of the narratives of progress, peace and reconstruction which returned in 1945. The bodies which Vichy rejected were assimilated back into French society under de Gaulle, though not always comfortably. Physical and spiritual rebuilding were the foci of post-war France, and these forces also played a role in the context surrounding Beckett's most important period of writing, as well as his participation in one of Ireland's most significant post-war charitable efforts, the recovery of Saint-Lô.

4

Beckett and Irish Neutrality

In January 1945, Beckett was informed by the Irish Legation in Paris that his family had not received much word from him during the war. 'BROTHER ANXIOUS BECKETTS WELFARE', his brother Frank had written to the Irish Legation in France, 'PLEASE WIRE REPLY AND ASK BECKETT TO WRITE' (*LSB II*: 9). Beckett had not been alone in his decision to leave Ireland on the onset of war. A number of Irish citizens volunteered in the British army or took on war work in Britain (Wills 2008: 4). This created great upheavals for many families and, for those like Beckett's, the loss of communications with loved ones further afield on the continent was a major concern. With the knowledge that he had not been home for five years to see his mother, Beckett made for Ireland at the end of April 1945.

Beckett's decisions to leave Ireland in 1939 and return in 1945, albeit briefly, have received mixed critical treatments. Some assessments have enjoyed the notion that Ireland's neutrality compelled Beckett to leave, particularly those which also situate his return to France and role in the French Resistance as a moral declaration against fascism. Lois Gordon offers an optimistic version of this view, suggesting that Beckett's left Ireland and joined the Resistance because he 'looked upon all of suffering humanity as his "friend"' (Gordon 1998: 140). While the experiences of his friends undoubtedly contributed to Beckett taking up Resistance work, the humanistic Beckett of Gordon's description seems somewhat idealized. Likewise, Beckett's remark that he could not stand by with 'arms folded' means that Ireland's neutrality has been read in Beckett criticism as national indifference at best, cowardice or callousness at worst, what James McNaughton sees as 'the process that allows people to irresponsibly assume they are outside of history' (2018: 40).

Yet the contention that Beckett rejected Ireland in 1939 (or 1945) on the grounds of neutrality surely misses the extent to which neutrality was a foregone conclusion in Ireland and conveys the debates over the policy as a binary one of for and against.[1] Neutrality would not have shocked Beckett, someone who kept himself well informed of Ireland's political policies even when abroad (*DF*: 187). Ireland's neutral position in international conflicts was made clear as early as the 1936 Italian invasion of Abyssinia. This was reaffirmed by Ireland's membership of the Non-Intervention Committee during the Spanish Civil War, a conflict to which Beckett played close attention (*PI*: 104–10). The war in Spain afforded Éamon de Valera the opportunity to spell out the 'moral doctrine' that would govern neutrality in the Second World War, that small nations should 'resist with whatever strength they may possess' the machinations of 'great powers' (qtd. in Teekell 2018: 19). Neutrality for Ireland was a matter of political independence and solidarity with other nations that had, at one time or another, been afflicted by conflicts they did not themselves provoke.

Neutrality was formally declared again on the outbreak of war (the 'Emergency' in Irish Free State vocabulary) in September 1939. Even though the policy was couched in the conservative, Catholic rhetoric of the Irish Free State – most famously emphasized in de Valera's 'dream of Ireland' speech in 1943 – the necessity of a neutral stance would have been of little surprise to even the surliest critics of the de Valera government. With a small defence force and a still emerging independent economy, intervention into the war would have not only tested Ireland's sovereignty from Britain but also crippled the nation financially. De Valera commented long after the war that his motivation for neutrality was also informed by the Irish experience of the First World War. 'I lost many good friends during the First World War and had no intention of doing so in the Second,' he told Terence O'Neill, prime minister of Northern Ireland (1963–9), in an echo of his anti-conscription address from 1918 in which he lamented the 'generous Irish youth' whose 'bones to-day lie buried beneath the soil of Flanders' (qtd. in Fisk 1996: 458).

While essays like 'Recent Irish Poetry' (1934) and 'Censorship in the Saorstat' (*c*.1934–6) demonstrate Beckett's rejection of the dominant political and cultural currents of the Irish Free State, the extent to which Ireland's neutrality compelled Beckett to leave for France at the outbreak of war has, I suggest, been overemphasized. After all, he had stated a full five months before war was declared that he would put himself 'at the disposition' of France in the event of invasion (*LSB I*: 656). To consider more fully Beckett's relationship to Ireland's

---

[1] For an analysis of Irish nationals writing during the war, see Anna Teekell's *Emergency Writing* (2018), a rich and varied examination of the ways in which Irish literature at the time conceptualized or responded to neutrality as a political and moral stance.

neutrality and the specific criticisms he directly and indirectly levelled at Ireland during this period, it is worth separating the military stance of neutrality from the methods of enforcement in Ireland at the time. It was not that neutrality allowed Irish 'people to irresponsibly assume they are outside of history'; it was that the Free State's censorship and propaganda processes made it difficult for people to get a full view of that history. Significant to this discussion are Beckett's review of Thomas MacGreevy's study of Jack B. Yeats (1945) and 'The Capital of the Ruins' (1946), the latter a text encoded with critiques of Irish wartime politics, but one which arose out of an opportunity – working with the Irish Red Cross – which was only possible because of the resources available as a result of Ireland's neutrality.

Neutral Ireland

Despite neutrality, Ireland's war years were far from peaceful. The nation suffered intermittent food shortages, declining employment and divisions between those who saw neutrality as a declaration of sovereignty from Britain by a small Catholic nation, and those who viewed the fight against fascism as one of moral importance. De Valera's government took the former view, and censorship was one of the primary tools used to enforce the policy. It came into immediate effect when neutrality was announced in 1939. Radio, film and published writings were all subject to censorship, chiefly those involving references to one side of the conflict triumphing in Europe, or external attempts to challenge neutrality (particularly from Britain). Propaganda also emphasized the moral and spiritual value of neutrality. Together, censorship and propaganda were identified as the twin methods of enforcement. On 23 January 1940, a memorandum by the Irish minister for the Coordination of Defensive Measures entitled 'Neutrality Censorship and Democracy' acknowledged the necessity of the strategy. 'In these days one of the most important weapons of war is propaganda,' the memorandum stated, though added the caveat that 'it behoves neutrals who want to remain at peace to walk warily in the zone of the propaganda war'. The conclusion was to 'ban the publication of statements which might endanger [Ireland's] neutrality' because 'in our country and in our circumstances it would be positively dangerous' to declare for either side of the war's combatants (qtd. in Fisk 1996: 560). Formal public debates over the matter were also suppressed because of a fear that division over neutrality could lead to another civil war.

Though there were some critics of the military implications of neutrality, it was the manner in which neutrality was enforced by censorship and framed as morally superior that provoked criticisms over isolationism and narrow-mindedness. These came from across the sociopolitical spectrum. The government presented neutrality as part of Ireland's post-independence spirit of national self-reliance, an ethical choice that accorded with the state's conservative, Catholic ethos: 'the sacred egoism of neutrality . . . implied sustained purity of soul – or at least of de Valera's fondly imagined Irish, Catholic soul' (Teekell 2018: 20). For those who found themselves excluded from this image of Irish citizenry, neutrality represented the 'virtual closing of the Irish Channel', as Elizabeth Bowen wrote in a report to the British Ministry of Information in 1940. The policy was the 'equivalent, for the more intelligent and Europeanly-minded people in Dublin and throughout Ireland, to a closing of the Burma Road' (qtd. in Fisk 1996: 409). A person's attitude to 'Europe' often dictated their attitude to neutrality.

However, Bowen's view of Dublin neglects the extent to which the city enjoyed a rise in its cultural status during the war. As Clair Wills suggests,

> Given the vociferous complaints about isolation, it's easy to overlook the fact that Dublin's bid for the status of European cultural capital was in some ways given a boost by the war. . . . [T]he outbreak of the war . . . produced an influx of 'refugees' to Ireland, who had a decisive, if ultimately short-lived, influence on aspects of Irish cultural life. (2008: 283)

Though writers such as Kate O'Brien left for London for war work, both in protest against what they saw as Irish parochialism and with a certain sense of individual responsibility, Dublin gained a new reputation for cultural activity, in part due to its relative safety. The city enjoyed an increase in art exhibitions influenced by European and modern artists, though this inevitably clashed with artists and politicians who cleaved more closely to official Free State cultural policy:

> Now London and Paris were fleeing to Dublin, transforming it from a provincial city into a European one, a beacon of creative freedom. . . . The battle between the moderns and the old guard had already reached a kind of climax in the Irish Exhibition of Living Art [IELA], a display of Irish avant-garde painting first held in 1943. . . . Responses to the 1943 show split along predictable nativist-versus-cosmopolitan lines. 'European influence was the dominant note,' said Con Leventhal, 'nothing that smacked either of insularity or narrow regionalism.' (Wills 2008: 284)

By comparison, an article in *The Father Mathew Record* condemned the artworks on show as 'affected, imitative, and empty' pieces of 'utter foreignness' (qtd. in Wills 2008: 285). The politics of 'national Irish art' raged ever strong in wartime Ireland.

These exhibitions carried on after the war. Beckett was typically scathing of the Dublin art scene, as evidenced by a letter to Georges Duthuit in August 1948 after he visited the IELA that year (*LSB II*: 96). Despite Beckett's lacklustre review, the IELA attracted many to Dublin during and after the war. Started in 1943 by the painter Mainie Jellett, the event was underpinned by many sensibilities that, regardless of his protests, were important to Beckett, especially a focus on challenging the dominance of mythology and folklore in modern Irish culture. Despite the battle lines drawn over native and international art, the annual exhibition achieved wide appeal. Thomas MacGreevy was among those who praised the 1943 IELA. Writing for *The Irish Times*, he particularly commended the number of female artists included in the roster.

Though debate abounded over neutrality in and outside of Ireland, it appears that the propaganda around the policy of neutrality was broadly successful among the general population. While the data is limited, according to one census eight out of ten citizens supported the policy (Fisk 1996: 413). There was also some cross-party support. Unionist MP Herbert Shaw observed in a memo to the British Foreign Office in January 1941 that the issue created nuanced meetings of political opinion:

> Nothing indeed impressed me more than the unanimity of Southern Irish support for the policy of neutrality as defined by Mr de Valera. I had expected to find it in the ranks of his supporters, and to a lesser extent those of the Cosgrave Party. I was surprised, however, to discover that even former Unionists, who were prepared without hesitation to send their sons into the British Army, held no other policy to be possible. (qtd. in Fisk 1996: 413)

Even Bowen eventually acknowledged the necessity of neutrality in Ireland:

> It may be felt in England that Ireland is making a fetish of her neutrality. But this assertion of her neutrality is Eire's first *free* self-assertion: as such alone it would mean a great deal to her. Eire (and I think rightly) sees her neutrality as positive, not merely negative. She has invested her self-respect in it. . . . One air raid on an Irish city would produce a chaos with which, in the long run, England would have to cope. (qtd. in Fisk 1996: 412, emphasis in original)

Sovereignty remained at the heart of neutrality, and the government presented the policy to be as much to do with cultural independence as with political or military strength.

Beckett and neutrality

Direct comments from Beckett on neutrality are scant. His later statement that he would prefer 'France in wartime to Ireland in peacetime' (Cronin 1999: 310) offers a broad sense of his position, though neutrality cannot be located in this directly. Neutrality was not peacetime. As we'll explore, it might be best to describe Beckett's position on neutrality as something like the following: neutrality was a necessary condition for a small nation such as Ireland, yet it was a policy that, unavoidably, symbolized what seemed already a widespread parochial and isolationist attitude. This is encapsulated in one of the few remarks by Beckett that seems to reference the neutrality policy, supposedly made on his return to Ireland after the war:

> Except for business trips into Dublin, Beckett was content to sit at home. All his cousins and aunts were anxious to see him, and there were interminable teas with enormous quantities of food. He seemed to abstain deliberately from eating, content with a single cup of tea and the thinnest slice of bread and butter. One of his cousins made a casual remark about a sumptuous tea table and was unprepared for Beckett's scathing reply. 'My friends eat sawdust and turnips while all Ireland safely gorges.' (Bair 1980: 287)

Evoking the relationship between hunger and plenty explored in the previous chapters, Beckett's remark imagines Ireland as a nation that had weathered the war with little concern. It is likely that Beckett's wealthy, middle-class family *had* remained in relative comfort during the war. But to see the plenty of a Foxrock table as the experience of the war for Ireland as a whole is to show where Beckett remained divorced from the majority of Irish experiences during the period. The very clear factor of class in this comment should be recognized so as not to damn Ireland's neutrality as a whole in order that it might fit with a desire for a certain picture of Beckett's political attitudes.[2] While Dublin and suburbs like Foxrock managed to maintain relative normality with access to food, fuel and even entertainment, much of Ireland suffered greatly at the hands of a warring world in which the nation had chosen to take no direct part:

> While hostile outsiders were suggesting that the country was both a peaceful haven and a hiding place for Nazi sympathisers, many ordinary citizens were facing poverty, destitution, even starvation. (Wills 2008: 237)

---

[2] It is this anecdote which precipitates McNaughton's remark on the Irish being 'outside of history' (2018: 40).

Though the 'bright lights' of the urban centres remained switched on, fuel and food were increasingly scarce through the war. Staples such as tea, wheat and coal were tightly managed with heavy fines for farmers or companies found to be doing less than their 'duty' in production efforts (Wills 2008: 237–8). Ireland also relied heavily on the major warring powers for trade. Britain, Ireland's largest trading partner, put pressure on the nation throughout the war to abandon neutrality and join the Allies, and one of Winston Churchill's persuasion tactics included limiting food and fuel trade in an attempt to starve Ireland into entering the war (Evans 2014: 22–3). Ireland's neutrality had a bleak underbelly, particularly for the poor.

'Tom seems happy & busy': Beckett, MacGreevy, national art and neutrality

With his return to Ireland after the war, Beckett was once again communicating with Thomas MacGreevy, his closest confidant of the 1930s. However, with the experience of the war alongside Beckett's further drift from Ireland in the late 1930s, their relationship had changed. During the war, MacGreevy had become even more invested in the relationship between Ireland's art and its politics. By comparison, Beckett firmly rejected how national politics could subsume art and artistic autonomy.

Soon after he had arrived back in Ireland, Beckett wrote to Gwynedd Reavey about MacGreevy's activities on the Dublin art scene:

> Tom seems happy & busy. He works a great deal with the Capuchins (art criticism) & is generally very active. Last time he was looking for a nice lavatory to change into his dinner jacket in, so that he would be wearing the right clothes for his discourse on Swift at University College. I think he is doing the kind of work he likes, for the kind of people he likes. (10 May 1945, *LSB II*: 10)

Though clearly pleased for his friend, Beckett's description is one of a professional scholar-critic, the role which Beckett had abandoned when he resigned from Trinity in 1931. Beckett's portrayal of MacGreevy is not dissimilar to the one he gave of T. S. Eliot to MacGreevy himself. Beckett saw Eliot's 'discourse' on Joyce in a Dublin lecture in 1936, and in 1937 he described Eliot as 'condescending, restrained & professorial' (*LSB I*: 536). The note on 'the kind of people he likes' signals too Beckett's awareness of MacGreevy's further gravitation towards an

Irish cultural climate that had largely left Beckett rejected or censored. Where Beckett found himself quite remote from the Irish cultural scene on his return in 1945, it appears that MacGreevy had benefited from the increase in artistic activity that had occurred in Dublin during the war.

Having returned to Dublin in 1941 from a London devastated by the Blitz, MacGreevy took up the role of art critic for *The Irish Times* and began writing for *The Father Mathew Record* that same year, a publication devoted to 'Irish culture, art and literature . . . from a Catholic point of view' (Schreibman 1999b). In 1942, MacGreevy joined the editorial board of *The Capuchin Annual* ('the Capuchins' in Beckett's letter), published by the Capuchin Order of Friars. MacGreevy's link with the Capuchins was facilitated by a Catholic discussion group in Dublin lead by Father Senan, editor of *The Capuchin Annual*. The group met 'in the Ritz café in Upper Abbey Street' and 'attracted writers and intellectuals', including MacGreevy, to discuss philosophical and political issues. Many discussions focused on socialist theory and how Catholicism could contribute to an alternative to 'the capitalist path to modernity' (Wills 2008: 353). Though *The Capuchin Annual* was run independently, the journal was considered by government officials to be among the key publications – alongside *The Bell*, the *Dublin Magazine* and the *Leader* – that should be exported 'for propaganda dissemination' to further promote neutrality as a virtue of a conservative Catholic Ireland, and to reaffirm neutrality as an ethical national stance (Cole 2006: 125). The latter was particularly crucial after the formally neutral United States joined the war in late 1941, putting renewed pressure on Ireland's own neutrality.

The war years seemed to clarify much for both Beckett and MacGreevy on the relationship between art and politics, and their views had grown even further apart when the conflict came to an end. Beckett wrote to MacGreevy regarding the latter's essay 'Dante and Modern Ireland' in 1948 in terms that indicate as much:

> Yes I received your <u>Dante</u> article and reading it was reminded of our talks 20 years ago in Paris. . . . I felt you constrained, as in all your work for The Record, and found myself wishing again you were writing more for yourself and less for Ireland. I know you are doing what you want, in a sense. But it must leave you often with a starved feeling. (18 March 1948, *LSB II*: 75; underline in original)

Beckett's message is clear: that MacGreevy had embraced a path that he could not follow. While Beckett saw in MacGreevy's work a sense of constraint after the war, this 'writing ... for Ireland' represented MacGreevy's increased confidence in the relationship between art, nationhood and faith.[3]

The strain in the relationship between Beckett and his friend is most visible in Beckett's 1945 review of MacGreevy's study of Jack B. Yeats. Though he praised MacGreevy's insights, Beckett challenged MacGreevy's identification of Yeats's national affiliations. He also used the review to outline his own position on the relationship between art and what he called 'the local substance' of history and politics:

> The national aspects of Mr Yeats's genius have, I think, been over-stated, and for motives not always remarkable for their aesthetic purity. To admire painting on other than aesthetic grounds, or a painter *qua* painter, for any other reason than that he is a good painter, may seem to some uncalled for. And to some it may seem that Mr Yeats's importance is to be sought elsewhere than in a sympathetic treatment (how sympathetic?) of the local accident, the local substance. (*Dis*: 96)

MacGreevy wrote the essay eight years prior to its publication, and Beckett read it at the time, offering encouragement but also noting his discomfort at the 'political and social analyses' of the piece (31 January 1938, *LSB I*: 599). That Beckett went ahead with the publication of the review in 1945 indicates how much his position had solidified after the war.

Before he published the study in 1945, MacGreevy added a preface which directly addressed the concerns his friend had made in 1938:

> I may be permitted to add that I do not feel called upon to apologise for introducing questions of either religion or patriotism in this essay or in writing about art anywhere. If art is concerned with religion and patriotism I do not see why art criticism should ignore them. And art is much more frequently concerned with them than is generally realised. (1945: 4)

Though not named here, MacGreevy elsewhere in the preface references Beckett and their discussions (14–15). MacGreevy's refutation of Beckett in public is indicative of the growing distance between the two friends. Beckett's submission of his review to *The Irish Times* likewise publicly affirms his suspicion of an emphasis on the identification of historical or political motivations for artistic expression or experience. The historical and political markers are not, for Beckett,

---

[3] The article in question is an example of such confidence, moving through the reception of Dante in Ireland, the effect Dante had on W. B. Yeats and MacGreevy's own reflections on his early encounters with Dante that were closely tied to his memories of Ireland (1948: 3–4). Beckett is unlikely to have warmed to this attempt to position one of his most favoured authors in terms of a nation from which he was increasingly distanced.

sufficient elements to account for Yeats's 'importance'. The position is aesthetic, but its frankness – notable in comparison to Beckett's otherwise often elliptical mode of writing in criticism – betrays a frustration which rings with Beckett's all too frequent encounters with art co-opted for political means, be it in Ireland, pre-war Germany or the propaganda of the war. Beckett's resistance to the 'local' also echoes the ambivalent attitudes to Ireland's moralistic politicking over neutrality which other modernist Irish writers also developed in the lead up to the war. In canto 16 of *Autumn Journal* (1938), Louis MacNeice describes mid-century Ireland as a 'tiny stage' where one can do 'local work which is not at the world's mercy'. A 'self-deception, of course', MacNeice concludes, for in Ireland 'there is no immunity either' (2007: 70–2). MacNeice, who worked for the BBC in London during the war, also had a difficult relationship with 'Emergency' Ireland. He saw neutrality as militarily necessary but rejected the 'soul-saving' rhetoric of its implementation, remaining wary of the binary thinking – 'neutral/war, Ireland/Europe', among others – that war brought about (Teekell 2018: 95–6).

MacGreevy's celebration of the political energy of Irish art was also a celebration of autonomy after colonization. In his essay, MacGreevy suggests 'the mind of the Irish people was centred on politics' (17) during Yeats's youth and that he carried this forward into his painting. For MacGreevy, Yeats's achievement is the incorporation of Ireland's politics and history into an art that MacGreevy deemed the first 'measure of self-expression in modern painting' (8). Such self-expression is connected, he suggests, to a vision of Ireland not defined by its politics yet unavoidably shaped by its particular history. For Beckett, 'national' is the confinement of art to the realm of material, historical and political particulars, whereas for MacGreevy it is a necessary aspect of artistic expression that can eventually lead to a collective spiritual awakening. This is why MacGreevy could at once be one of the most vocal defenders of the Irish Exhibition of Living Art, a distinctly modern (and modernist) art movement, and the more traditional state-sanctioned forms found in the pages of *The Capuchin Annual* and *Father Mathew Record*; these were all forms of expression achieved in and by Ireland.

MacGreevy's sense of religious and national sensibilities were based on two principles: that God's grace could only be received when people were united as both a nation and a community; and that Catholicism provided Ireland with a network of historical and cultural connections in Europe that could supplant the lingering influences of British colonialism. MacGreevy's republicanism manifests as a pro-European sensibility, one in which a rejection of British influence was not just the pursuit of self-governance but the pursuit of greater harmony with continental Europe. Take, for example, his 1943 *Father Mathew Record* article on Henry Morris's essay 'The Iconography of Saint Patrick' in which MacGreevy praises Morris for drawing attention to Saint Patrick's importance to a collective spiritual sensibility shared by Ireland and the Catholic nations of Europe. Again, such writing accords with state neutrality propaganda during the war, which frequently located Ireland among a cluster of other small European nations that had adopted neutrality – many of which were Catholic (Teekell 2018: 72).

The drift between Beckett and MacGreevy, then, was in part tied to MacGreevy's gravitation towards an official cultural politics devoted to nationhood and Catholic conservatism, one which, during the war, powered the neutrality policy. MacGreevy's one published comment on Ireland's neutrality – that it was a 'clinching re-affirmation of the Irish nationhood' (qtd. in Wilson 2013: 86) – squares as much with his own politics as it does official Free State discourse on remaining neutral. By contrast, Beckett saw the 'kind of work' undertaken by MacGreevy and other Irish nationalists as an intellectually justified parochialism, one infused with official Catholic moralizing. Beckett's 1945 review of MacGreevy has been described as part of his rejection of 'an exclusivist Free State cultural agenda that was defining itself increasingly in Catholic and nationalist terms' (Kennedy 2004: 67). In this sense, it is also a rejection of the 'cultural agenda' which propped up neutrality. Government policy was chiefly focused on the '"morality" of neutrality' (Teekell 2018: 21). State-sanctioned culture derived from the Irish Revival was twinned with censorship as the 'primary weapon[s]' in making neutrality part of the moral fabric 'of a conservative, Catholic, and insular Ireland' (Teekell 2018: 21). Beckett rejected wholesale the Revival's folkloric nationalism and what he called in 1934 the 'stuff of song' which obsessed Revival poets (*Dis*: 71). He also rejected the moralizing discourse that the Irish Free State brought to its cultural agenda, particularly through censorship, what he called the 'sterilization of the mind' (*Dis*: 87). Although Beckett was not present in Ireland during the war, his rejection of MacGreevy's spiritual and political perspectives on art set him at odds with the same sensibilities that governed the neutral policy.

'The human heart itself': MacGreevy and Beckett on humanism

The 1945 review of MacGreevy's Yeats study is also indicative of Beckett's further rejection of the language and intellectual framework of humanism. Beckett had described MacGreevy's poetry in the 1930s with the phrase 'humanistic quietism' in a review that was largely complimentary of MacGreevy's work (*Dis*: 68–9). However, as Andy Wimbush argues, Beckett's rejection of 'anthropomorphization' in letters to MacGreevy himself during this period suggests that 'Beckett's attribution of "humanism" to MacGreevy may not exactly be a note of praise' (2014: 204).

MacGreevy's humanism was of a religious kind, one again articulated through the lens of Irish nationhood. MacGreevy locates in Yeats's paintings 'the Ireland that matters', and what 'matters' in Ireland and its art is '[t]he classical trinity of the true, the good and the beautiful. That trinity constitutes the part of the Kingdom of God that even profane philosophers allow to be within us' (1945: 6). This 'trinity' is not just in Ireland, however. For MacGreevy, Ireland and its art represents only one instance of the 'essential elements' that are within 'every place in which there are human beings' (5). This religious humanism is central to MacGreevy's essay:

> Ireland was more than adult in experience of unpleasant reality and the opportunity to develop a greater leaven of humanism, of sympathetic imagination, in the make-up of the people, was overdue. Now it has come. And for the present at any rate, there seems to be no danger of its leading to any divorce from reality, to any of the fake mysticisms. It should on the contrary, make for a more comprehensive grasp of reality, a deeper and wider understanding of essentials in living, and for the expression of that understanding in art. (32)

Suggesting that communion with God is made possible by the communal possibilities of nationhood, MacGreevy's is a clear intersection of religious and humanist sensibilities that stands quite apart from Beckett's fidelity to a 'rupture' (*Dis*: 70) between what MacGreevy calls an artist's 'subjective world' and 'the objective everyday scene' (1945: 31). Yet the everyday, as we have seen, was under specific duress during the war, and MacGreevy's discussion of the everyday is part of a larger argument about how warfare necessitates that a modern Christian humanism arise out of the proper contemplation of artwork in both national and personal contexts:

> Man's life on earth is a warfare, to-day no less than three thousand years ago, and the Caesars and would-be Caesars who claim to be able to establish peace are not the least of the causes of that warfare.... In such a world, the intelligent man cannot but realize that there is only reassurance to be drawn from the deeper contemplation of the Kingdom of God, of the truth, goodness and beauty, that are to be found for the searching even within the human heart itself; that he must

inevitably return from that contemplation with a renewed and steadied sense of the eternal, simple values in living.... Withdrawal is only dangerous when it is dictated by cowardice or by egotism, by the desire to pose as an *indifférent* or as an infallible expert on the unseen.... In the case of Jack Yeats there is obviously no such danger. He takes all his human values into his subjective world, his sense of humour no less than his capacity for sympathy. His imagined scenes are all potentially true. And, then he returns from them to paint the objective everyday scene – with even greater mastery than before. (1945: 31)

MacGreevy's language of 'withdrawal' and his dismissal of the 'expert on the unseen' seem further barbs aimed at the likes of Beckett. His point, ultimately, is that a 'pose' is of little use when life is warfare. For MacGreevy, the fullest acceptance of the religious possibilities of artistic contemplation may open up avenues for peace and 'sympathy'.

Beckett was increasingly unable to accommodate such ideas after the war. During this period, his critiques of humanism crystalized further. He moved away from the language of 'anthropomorphism' found in his attacks on humanist discourse and realist art in the 1930s and adopted instead the terms 'human' and 'humanity' in response to the cultural commentaries circulating at the time in Ireland and France alike. While the 'human' is not a direct subject in Beckett's review of MacGreevy's study, Beckett's bristly response to the political dimensions of MacGreevy's study evinces a rejection of such terms because they deviate from the 'aesthetic grounds' Beckett saw as the only mode of artistic encounter.

The publication of Beckett's review of MacGreevy also coincided with the composition of his short critical study of Bram and Geer van Velde's paintings, 'La Peinture des Van Velde ou le monde et le pantalon' (The painting of the van Velde brothers or the world and the pair of trousers), in the summer of 1945 (Cohn 2001: 125), a text in which post-war humanism is an explicit concern. In his analysis of the van Veldes' paintings, Beckett suggests that both artists are focused on 'la condition humaine' (the human condition), each seeking a way out of the desire to situate that 'condition' in time: 'A quoi les arts représentatifs se sont-ils acharnés depuis toujours? A vouloir arrêter le temps, en le représentant' (For what have the representative arts always thirsted? To want to stop time by representing it) (*Dis*: 126; trans. Brazil 2013: 93). History has not stopped, however, and Beckett identifies 'the human' as a term which has entered European post-war intellectual and artistic debates with 'une fureur jamais égalée' (an unrivalled fury) (*Dis*: 131). The arrival of this post-war humanism is a part of a pattern of historical trauma because 'human', Beckett suggests, '[c]'est là un vocable, et sans doute un concept aussi, qu'on réserve pour les temps des grands massacres. Il faut la pestilence, Lisbonne et une boucherie religieuse majeure, pour que les êtres songent à s'aimer, à foutre la paix au jardinier d'à côté, à être simplissimes' (a word, no doubt a concept too, that has to be reserved for times of huge slaughters. One needs the pestilence, Lisbon and a major religious butchery for people to think of loving one another, of leaving the neighbouring gardener in peace, of being radically simple) (*Dis*: 131; trans. Rabaté 2016: 18). Beckett inserts the war of the 1940s into a history of traumas which take in famine, wars of religion and the devastation of Lisbon in 1755. Prior to this essay, Beckett's references to Lisbon – in the 1938 poem 'ainsi a-t-on beau' (*CP*: 98) and in Arsene's 'short statement' (*W*: 31–5) – allude to Immanuel Kant's supposed rejection of teleologic optimism following the city's destruction (Carville 2018: 11). In 'La Peinture', Beckett expands his view, with the Lisbon earthquake placed in a continuum of historical episodes in which the promises of humanistic progress are repeatedly debased. Going one step further, Beckett registers the dependency of the concept of the 'human' on such traumas to give it substance or viability, and argues that the language of 'humanity' is most in circulation when 'butchery' and 'slaughters' are rife in the world. A year after he wrote 'La Peinture', Beckett would add the destruction of Saint-Lô to the list of 'humanity''s failures.

We will look further at the French context of the van Velde essay in Chapter 5, but Beckett's engagement with MacGreevy in 1945 is important to understand the wide scope of Beckett's published confrontations with humanism in the post-war moment. While MacGreevy saw the machinations of 'Caesars' as the catalyst for greater humanistic spirituality and as a foundation for future national and international artistic and intellectual unity, Beckett found 'the "human"' to be an idea that was only ever coupled with 'huge slaughters'. Set in opposition to MacGreevy's religious-humanist understanding of art, Beckett's 'profane philosoph[y]' (MacGreevy 1945: 6) was that artists like Yeats bring 'light ... to the issueless predicament of existence' (*Dis*: 96). Beckett's image of illumination has traces of the kind of hopeful proposition that MacGreevy's 'leavened' humanistic imagination conjures. However, Beckett celebrates what he identified as Yeats's representation of the fundamental incoherence of reality. The turmoil of the war all but confirmed that incoherence, and intensified Beckett's view that the 'rationalisation' (*GD*: 87) of art through political interpretations nullified its value.

Saint-Lô, 'a heap of rubble'

New property legislation in France forced Beckett to leave Ireland in the summer of 1945. To keep his flat in Paris, he had to secure paid employment in France.

In the July, Dr Alan Thompson informed Beckett of a hospital project destined for Saint-Lô in northern France. The Irish Red Cross was to build a temporary hospital that could provide assistance and healthcare to those rebuilding the town following the D-Day bombings. Beckett took on the roles of storekeeper, interpreter and ambulance driver. He left with Thompson and the other members of the advanced party in August 1945.

The Irish Red Cross chose Saint-Lô as the site for its temporary hospital because of the scale of destruction the town sustained from Allied and German forces during the D-Day assault. Saint-Lô was a strategic stronghold for the occupying forces, and it took seven weeks for the Allies to take control at the cost of 11,000 American lives as the town changed hands between the Americans and the Germans. The cathedral, surrounding ramparts and countless buildings were all destroyed (Figure 8). When the Nazi forces had learnt of the Allied plans to bomb the occupied northern French territory, they ordered all civilians to remain where they were, threatening arrest and execution should any try to flee (Gaffney 1999b: 4). This contributed to the loss of nearly 1,000 lives in Saint-Lô, a smaller number in comparison to others in the region (2,000 were killed in the bombing of Caen, for example), but it was the scale of physical damage which drew the Irish Red Cross to Saint-Lô. The Red Cross arrived to find the town's

Figure 8 'Saint-Lô: Bombardement de 1944' © Conseil Régional de Basse-Normandie/National Archives USA.

buildings nearly all levelled and the populace reeling from the air and ground assaults: 'survivors have vivid memories of the sights, sounds and smells of that infernal week when Saint-Lô burned . . . everywhere there was a ghastly smell of sulphur and burnt flesh' (Gaffney 1999b: 7). While both sides bombed the town, it was the American bombers which many citizens most clearly recalled (Gaffney 1999b: 22). Beckett wrote to MacGreevy soon after he arrived that

> St. Lô is just a heap of rubble, la Capitale des Ruines as they call it in France. Of 2600 buildings 2000 completely wiped out, 400 badly damaged and 200 'only' slightly. It all happened in the night of the 5th to 6th June. It has been raining hard the last few days, and the place is a sea of mud. (19 August 1945, *LSB II*: 18)

He was clearly sceptical of the official language used to describe the town. Those 'slightly' damaged buildings included homes with walls missing and collapsed roofs under which unlucky citizens were trapped or dead.

The Saint-Lô hospital project developed through a series of negotiations between the Irish government, the Irish Red Cross and the French. The Red Cross had been planning to deliver assistance in Europe since 1943. However, the process of bringing aid to France was somewhat tense at the end of the war, as the French government had ordered the replacement of all ministers from neutral nations who had served as diplomatic liaisons with the Vichy regime. Seán Murphy, with whom Beckett had dealings in 1943 over his identity papers, was kept on because he was appointed before the war, and it is possible that the hospital aid project helped Murphy keep his position (Gaffney 1999b: 17). The French ambassador to Dublin was in no doubt that the whole process was an attempt to shore up political ties between Ireland and France, though he acknowledged the ambitions of the project represented the 'most significant' political gesture 'imaginable, within the framework and the boundaries of the neutral stance' (qtd. in Gaffney 1999b: 18). The project was also an exertion of Irish independence designed to forge links that circumvented a dependence on British trade or politics.

However, the Saint-Lô hospital was plagued by issues due to a strain between the local French community and the Irish hospital staff. 'Obscure tensions' was Beckett's phrase (*LSB II*: 18). Despite this, Eoin O'Brien describes Saint-Lô as a 'spiritual exodus' from Ireland for Beckett, suggesting that Beckett discovered once and for all his allegiance to France (1986: xxv). Perhaps so, but the project represents a significant (if relatively short) period in which Beckett worked with and alongside a diverse group of Irish citizens drawn from all walks of life, including figures like Arthur Darley, a Catholic surgeon, and the storekeeper assistant Tommy Dunne for whom Beckett bought rosary beads when out at a French market (Gaffney 1999b: 41).

Beckett's most direct response to the Saint-Lô project is found in the radio script 'The Capital of the Ruins'. At first glance, the text is a fairly straightforward account of the Saint-Lô experience. In fact, the text is a politically engaged, subtle piece of war writing that also addresses the cultural and political conditions of neutral Ireland. Before analysing the piece's content, though, it is necessary to establish the archival and historical details available for 'The Capital of the Ruins', as the record is somewhat inconsistent. Indeed, 'The Capital of the Ruins' is one of the least well-documented of Beckett's texts. It also represents the most direct form of war writing in Beckett's canon.

'The Capital of the Ruins': A partial history

At some point in the first half of 1946, Beckett was invited or commissioned to write a radio script for Radio Éireann (now RTÉ) detailing the project in Saint-Lô; he had finished his contract with the Irish Red Cross on 1 January 1946. 'The Capital of the Ruins' was the result, named after a pamphlet of photographs of the ruined town. The text has appeared in a number of editions with varying contextual details. Discovered in the archives of RTÉ in 1983, the typescript, which is signed by Beckett with the date 10 June 1946, contains edits from multiple origins, as confirmed by Beckett after S. E. Gontarski sent him a copy in July 1983 (*CSP*: 286).[4] The text has been published with introductions by Eoin O'Brien in *The Beckett Country* (1986), by Dougald McMillan in *As No Other Dare Fail* (1986) and *As The Story Was Told* (1990), and by Gontarski in *Complete Short Prose* (1995), all with various incorporations or exclusions of the edits found on the typescript, and all with different information on the text's history and possible broadcast. In *The Beckett Country*, O'Brien writes that 'On 10 June 1946, Samuel Beckett . . . wrote an account of the Irish Hospital for broadcasting to the Irish people on Radio Éireann' (1986: 333). McMillan takes 10 June 1946 to be the date of broadcast: 'The following script published here for the first time, was read by Beckett on Radio Erin on 10 June, 1946' (1990: 84). As Gontarski shows, any broadcast of the script is undocumented by RTÉ, with neither fee cards nor correspondence included in the archives (*CSP*: 286). The date on the typescript is

---

[4] Gontarski confirmed to me in private correspondence that he sent Beckett a photocopy of the text and that Beckett's reply printed in *CSP* was made with the photocopy in his possession.

likely the date of Beckett's completion of the text or, more likely, his submission of the text to RTÉ, since the date is repeated in another hand in the top right corner of the first typescript page, probably confirming receipt of the script.

The text's archival history also requires clarification. After the typescript was found in the RTÉ archive in 1983, Seán Ó Mórdha showed the document to Eoin O'Brien (O'Brien 1986: 385) who published the text 'in full incorporating all the manuscript changes in Beckett's hand' (333), though some changes are not Beckett's, as discussed below. The original remains part of the RTÉ archive holding, now managed by University College Dublin, and at least two photocopies were made on its discovery. One photocopy was sent by John Calder's secretary Anna Menmuir to Barney Rosset on 7 November 1986 along with a copy of 'neither', both now held at Boston College.[5] A second is in the Beckett International Foundation archives at the University of Reading (UOR MS 2905), part of a donation made by Beckett in 1987. Gontarski also had a copy which he sent to Beckett, as noted earlier. Phyllis Gaffney cites another copy among the papers of Mary Crowley (1999a: 260), the Saint-Lô hospital matron. However, my correspondence with Eoin O'Brien and Mary O'Doherty, the archivist managing Crowley's papers at the Royal College of Surgeons in Ireland, suggest that this is not the case. In a 1972 interview with Deirdre Bair, Crowley does not mention the script (HRC MS-5124, Container 1.6) and, until further evidence can be found, this copy should be either discounted or considered lost.

Of the two extant copies, the UOR photocopy is unique as it was edited in red pen after the copy was made. I suggest that this version is in fact the one sent to Beckett by Gontarski in 1983 after the initial discovery of the text. Many of the edits in red pen are concerned with the revisions made by other 'hands' on the original, to which Beckett drew Gontarski's attention in his correspondence. Most of the changes or deletions on the photocopy are marked with 'STET'. The capitalization makes it difficult to confirm that the red pen edits are definitely Beckett's. However, 'stet' is a notation Beckett was accustomed to using,[6] and it is highly unlikely that an RTÉ staff member edited the text on its discovery in 1983. Given that Beckett also made a point of noting to Gontarski that the typescript had been edited by people other than himself, it is highly likely that the red pen edits are Beckett's. The red pen edits restore Beckett's original wording and punctuation, as well as adding circumflex accents to the *o* of

---

[5] I thank James Little for this information.
[6] Beckett's use of 'stet' is most common when he is editing on typescripts. Examples can be found in the typescript drafts of *Fin de partie* (BDMP *Fin*, MS OSU RARE 29/5/11r) and in the translation drafts of *Molloy* (BDMP *Molloy*, MS BRML NWWR 2/38/08r), *Malone Dies* (BDMP *Malone*, MS WUMSS008 2/47/51r) and *The Unnamable* (BDMP *The Unnamable*, MS HRC SB 5/10/01r–111r). He also uses it during work on typescript drafts of *Stirrings Still* (BDMP *Stirrings Still*, MS UoR 2935/3/4).

Saint-Lô throughout. It is not this copy that informs the *CSP* version of the text, the last published version, which retains several of the edits by other 'hands' first included by O'Brien such as the deletion of the phrase 'no offense meant' (UOR MS 2905/1r) and the elocutionary commas added on the third page (UOR MS 2905/3r). Some of the *CSP* variants are errors introduced in Dougald McMillan's 1986 and 1990 editions, as Gaffney notes (1999a: 265), in particular the error 'human conditions' for 'human condition' and 'cures' for 'cured', which are reproduced in *CSP*. There are several more errors carried forward across the text's publication history, as well as the inclusion of further edits not made by Beckett such as the deletion of 'there' in the phrase 'there where', and the edit of the phrase 'present circumlocution'.[7]

On the question of broadcast, Gaffney locates a 'Paris Newsletter' RTÉ segment running throughout the summer of 1946. On 10 June, there is a 'Letter from Paris' listed in the schedule which Gaffney speculates could have been 'The Capital of the Ruins' (1999a: 260). However, if these newsletters were submissions or broadcasts from Paris to Dublin, correspondence from Beckett between 25 April and 19 June place him in Dublin during this period (*LSB II*: 29–37). The lack of RTÉ record remains the clearest indication that the text was not broadcast. The reason for this will likely remain unknown. Gaffney's notion that the censorship in Ireland of Beckett's work played a role is possible given the recent neutrality censorship, which came to an end for RTÉ on 11 May 1945. One would suspect that Beckett's censored status would have been dealt with at the point of the text being commissioned – unless it was commissioned by the Red Cross, rather than by RTÉ directly. There is the possibility that the text was ultimately dismissed by the RTÉ talks organizer Roibeard Ó Faracháin who, in 1940, had made known his commitment to representing the 'Real Ireland of Today' – 'the Catholic, pious, rural, and parish-based one', as Wills describes it (2008: 353) – on state radio. That Ó Faracháin saw the text is evidenced by his initials on the first page of the typescript, as Gontarski also acknowledges (*CSP*: 286). It is possible that Ó Faracháin's political and cultural sensibilities may have played a part in the lack of broadcast.

Beckett and war reportage

Since its first publication, 'The Capital of the Ruins' has most frequently been examined for the turn to 'humanity' in its second half. Darren Gribben suggests

---

[7] See Davies (2017) for a full discussion of the edits and Beckett's corrections.

the text is a 'barometer' by which the subsequent work can be measured as a Beckettian 'presentation of humanist optimism' (2008: 265). Lois Gordon identifies the text as the documentation of Beckett's 'pride in joining his Irish kinsfolk' and his 'confidence in his observations of human nature and a realisation of his own personal courage' (2013: 122).

Yet as a report designed to reflect on its author's eyewitness experience of the Saint-Lô project, 'The Capital of the Ruins' is first and foremost a piece of war reportage, one that makes use of the structures and tropes of the war report as a genre in its own right. Specifically, the text rests on a tension between the statement of the everyday nature of the Irish Red Cross Hospital project and a consideration of the 'condition' of the post-war 'universe'. Just as the everyday is a powerful dramatic force in a text like *Waiting for Godot*, so the everyday is a key element of the war report genre in its 'commitment to shared information and a recognition of the importance of being there' (McLoughlin 2010b: 55). The text presents itself as a carefully constructed piece of reportage, beginning with a factual account of the conditions of the hospital, the sparse supplies of linoleum, the methods of heating and provision of electrical supply (*CSP*: 275–6). These are a 'few facts, chosen not quite at random' which are paired with descriptions of the diseases and malnutrition affecting the hospital's patients (*CSP*: 276). However, despite mention of people working on the project, the piece does not evolve into a human-interest story in the journalistic sense (though Beckett plays with the presence of 'human interest' in its vocabulary). Instead, the text contends that the everyday itself has 'become provisional'. Food and medicine supplies change daily, Beckett reports. The physical landscape transforms as mud accumulates, structures collapse and 'children play with detonators' (*CSP*: 276), intimating the potential for random suffering at any moment. Beckett even acknowledges how 'painstakingly anonymous attempts' had been made in Ireland (*CSP*: 276), or what McMillan identifies as public 'disparagement of the project' in the conservative Dublin press (1990: 84), to discredit the food and fuel supplies. Such false reports created a provisionality around the perception of the project's successes, obscuring the reality of the project for political purposes. Beckett uses these 'not quite' random facts to assure his potential listener of his eyewitness report, leading to the gravitas of the statement that 'Saint-Lô was bombed out of existence in one night' (*CSP*: 277). The assuredness of the statement at first conceals its deeper implications. In it, Beckett is roundly dismissing, and thus correcting, 'the opinion generally received, that ten years will be sufficient for the total reconstruction of Saint-Lô' (*CSP*: 277). Considering the rubble was, two years after the bombing, still being moved 'literally by hand' by the 'population of German prisoners of war, and causal labourers' without the 'benefits of bulldozers' (*CSP*: 277), Beckett's conclusion sounds reasonable.[8] Chilling as Beckett's assessment may be in its even-handed tone, it demonstrates an attempt to present the aftermath of the war as accurately as possible, giving weight to his judgement of the time it will take to rebuild the town. As Kate McLoughlin writes, 'such representation might not stop future wars, but it can at least keep the record straight' (2010a: 1). In turn, however, Beckett was well aware of the ways in which language had been used to sway minds during the events that caused Saint-Lô's destruction. He caveats his statement by giving his relation to the hospital project – 'a retiring and indeed retired storekeeper' (*CSP*: 277) – to make clear that he is both eyewitness and predisposed to a given perspective on the project. This too is a recognition of the mechanics of war journalism, and Beckett does his due diligence in the process, suggesting that his perspective as eyewitness adds authority to his view on the 'opinion generally received' about Saint-Lô's reconstruction; his record is, he implies, as 'straight' as it can be. The language of journalism and reportage, 'like all potential abuses of the rhetorical power imbedded in language' (Bolton 2016: 87), is to be treated sceptically, for it has 'become provisional' alongside every other aspect of living in the wake of total war. Beckett treats seriously the onus on his report for authenticity and transparency, particularly necessary since Irish neutrality had involved the censorship of information from the war zones in Europe. The management of reports from the continent could be one source for the 'disparagement' to which McMillan alludes. Beckett's attempt to 'keep the record straight', as McLoughlin calls it, is a confrontation with the ideological forces that would see the record abused, obscured or destroyed, be it in the Irish press or state documentation.

In closing his report, Beckett states that Saint-Lô presented to him a 'time-honoured conception of humanity in ruins' and an 'inkling of the terms in which our condition is to be thought again' (*CSP*: 278). The optimism frequently located 'The Capital of the Ruins' in scholarship by Gordon, Gribben and others is tempered by Beckett's implication that the image of 'humanity in ruins' is so familiar that it borders on 'time-honoured' banality.[9] Likewise, as Beckett wrote in his essay on the van Veldes, even a discussion of 'humanity' is itself banal, a placebo notion for moments of historical trauma deployed to occlude the reality

---

[8] Katherine Weiss surely overestimates Beckett's 'true generosity and forgiveness' when he includes the German prisoners in his account (2009: 159). They are facts of the situation just like the limited supply of linoleum or the recurrence of accidents.
[9] 'time-honoured | time-honored, adj.' (*OED Online*). Beckett's interest in the ways in which wars are patterned across history can be found in works like *Mercier et Camier* and the drafts of *Fin de partie*, as will be discussed in Chapter 6.

of suffering. Crucially, moreover, the 'condition' to which Beckett refers has most often been identified as the 'human condition', a universalizing notion of a common human experience. But this is a report on a hospital, and the language is medical. In hospitals, a 'condition' is an illness, an ailment. 'Our condition' is 'our illness'. If that 'condition' is to be 'thought again', it is with diagnosis and careful study, just as the war report attempts to do as a genre. Beckett the eyewitness writes with an awareness that his report will not 'stop future wars', yet he remains committed to keeping 'the record straight' in the face of an empty rhetoric of 'humanity' or the political idealism of national spirit.

The movement from the everyday of the hospital to the condition of humanity itself exemplifies another critical element of war writing that McLoughlin identifies: the use of 'techniques and tools' which can 'dismantle accounts of war that are distorting or deceitful' (2010a: 1). This is true of war reportage as it is of war fiction, and as we saw in Chapter 3, though we cannot so easily call his writing 'war fiction', Beckett's works frequently take to 'dismantling' the 'deceitful' methods and values at the heart of political rhetoric and ideology such as that which propped up Vichy, notably in the cult of Pétain. In Beckett's hands, the classical ideal of athletic masculinity is made meagre and weak, piety for the 'Lion of Verdun' becomes pity for the 'poor old misled man',[10] and grand philosophizing over 'humanity in ruins' is juxtaposed with the reality of children playing with explosives.

'The Capital of the Ruins' achieves its 'dismantling' in part by reincorporating the language of recovery: the 'provisional', 'Reconstruction', the discharge of a 'function', prosperity (*CSP*: 277–8). The text recycles administrative vocabulary to demonstrate that the 'liberation' of Saint-Lô involved obliteration, by not only the Germans but also the liberating forces. Beckett's most stinging indictment of official rhetoric in 'The Capital of the Ruins' comes when he turns to his own line of thinking on the 'provisional universe'. He reveals his underlying sense that ideas of reconstruction and prosperity hide the fact of the matter: time will not be enough to heal Saint-Lô from the devastation it experienced, devastation that was meted out not only by its occupiers but also by its saviours. Physical rebuilding does not do away with historical memory or the smell of sulphur and flesh (Gaffney 1999b: 7). Reconstruction and prosperity are the language of those who caused the town's devastation, a vocabulary used, as Marina MacKay writes, 'when the unjustifiable has to be justified through a vocabulary that

---

[10] Beckett had a long-standing interest in the pity/piety pun, first found in 'Dante and the Lobster' – 'why not piety and pity both?' (*MPTK*: 13).

renders invisible the brutally violent phenomena it purports to name' (2009: 5). It was with the vocabulary of 'liberation' and 'victory' that the Allies bombed Saint-Lô, and it is against this rhetoric that Beckett states that ten years will not 'be sufficient for the total reconstruction of Saint-Lô' (*CSP*: 278).

The 'chaos' Beckett described in his 'German Diaries' and the 'provisionality' noted after his experiences of Saint-Lô are apiece. The only thing that can truthfully be asserted in the 'provisional' scene presented by the hospital at Saint-Lô is the 'flotsam' (*GD*: 87) of its location: 'this will have been in France' (*CSP*: 278). All else, from narratives of recovery to the prospect of communal aid, is provisional. In these terms, Beckett's report is not simply a 'glimpse at a population that refuses to allow the ruins of their town [to] destroy their humanity' (Weiss 2009: 159). From the sight of children playing with detonators to the rubble of previously standing buildings, it extrapolates a 'conception' which is 'time-honoured': war is suffering, recovery is not the end of suffering, and, as Beckett made clear in his piece on the van Veldes, the rhetoric of 'humanity' is ultimately of little value. Though different wars depend upon different factors – '[the] historical moment, *casus belli*, political and cultural disposition of the sides involved, type of terrain, professional or conscripted armies, weapons technology' (McLaughlin 2010a: 1) – the vision of 'humanity in ruins' remains 'time-honoured'. The everyday gives war historical fixity, defining its character and conditions; the occurrence of war, though, is the facticity of humanity.

Not for broadcast: A Beckettian polemic?

Alongside the everyday nature of recovery in a recent war zone, 'The Capital of the Ruins' is indexed to a specific Irish context. This has seldom been discussed in scholarship on the text, though McMillan briefly notes its potential political implications: he describes the radio script as 'a rare piece of polemic' that is 'attempting to correct Irish parochialism', but does not extrapolate further (1990: 84). Given that there was a recurring scepticism towards reports from Europe in the Irish press during the war, as well as a certain cynicism towards post-war charitable projects, and with the conditions of Ireland's wartime neutrality in mind, there is more to be said on the piece's position as a corrective 'polemic' than has previously been considered.

Wartime censorship in Ireland came to an end in May 1945. British footage of devastation on the continent circulated more freely, as did images of the concentration camps released by British, US and Russian sources. The reports of the camps were disputed by some in Ireland as Allied propaganda. Having lost friends and Resistance colleagues to the camps, Beckett would not have been sympathetic to this pernicious yet inevitable outcome of five years of censorship and scepticism towards British intentions. An exchange in *The Irish Times* in May 1945 is indicative of the situation. On 14 May, the paper published a letter from one Senata Woods who wrote of 'dismay' at how 'the general public doubt the truth of the articles and photographs which have been published in the leading British newspapers about the atrocities committed by the Germans in the concentration camps in Germany' (qtd. in Brown 2015: 190). Woods suggested an Irish delegation be sent to the camps. A reply to Woods was published on 16 May:

> [i]f we are to celebrate the removal of the censorship by washing other countries' dirty linen in our public press, why not send the party of ghouls to India, China, Palestine or Russia? . . . Now that the war is over, there is a real task before us – that of building the peace. We now need to strengthen our confidence in human nature, not undermine the last tottering ruins of it. It would be more encouraging at this point to be shown the great things of which mankind is still capable; there is already too much evidence of its failings. (qtd. in Wills 2008: 399)

As Wills argues, for some this defiantly humanistic response was a mark not of decency but of the dangers of neutrality:

> This wish to hold back stories of the horrors of the war was echoed by numerous journalists and commentators in the final weeks of the conflict. . . . It was the kind of attitude that seemed to confirm the complaints of people as far apart politically as Elizabeth Bowen and Francis Stuart: that neutrality had bred insensitivity and complacency. (2008: 399)[11]

Given this context and the scepticism expressed in 'The Capital of the Ruins' towards a speedy recovery in Saint-Lô, Beckett's repeated turn to the notion of the 'human condition' may not be as optimistic as critics have suggested. While the text might exalt 'the comfort to be drawn from the inward human capacity to surmount circumstances of the utmost gravity' (Gordon 1998: 201), the text's political commentary addresses the effects of a neutrality governed by censorship.

As the war came to a close, press coverage of the devastation in Europe prompted several organizations to pursue aid projects, including the Irish

---

[11] A. J. Leventhal was among the critics of this outcome of neutrality (Brown 2015: 192).

Red Cross. Saint-Lô was chosen not only for the devastation it endured but for the press coverage it received in Ireland and Britain. Gordon writes that '[m]ost Dubliners would have been keenly aware of the devastation suffered by Saint-Lô' since *The Irish Times* 'closely documented Saint-Lô's heartrending ordeal' (1998: 190). While neutrality had hit Ireland's resources, donations to charities committed to overseas aid such as the Irish Red Cross had continued, complicating the picture of self-serving wartime isolation generated by anti-neutrality discourse.

Upon arrival in Saint-Lô, however, Beckett had been more dismayed than charitable, as shown by a letter to MacGreevy on 18 August 1945:

> We have been quite misinformed by the French Red X and the whole thing is disappointing. It is complicated further by all kinds of obscure tensions between the local medical crowd and the Red X people in Paris. We have the impression that the locals would like stuff, but don't want us (very reasonable attitude). . . . The apparent apathy doesn't irritate me as it does the other two [Alan Thompson and Colonel McKinney], whose reaction to the people is more or less the classical anglo-saxon [*sic*] exasperation. It is a tune of which I am tired. (*LSB II*: 18–19)

Though hardly renowned for its musicality, 'The Capital of the Ruins' contains several traces of the 'tune' that tested Beckett's patience. As well as functioning as a report on the town's devastation and a piece of war writing from the heart of France's recovery operation, the text is also a serious evaluation of Irish politics from the period, one that implies that the charity of the Irish Red Cross was not matched by cultural and political attitudes which remained dominant in Ireland.

One of the more critical phrasings is revealed by attention to the typescript. As published, Beckett's summary of the hospital is as follows:

> The hospital is centrally heated throughout, by means of coke. The medical, scientific, nursing and secretarial staff are Irish, the instruments and furniture (including of course beds and bedding), the drugs and food, are supplied by the Society. (*CSP*: 276)

The typescript shows that Beckett wrote the phrase 'no offense meant' after the word 'scientific' which was subsequently deleted by an editor at RTÉ (UOR MS 22905/1r). The phrase is included in McMillan's editions of the text where the RTÉ deletion is ignored, but does not appear in Gontarski's *Complete Short Prose* version. Beckett applied a 'STET' on the UOR copy, restoring the phrase. Emphatically positioned after 'scientific', the phrase reads as an apology for the mention of the word 'scientific' in a broadcast on Irish state radio, a barb that makes scientific practice commensurate with a kind of attitude and policy that is lacking and even 'offensive' in Ireland, recalling Beckett's acknowledgement of banned scientific works in 'Censorship of the Saorstat' (*Dis*: 88).

As he moves through his description of the hospital's materials, Beckett addresses his prospective listener, anticipating their listening habits and reactions to a report from a place made all the more remote by the recent neutrality censorship. In the process, he makes reference to the 'rare and famous ways of spirit' of the French, alluding to the fundamental difference between peoples that war and its devastation creates:

> That the operating-theatre should be sheeted with an expensive metal, or the floor of the labour-room covered with linoleum, can hardly be expected to interest those accustomed to such conditions as the *sine qua non* of reputable obstetrical and surgical statistics. These are the sensible people who would rather have news of the Norman's semi-circular canals or resistance to sulphur than of his attitudes to the Irish bringing gifts, who would prefer the history of our difficulties with an unfamiliar pharmacopoeia and system of mensuration to the story of our dealings with the rare and famous ways of spirit that are the French ways. (*CSP*: 276)

This is one of the more convoluted passages (in a text that would already be a difficult listen for any audience), in which Beckett marries the Homeric 'bringing gifts' metaphor with the oddly academic specificity of regional French ear shape and 'resistance to sulphur', an allusion, direct or not, to the smell of sulphur which lingered in Saint-Lô from the bombs and leaking gas pipes. Again, the text draws on a scientific lexicon to address the prospective Irish listeners, mocking a preference created by neutrality radio censorship for nature documentaries, quiz programmes and detached statistics rather than war reports from Europe.[12] The implication, though, is scathing, suggesting that Irish ears have become deaf to the events of the war and accounts of continental recovery, a critique of the fallout of Irish neutrality policy and the dominance of 'sensible people' over how the war was portrayed in Ireland.

A second bracketed comment later in the text again mocks the insularity Beckett saw in post-independence Ireland, a notion seemingly confirmed by the discourse surrounding neutrality. This comment revolves around the perceived difference between the French and the Irish working on the project:

---

[12] Successive audience surveys show that the programme 'Question Time', launched in 1938, which toured Ireland and broadcast from different locations, was the most popular radio programme in Ireland during the war (Morgan 2001). Beckett's allusion to French ear canals may be an obscure reference to the gamification of knowledge on 'Question Time'.

> What was important was not our having penicillin when they had none ... but the occasional glimpse obtained, by us in them and, who knows, by them in us (for they are an imaginative people), of that smile at the human [condition] as little to be extinguished by bombs as to be broadened by the elixirs of Burroughes and Welcome [sic], – the smile deriding, among other things, the having and the not having, the giving and the taking, sickness and health. (*CSP*: 277)

The French would need an imagination to find in the Irish 'that smile at the human condition', Beckett proposes. In part, perhaps, this is because 'that smile' is one generated by 'bombs' which the Irish had not experienced. Regardless, the text implies a separation between the Irish and the French during the project, recalling Beckett's private frustrations in correspondence sent on his arrival in Saint-Lô. 'It would not be seemly', Beckett continues in his radio script, 'to describe the obstacles encountered' between the Irish and the French, or 'the forms, often grotesque, devised for them by the combined energies of the home and visiting temperaments' (*CSP*: 277). He acknowledges, however, that the two had in some sense come together in the project: 'It must be supposed that [the obstacles] were not insurmountable, since they have long ceased to be of much account' (*CSP*: 277). Given the implication that these difficulties were surmounted, Beckett's critique is directed elsewhere, at the prospective listener in Ireland, the collective 'us' of the presumed audience. This rhetorical sleight of hand critiques not the Irish in France but the Irish in an Ireland under censorship, particularly those who sought a language of 'human nature' and its redemption while the realities of the war's aftermath remained rubble and ruins.

As the piece draws to a close, Beckett intimates a more contemplative approach to recent history, yet it is here that he encodes his most direct attack on Irish Free State cultural politics:

> When I reflect now on the recurrent problems of what, with all proper modesty, might be called the heroic period, on one in particular so arduous and elusive that it literally ceased to be formulable, I suspect that our pains were those inherent in the simple and necessary and yet so unattainable proposition that their way of being we[] was not our way and that our way of being they[] was not their way. It is only fair to say that many of us had never been abroad before. (*CSP*: 277)[13]

---

[13] I have used empty square brackets here to indicate Beckett's 'STET' in UOR MS 2905/3r of the punctuation added in by another hand. *CSP* keeps the punctuation added by another hand.

The phrase 'the heroic period' undoubtedly evokes the war and the 'heroic' effort required to rebuild France after a war that 'ceased to be formulable'. However, the phrase 'the heroic period' is also a reference to Standish O'Grady's *History of Ireland: Heroic Period* (1878). Mocked in Beckett's 1934 essay 'Recent Irish Poetry', O'Grady's approach to Irish history underpins much of the emphasis on Irish national culture that Beckett attacked throughout the 1930s, and which was used to maintain neutrality. For O'Grady, 'history' is a 'flower' of a 'heroic' kind in Ireland, one dominated by 'great heroic personages of a dignity and power more than human' (1878: n.p.). For Beckett, such a rhetoric of national heroism represents the 'recurring problems' that separated the Irish Free State from the reality of the recent war. Directed at an imagined Irish audience shaped by five years of neutrality propaganda, 'The Capital of the Ruins' offers a commentary on the perceived implications of neutrality at the time and what Beckett writes off as the ongoing insularity of Irish national attitudes as generated by Irish Free State governance. The text's conclusion is that the 'pains' of the project are symbolic of an inward-facing national attitude – a result of the fact that 'many of us had never been abroad before'. Already implying a lack of cultural experience among the project's staff, the phrase also employs the double meaning of 'abroad': both being in a foreign country and being outside or away from one's home ('abroad', *OED Online*). A subtle difference, it nonetheless indicates a certain insularity that Beckett attributes to the intended Irish listener, encoded within a description of the Saint-Lô workforce. The latter definition appears in 'The Expelled', a contemporaneous text to 'The Capital of the Ruins', as the narrator closes his story by describing his patterns of travel out in the world: 'When I am abroad in the morning I go to meet the sun, and in the evening, when I am abroad, I follow it, till I am down among the dead' (*ECEF*: 16). In *All That Fall* (1957), Maddy Rooney sets out the dilemma of being 'abroad' in a manner far more reminiscent of 'The Capital of the Ruins': 'It is suicide to be abroad. . . . But what is it to be at home . . . a lingering dissolution?' (*CDW*: 175). Maddy implies that venturing outside and away from the homestead is death by one's own hand. The sinister alternative, though, is the slow decay at home. Neither is preferable, both lead to death, but to remain at home is to invite or embrace a protracted decline.

Finally, 'The Capital of the Ruins' concludes its subtle yet spiky appraisal of state-authorized parochialism in its closing confirmation that any 'vision' or 'inkling' of 'humanity' – even one 'in ruins' – is only to be found outside of Ireland. The impact of this, Beckett writes, will see the project remembered as 'the Irish hospital', but, crucially, the experience of being 'abroad' and of 'humanity in ruins' will 'have been in France' (*CSP*: 278).[14]

While we do not have direct remarks from Beckett on Irish neutrality itself, this reading of 'The Capital of the Ruins' finds in it a political undercurrent that admonishes how neutrality was enforced through an insular politics of censorship and cultural nationalism, denying the Irish public access to a world beyond their borders. In turn, the text adopts a language of collective 'pains' to provoke a reconsideration of insularity and parochialism. By pivoting upon the concept of a 'glimpse' of a 'human condition' that might be 'thought again', the text points towards the prospect of a more open national attitude. Yet it also subjects to scrutiny the ways that a rhetoric of humanist solidarity in Ireland (and elsewhere) had the potential to isolate the populace and downplay the reality of the ruins in Europe, masked through appeals to a historically blind desire to focus instead upon what the 16 May 1945 letter to *The Irish Times* called the 'great things of which mankind is still capable'. The veiled critique of Irish policy in 'The Capital of the Ruins' rests upon an ambiguity of encoded language that also produces a legitimate, sympathetic response to the horrors of the systematic devastation of modern warfare symbolized by Saint-Lô.

Beyond the political and historical triangulations of the text, 'The Capital of the Ruins' does constitute a signpost for the work that was to come, though the nexus of the post-war everyday and Irish political conditions leaves 'optimistic' views about the text's 'humanism' without much foothold; Beckett's distaste for post-war humanism, introduced earlier, is discussed further in Chapter 5. While it may be an overstatement to suggest that Saint-Lô can be figured directly within the various landscapes of Beckett's post-war work, it is certainly the case that this destroyed yet inhabited terrain, hostile yet still life-sustaining, is evocative of many of the vistas we encounter in Beckett's post-war worlds, both in the immediate aftermath of the war and later in his career. Even the nowhere of later texts are 'place[s] of remains' in which 'amidst his ruins the expelled' can be found ('For to end yet again,' *TFN*: 151).

When Beckett put his experience of Saint-Lô into creative form, the project prompted one of his most poignant engagements with the war, the poem 'Saint-Lô', a quatrain of only twenty-one words in which the River Vire courses its way through the shadows of historical and future trauma. Though geographically situated through its title and mention of the 'wind[ing]' Vire river, the poem

---

[14] See Gibson (2013) for a discussion of the ways in which this tension between the Irish and French elements of the Saint-Lô experience has particular importance for the Franco-Irish dynamic of *Mercier et Camier*.

evokes a history of chaos, of militaristic 'havoc', in which the 'old mind' is defined by its relationship to 'ghost[s]' and the prospect of the 'unborn', a term that plays upon a duality which conjures both those yet to be born into a world of 'other shadows' (*CP*: 105) and those who have died and returned to the 'sea of mud' which plagued the project (*LSB II*: 18). 'The Capital of the Ruins' consciously avoids mention of the dead, while the poem is haunted by them. In Saint-Lô, alongside the politicization of recovery, liberation and even charity, Beckett was confronted with the realities of the war, with those quite literally 'unborn' by the violence required to bring freedom to the town.

5

The Language of Recovery
Beckett and France after the Liberation

After ending his contract with the Irish Red Cross, Beckett took up residence again in Paris. Beckett's return to the city in January 1946 coincided with the first year free of official warfare in French territory since 1940, the first year that was formally 'postwar' for the country. This chapter puts Beckett's creative and intellectual activity into dialogue with the various activities and proclamations by the governing forces of post-war France, chiefly Gaullists and the French intellectual elite who attempted to make sense of the chaos of the war and its shadow over the years that followed.

Though Paris was not destroyed like towns such as Saint-Lô, the 'universe' of post-war recovery remained tinged by the provisional. It was found even at the level of the French government. Between 1944 and 1946, France was governed by the Gouvernement provisoire de la République Française (GPRF; Provisional Government of the French Republic). Styled as an interim governing body, the GPRF set to putting French recovery in motion. Alongside physical rebuilding and economic recuperation, the provisional government and subsequent Fourth Republic pursued state justice in a series of high-profile cases against Pétain and his cabinet, as outlined in Chapter 3. The nation seemed to thirst for vengeance after four years of oppression. Citizen justice was also widespread, with 311,263 accusations of collaboration submitted to the courts (Jackson 2001: 578). Trials took place soon after the nationwide *épuration sauvage* in which known (and sometimes presumed) collaborators were beaten, tortured or even killed. Reprisals were particularly harsh against women who had entered into relationships with German soldiers, or who had become pregnant by them, regardless of consent. These purges are now infamous for the retaliatory shaving of women's heads as both acts of violence and marks of social ostracization (Jackson 2001: 580–2). The public trials of figures like Pétain were in part designed to direct public anger away from such vigilante justice.

The France to which Beckett returned was fragile. Material hardship continued as wartime restrictions were reinstated at various points to aid the struggling infrastructure of the country. The Paris of 1946 was awash with 'disappointment, disillusionment and depression' (*DF*: 353). The capital had survived the war mostly intact, but Vichy's authoritarian traditionalism and collaboration with the Nazis were at the forefront of national consciousness, and the ongoing trials and cycles of purges kept Pétain's government in full view for much of the second half of the decade. The very idea of 'France' in the post-war moment was in flux. Jean Guéhenno finished his war diary with a mixture of hope and trepidation: 'France is beginning again' (25 August 1945, *DDY*: 272).

Later in life, Beckett was reticent about his war experiences. His off-hand remarks about his work for the Resistance have most often been read as a turn of modesty on his part – 'boy scout stuff' (*DF*: 303) – and as a signal of his ardent desire not to see his life overshadow his work, as discussed earlier. Beckett's sentiments in letters to friends following his return to Paris, though, suggest that he was disillusioned by the France in front of him, one strikingly distant from the country for which he and many Resistance members had fought. The Resistance had been incorporated into the post-war recovery of the nation, mythologized by de Gaulle to present a narrative of a coherent nation of 'true' French citizens. The material conditions reflected the disruption of the moment and undermined much of the optimism of Gaullist rhetoric. 'Life in Paris is pretty well impossible,' Beckett wrote to George Reavey from Saint-Lô on 31 October 1945 (*LSB II*: 24). Two years later, he wrote to Thomas MacGreevy on 24 November 1947 detailing the material conditions of the city:

> The winter is setting in now in Paris. No heating in this house for the 6th year in succession. Things are very bad, with a badness that won't lead anywhere I fear, perhaps only, after an ineffectual skirmish, to French Yankeeism and then war. (*LSB II*: 65)

Beckett's sentiments are far from the images of heroism that de Gaulle and other political figures turned to in public speeches, and they reflect the widespread feeling that France was on the brink of plunging back into violence, even civil war (Creswell and Trachtenberg 2003: 9). In the late 1940s, it seems Beckett saw further conflict as the likeliest outcome of the conditions in France, and he maintained a healthy suspicion of programmes designed to aid the nation, be they the 'Yankee' Marshall Plan or organizations like UNESCO for which he produced translations on commission, though he deemed UNESCO 'impossible to have any sensible dealings with' and lampooned their method of declaring all work 'urgent-top-priority' (Beckett to Duthuit, 12 January 1951, *LSB II*: 224).

De Gaulle's rhetoric maintained the myth that France was 'liberated by itself', compartmentalizing Vichy as a traitorous minority. With little recognition of either the collective efforts of the Allies and the multi-national Resistance groups, or the realities of Vichy and the violence of the post-war purges, de Gaulle pursued a vision which 'sprang solely from his imagination' because of 'the need to limit the repercussions of the war, and because rival political forces attempted to exploit an ambivalent heritage to their own advantage'. As a result, 'collective memory of fresh events quickly crystallized around a small set of central ideas and images' (Rousso 1991: 16). The post-war purges and trials seized on de Gaulle's conception of Vichy as an anomaly in French society and politics. However, many of the trials were unsupported by a notable portion of Resistance members. Jean Cassou, a Resistance fighter, wrote in 1953 that

> The judgements of the courts were generally nothing but shams, which never got to the heart of what was fundamentally a simple issue. No one learned anything from the trials of Pétain and Maurras, neither those unwilling to learn nor those who needed to learn. (qtd. in Rousso 1991: 21)

Beckett's own negative remarks about France's recovery in the 1940s and his later apprehensions when discussing his Resistance work indicate that he was wary of the narratives France embraced as it recovered from the war, including those involving the Resistance. We know from his 'German Diaries' that Beckett was particularly sensitive to historical fabrication. As noted in Chapter 2, his description of the 'forget and forgive' post-war sentiment in France in his response to Arland Ussher's anti-French nationalism essay 'The Meaning of Collaboration' shows this sensitivity did not abate after the war (11 December 1946, *LSB II*: 47). To Beckett, the leaders of the liberation were at least guilty of political grandstanding and, more perniciously, risked an historical blindness that would allow the nation to abandon any memory of Vichy or collaboration. With two world wars in living memory for so many citizens, the notion that nothing had been learnt from the atrocities of the conflicts sat heavy on France's collective consciousness, compounded by the Gaullist attempt to omit Vichy from the history of the nation.

Henry Rousso argues that Gaullist blindness to the 'fresh events' of the war and the liberation induced an unfinished mourning in France leading to a 'Vichy syndrome', which occupied French historical consciousness for decades to come (1991: 10–11). The discourse around Pétain during and after his trial contributed significantly to this 'syndrome' as, throughout his trial, Pétain's defence team emphasized his services in the First World War, and the elderly marshal was presented as the shield that had held back German military ambitions, just as he had done three decades earlier. Pétain claimed that he had protected France by tempering the racial violence of the occupiers. The trial was fraught with difficulties in both legal and moral matters:

> Certain issues remained taboo. Although in the preliminary hearings Pétain was tackled on the origins of Vichy's racial laws, the question of Jewish persecution did not feature prominently in the proceedings, an indication that in the *après-guerre* few were prepared to admit or come to terms with the part played by Vichy in the Holocaust. Rather most of the arguments centred on the armistice and foreign policy. (Atkin 1998: 194)

Pétain attempted to sway the court by questioning its legitimacy. He declared, 'It is to the French people that I have come to make my account. The High Court, as constituted, does not represent the French people, and it is to them alone that the marshal of France, head of state, will address himself' (qtd. in Atkin 1998: 194). While Pétain and other members of the Vichy elite stood trial in the French courts, the purges swept through the nation, and all the while France attempted to rebuild its politics, its culture and its physical infrastructure.

Despite his trial, exile to the Île d'Yeu and inglorious death on the island in 1953, Pétain's legacy in France remained a complex issue in the decades following the liberation. This was made no more apparent than when de Gaulle laid a wreath on the tomb of Pétain in 1968. As Michael Curtis writes, de Gaulle claimed that he was 'paying homage to "the victor of Verdun"', not to the head of the Vichy state, and de Gaulle's successors continued to lay tributes to Pétain until 1992 (2002: 73).[1] Such a tribute is indicative of de Gaulle's attempts to compartmentalize Vichy outside his narrative of French history, which included Pétain's role in the First World War but ignored his collaboration in the Second. Pétain remained an important part of the French history that de Gaulle saw as imperative to rebuilding France, sustaining the cult of Pétain that had anchored the Vichy regime.[2] De Gaulle commemorated Pétain for his legacy

---

[1] In 2018, President Emmanuel Macron drew criticism for suggesting Pétain be celebrated as a war hero as part of the anniversary commemorations of the First World War.

[2] The strange cultism that Pétain's celebrity and legacy invited continued into the post-war period. This was perhaps best represented when a small faction of ultra-Pétainists attempted to fulfil the marshal's dying wish: to be buried alongside his troops rather than his place of exile on the Île d'Yeu.

as the 'hero of Verdun' without reference to his role in Vichy. For de Gaulle, rebuilding national identity required refashioning historical fact, a major aspect of the 'Vichy syndrome' of post-war France.

Vichy was imagined as a digression in, rather than a product of, French history, and the provisional government and Fourth Republic drew on de Gaulle's rhetoric of French unity to combat the lingering sense that Vichy had been condoned, even welcomed, at the point of defeat in 1940. Various post-war conceptions of humanism were central to this notion of unity, many of which were underpinned by a faith in the democratic, rationalizing project of nationhood derived from the French Enlightenment. Drawing on the work of French historian Jean Lacouture, Andrew Gibson frames de Gaulle's post-war political vision as one that required 'rationalization in general' following years of barbarism – itself its own kind of rationalization – 'and rational planning in particular'. 'In the postwar years', Gibson argues, 'this would be ever more closely bound up with the emergence of a new technocracy and a new kind of French bourgeoisie' (2010b: 4). For de Gaulle, this was necessary to rid the nation of the forms of nationalism – monarchist, anti-democratic, fascist, among others – which had allowed France to fall into the clutches of Vichy. In part, Beckett's scepticism resulted from the fact that de Gaulle's logic of a 'true' France mirrored that of Pétainism's bid for traditionalism, though this had been rationalized by the apparently self-evident decadence of the Third Republic and threat of 'undesirables' to France itself.

Nevertheless, Vichy and Gaullism alike called upon the reorientation of the individual subject to that of a national subject. The national subject – the 'true' French citizen – was defined by their ability to make moral or ethical choices for the good of the nation. Such actions could be carried out 'in the name of' France, including acts of violence (the post-war purges) or exclusion (Vichy's racism). For Gaullism, the collective unity of France was necessary to a narrative of nationwide resistance against occupation. Beckett's post-war narrators reimagine this logic with macabre humour, most startlingly, perhaps, in 'The Expelled': 'They never lynch children, babies. . . . I personally would lynch them with the utmost pleasure, I don't say I'd lend a hand, no, but I'd encourage the others and stand them drinks when it was done' (*ECEF*: 8). The image of lynching is as evocative of wartime horrors as it is the post-war purges. It is both grimly humorous and horrifying, containing within it the

In 1973, 'a band of right-wing fanatics took matters into their own hands, digging up the body and heading off for Verdun. The marshal's remains were eventually discovered in a garage outside Paris, and returned to their island resting-place, where they remain to this day' (Atkin 1998: 196).

way in which the language, even the celebration, of unity and the collective can conceal violent urges and actions.

Beckett and the politics of post-war humanism

The attempt to reconstruct France through a set of values that were both universal and French – encapsulated in the restoration of the *Liberté, Égalité, Fraternité* motto – was symbolized by de Gaulle. Though he resigned in 1946 at the creation of the Fourth Republic, the ideals of Gaullism carried forward and allowed for de Gaulle's return in 1958. Central to Gaullism was the notion of the strong state comprised of individuals defined by their relation to 'Frenchness', and on this count, like Vichy, Gaullism required the definition of a 'true' France and French identity. Despite some surface conceptual overlaps in its notion of the state, Gaullism rejected Communism wholesale, a source of much tension in the post-liberation years. For de Gaulle, France is 'an indomitable entity, a "person" with whom a mystical dialogue was maintained throughout history' (Berstein 2001: 307). Vichy had brought shame upon this 'person', but de Gaulle asserted that French unity would heal the country:

> We are living through moments which transcend each of our poor lives. . . . All the men who are here today and all who hear me elsewhere in France know that this warlike duty demands national unity. . . . The nation well knows that the sons and daughters of France – all the sons and daughters except for a few unhappy traitors who gave themselves over to the enemy and who are tasting or will taste the rigours of the law – yes! All the sons and daughters of France must march towards France's goal, fraternally and hand in hand. (1944)

Gaullism was also a humanist ideology which appealed to the heritage of the Enlightenment in its values, particularly on the matter of human rights and freedoms of the individual. In parallel, the post-war years saw a surge in different conceptions of humanism across the political and philosophical spectrums in France, as intellectuals attempted to grapple with the violence and chaos of the war. Though the racial identity politics of Nazism and Vichy had been defeated in the liberation, what Molloy terms the 'relentless definition of man' (*M*: 38) was an essential intellectual focus in post-war recovery.[3]

---

[3] I use 'human' and 'humanity' throughout this chapter. 'Man', 'mankind' and other gendered formulations are used only in quotations.

'Liberal' humanism is a particularly apt descriptor of the culture of post-war France which arrived with Gaullism, adopted after the liberation to a resounding celebration of freedom, rationality and progress. It is in this context that Beckett begun his most productive period of writing: the famous 'siege in the room' (Bair 1980: 294). Paris's post-war culture of humanism surrounded Beckett. As Andrew Gibson emphasizes, 'Order, unity and unanimity, reason and rationalization, purification and exaltation: these values had a determining effect both on the immediately postwar French society in which Beckett produced his greater works, and on its dominant discourses' (2010b: 6). For Beckett, however, this humanism was, Gibson writes, 'a failure of sensibility and intellectual courage' (2010a: 124). Such failure is inscribed into the recurring denigration of 'man' in Beckett's post-war writing, and becomes all the more politically potent when we consider just how pervasive humanism was in post-war French culture.

The turn to humanism was a conscious attempt from all corners of the political and intellectual establishment to bring a renewed set of values to France during a period when social and political unity was low. For France, as Michael Kelly argues, this was of particular importance given the diminished status of the French Catholic Church after its alignment with Vichy. The Church's reduced standing forced the 'political and intellectual elites' to 'look elsewhere' for stable foundations for meaning. Humanism 'emerged suddenly and unexpectedly as the uncontested framework of values within which the debates and struggles of the period were expressed' and became, 'in effect, the conceptual form of French universalism' (Kelly 2004: 127, 153). From the liberation of Paris in August 1944 onwards, humanistic rhetoric was enshrined in French public life. In a bid to banish Vichy authoritarianism from French thought, de Gaulle quickly reinstated the Déclaration des droits de l'homme et du citoyen (Declaration of the Rights of Man and of the Citizen), which was subsequently incorporated into the Fourth Republic's official constitution. According to Gaullism, the Resistance was dedicated to the 'rights of man' (Gildea 1996: 64) and, as Gibson writes, 'those who participated in the Resistance, whether Republican, Communist, Socialist, monarchist or other', were imagined to have 'shared the values involved in this ideology, signed up to them and gave them pre-eminence for the duration of the war' (2010b: 6).

Jean-Paul Sartre's famous lecture 'L'Existentialisme est un humanisme' (Existentialism Is a Humanism) at Club Maintenant in October 1945 certified humanistic existentialism as the de facto philosophy of the Fourth Republic, and

Sartre its philosopher.[4] Sartre was keen to publicly defend existentialism against accusations of nihilism, and to legitimize a truly atheistic moral framework. He was all too aware of the trappings that the label of humanism could entail, and that unchecked humanistic proclamations could become a 'cult of humanity' which ends 'shut-in upon itself' and 'in Fascism' (1980a: 368). Sartre's aim was to style existentialism as a viable mode of thought which would not descend into essentialism and could, by extension, protect French intellectual life from a cultism that could give way to fascism's biopolitical rationalizations. Sartre's desire to recoup 'humanism' as a concept for existentialist discourse demonstrates the heightened political charge the term carried at the time.

This appeal to humanism went far further afield, though, as cultural and political factions began to grapple for power.[5] The Catholic periodical *Temps présent* published a series of lectures in 1946 under the title 'Les Grands appels de l'homme contemporain' (The great appeals to modern man). In 1947, Martin Heidegger's 'Letter on Humanism' and Maurice Merleau-Ponty's *Humanism and Terror* were published. The former contends with the ontological structures of thought in humanism in the post-war French context, the latter with the extent to which humanism was still present within the Communist project, despite the violence and terror in the USSR. For Beckett, France's post-war humanism was all a variation on the same theme, what *The Unnamable* calls 'all that balls about being and existing' (*U*: 63).

The humanist ideas and ideals of the post-war period recur as an object of enquiry in Beckett's writing, often through a scathing critique or parody. As noted in Chapter 4, Beckett declared 'human' a word used only in 'times of huge slaughters'. He also called it 'a word that is being bandied around today with an unrivalled fury. Just like dum-dum bullets' (*Dis*: 131–2; trans qtd. in Rabaté 2016: 18). The dum-dum bullet expands on impact, stopping the target faster as the bullet's energy transfers into the wounded body. Beckett overlays the bullet's damage pattern onto the post-war French art scene: 'art should not need cataclysms to be able to be practiced. The damage is already considerable. With "this is not human", one has said it all. Throw it to the garbage can. Tomorrow

---

[4] Graham O'Dwyer goes so far as to argue that de Gaulle's understanding of the 'authentic' French individual in relation to the 'authentic' French state, and the role of the former in the creation of the latter, was Sartrean. Rather than claiming there to be an overt use of existentialist philosophy in de Gaulle's political thinking, though, O'Dwyer suggests that 'once we reconcile ourselves with de Gaulle's ontological understanding of France and nations in a wider sense we may see the strain of existentialism that courses through his foreign policy' (2017: 129).

[5] Michael Kelly writes that 'the postwar humanist upsurge can be seen in the plethora of books published with some variant of *l'homme* or *l'humanisme* in their title. A handful of such books in 1945 was followed by three times as many the following year' (2004: 142).

one will require that *charcuterie* be human' (Ibid.). The term 'human' continues to wound, Beckett argues, long after it has been used.

Beckett's scepticism towards post-war humanism and a vocabulary of the 'human' was not an isolated concern, nor was it limited to France. Writing in *Horizon* in 1946, George Orwell identified 'human' as one of the terms in contemporary art and literary criticism that was 'completely lacking in meaning' (1957: 148). In France, the abstract painter Camille Bryen and playwright Jacques Audiberti[6] developed what they termed 'abhumanism', a philosophical position that rejected the reifying narrative of the human in Enlightenment humanism and emphasized parody and playfulness. The philosophy was closely related to Dada and surrealism, and Bryen and Audiberti published their thinking in 1952 in a text entitled *L'Ouvre-Boîte: Colloque abhumaniste* (The can opener: An abhumanist colloquium). Painting that disrupted notions of anthropocentricism (like that of the van Veldes) was of major importance to the abhumanists, as was any art form that could 'liberate' humanity 'by abandoning pretensions of grandeur' and return it to its 'humble place in the universe' (trans. in Slavkova 2003: 321). The abhumanists emphasized that the human 'should turn to vitalizing accomplishments – joy, pleasure, sex, art – without justification, without noble end, without premeditation' (trans. in Slavkova 2003: 321). This emphasis on 'vitality', on life itself, was juxtaposed with the ferocious and devastating violence of the First and Second World Wars, and like Beckett the abhumanists abhorred the emergence of 'humanity' at times of great violence. As in Beckett's post-war work, the abhumanists relied heavily on humour, puns and caricature in their send-up of modern humanism:

> Man is intoxicated by anthropophagy. Beneath the white medical caps, beneath the big literary bonnets, under the political top hats, man continues to graze on man to digest the explanations, melodies, parodies, hominal sexualogies [*sic*]. (trans. in Slavkova 2003: 321)

Like Beckett's image of 'mouton sacré' in his van Veldes essay (*Dis*: 14), the abhumanists were concerned not only with the artistic implications of a naive and reifying humanism but also with its implications for turning the human into a passive herd animal. Angela Moorjani has read *Molloy* in terms of an 'ahumanism' which very much accords with the post-war abhumanist project. Noting the text's recurrent use of the image of the bicycle as a 'displaced reference' to the Second World War, brought about by the mention of Nazi leader Hermann

---

[6] Audiberti was an admirer of Beckett's theatre, particularly *En attendant Godot* (Graver and Federman 2005: 8).

Goering when Moran taunts his son (*M*: 149), Moorjani identifies this treatment of history in conjunction with the text's recurrent attack on conceptions of 'man' as an assertion of 'the writer's role' in 'chip[ping] away at the humanistic past' (Moorjani 2013: 94), one energized by the post-war political clamour over humanism in the light of Nazism's 'definition of man' in its extermination policies. Such a reference finds its disruptive power through an abhumanist mode of playful invocation, treating the recent past with derisive irreverence.

Throughout the late 1940s and early 1950s, Beckett remained engaged with (and critical of) the entrenched humanism of post-war France, particularly in his reading of journals and magazines. This was augmented by his work for Georges Duthuit's revived *Transition* journal. Beckett provided translations for Duthuit and was the architect of the *Three Dialogues* on contemporary art.[7] As announced by the editorial statement of its first issue, the journal endeavoured to re-establish the international significance of French culture after the insularity of Vichy by bringing together diverse and divergent strains of French culture and politics:

> The object of TRANSITION *Forty-eight* is to assemble for the English-speaking world the best of French art and thought, whatever the style and whatever the application. So it is that our first number presents an atheist philosopher like Sartre, wrestling with Breton and the surrealists; a learned Catholic like Gengoux; Jean Wahl, the lucid, hesitant believer; Artaud, pain-haunted rebel and solitary. Their divergences are strident, and it would be odd if men exploring the same Stygian cave did not sometimes come into collision. (1948: 5)

Duthuit's magazine was keen to mark itself as a crucible for 'the best' French thought, and its emphasis on 'collision' marks its achievement in unifying diverse French thought through exchange. By contrast, Gaullism's rhetoric of French unity failed to conceal its narrow perspective on the war and on French national life.

Nevertheless, *Transition* often includes pieces devoted to new, rethought or rediscovered humanisms, particularly from the existential and surrealist stables. For Beckett, the humanisms of figures like Sartre and André Breton represented in *Transition* were 'pernicious':

> From your Sartre-Breton equation one may indeed emerge, I think, into a pure air of grandeur, distinguished conation and utilitarian splendor, in which an end is made of the pernicious illusion in which they are at one, in which people everywhere have always been at one (I can hear you groaning), the illusion of the human and the fully realized. (27 July 1948, *LSB II*: 86)

---

[7] For a discussion of Beckett's work on paintings and the intricacies of the art world at this time, see Carville (2018: 182–213).

Beckett's concern with the 'illusion' of 'the human' echoes the problem raised by Fernand Robert in *L'Humanisme: Essai de definition*, published in Paris in 1946:

> At the end of the Second World War, the word humanism is a fashionable word. Honouring the human person, and basing morality and politics on the respect due to him, is one of the strongest leanings of public opinion, and consequently one of the main themes in all the programmes of parties and sects. . . . [W]ith a modicum of rhetorical ingenuity, it is possible to dress up almost any doctrine as a humanism, simply by showing – and one can show this about all of them – that it concerns Man, and that it is important to Humanity. (trans. in Kelly 2004: 142–3)

The humanism label became a legitimizing one in post-war Paris. For Beckett, this was 'pernicious' in its nullifying effects on art and its reception, making sheep of those who absorbed the rhetoric of humanity wholesale.

Such a scepticism towards humanistic idealism finds its way into other aspects of Beckett's work at the time. His frequent complaints over working for UNESCO on Octavio Paz's *Anthology of Mexican Poetry* during the period, for example, falls more concretely into place as part of his general post-war apprehensions (*LSB II*: 72). What Beckett identified to Israel Shenker in 1956 as the method of 'ignorance' and 'impotence' that fuelled his work from 1946 onwards (Graver and Federman 2005: 162) sits squarely opposed to the well-publicized 1946 programme of 'Fundamental Education' put forward by UNESCO:

> As part of its efforts to create the conditions of 'mutual understanding' deemed necessary to avoid a third World War in the twentieth century, UNESCO proposed a 'radical revolution' in the name of 'human betterment' and the 'spirit of brotherhood', entreating the literate world to 'launch' a global humanitarian 'war on ignorance', with an especial 'attack on illiteracy'. (Slaughter 2007: 278)

By contrast, Beckett's championship of ignorance counters the extent to which 'human betterment' could be defined with strict parameters of knowledge, a process which rings of the civilized-uncivilized dichotomy central to imperialist, even fascist rhetoric. In UNESCO's formulation, knowledge will prevent war, but only if a metaphorical war is conducted on ignorance, particularly nations or cultures unwilling (or, more likely, unable) to redress social imbalances caused by deficiencies in the kinds of education lauded by the West.[8]

---

[8] For a reading of the 'neo-imperialist' dimensions of UNESCO's cultural agenda, see Brouillette (2019). For a discussion of the political factors involved in Beckett's translation project, see *PI* (118–20).

Writing again to Duthuit in the spring of 1950, Beckett remarks that he had 'read with wonderment Breton, Patri, Péret in *Combat*' and concluded that it was 'flowery stuff'. André Breton, who had managed to escape Vichy persecution and spent the war in the United States, was a figure whose humanism did little to convince Beckett of its weight or significance:

> Noted in Breton the singularly powerful image of the ship of humanity cast adrift by its navigator on to the 'definitive reefs'. To wait until the atomic age before feeling really worried, that is indeed surrealist. And that certainty of spring that did his heart good in the worst moments of the Occupation. Lucky thing. (*LSB II*: 196)

The notes in *Letters II* identify the Breton passage to which Beckett refers:

> En ces premiers jours de printemps, me revient à l'esprit une des rares idées secourables à quoi je parvins à m'accrocher aux pires jours de la dernière guerre : tant de dévastations ne pourraient rien contre le retour du printemps, assez grand magicien pour prêter un sourire aux ruines.
>
> (In these early Spring days, I am reminded of one of the few helpful ideas that I contrived to hold on to in the worst days of the last war: the many devastations could do nothing to stop the return of Spring, a magician great enough to lend a smile to ruins). (trans. in *LSB II*: 199)

Though Beckett would likely have found some appeal in the alienation of the human from nature and the movement of time here, Breton's optimism over the ruins that Beckett encountered first-hand seems to have been less convincing. Nevertheless, Beckett uses a similar image in Molloy's rejection of the humanist education he was put through, concluding that '[i]n the end it was magic that had the honour of my ruins, and still today, when I walk there, I find its vestiges' (*M*: 38).[9]

As his letters to Duthuit, Reavey and MacGreevy during this period make clear, Beckett was wary of humanist narratives of hope or progress as France navigated the threat of civil war and the onset of the Cold War. One of the major contributions to these tensions was the popularity of Marxist thinking in the post-war period, opposed by Gaullism but championed by many left-wing intellectuals. Beckett's writing takes to task the Marxism of Paris in the late 1940s on several occasions in his writing, each one with an eye to the wider context of humanist discourse which held sway at the time.

---

[9] Beckett's choice of 'ruins' in the English translation is worth noting in this regard, given that the original '*décombres*' translates more conventionally as rubble.

Violence and progress: France, humanism and post-war Marxism

Following the liberation, there was a constant tension between the Fourth Republic and the Parti Communiste Française (PCF; French Communist Party). The PCF had formed a major part of the Resistance and was initially included in the governance of post-war France. This ended in 1947 with the expulsion of the Communists from the coalition. Gaullism became the official doctrine of the Fourth Republic's government, as did anti-Communism. France then joined the Cold War against Soviet Russia, formalized with the founding of NATO in 1949. Meanwhile, intellectual Marxists continued to espouse the promise of Marxist and Communist thinking, but this became increasingly difficult as the atrocities of Stalin's brutal regime continued. Those who either supported the USSR or remained silent on the matter stood on increasingly dubious ground as the Iron Curtain came down over Eastern Europe. It took the invasion of Hungary by the Soviets in 1956 for Sartre to denounce the Soviet Union.[10] Nevertheless, he continued to believe 'Marxism the one philosophy of our time which we cannot go beyond' (1980b: 369) and, in the light of Soviet atrocities, attempted to position existentialism as a complimentary system of thought that could redeem Marxism's absorption into the Soviet Union's authoritarianism.

Beckett's aversion to the intellectual and political dominance of Marxism after the war is marked out explicitly in two instances: in *Eleutheria* in the character of Dr Piouk and in 'The End' as a man berates people from the top of a car. Jackie Blackman (2008) locates these allusions in Paris's post-war intellectual debates, reading *Eleutheria* as a direct parody of Parisian intellectuals espousing the merits of Marxism while blind to the reality of violence in the Soviet state. For Blackman, Dr Piouk is modelled on Sartre. The text requires closer analysis in these terms, though, and should be more firmly situated in the wider context of the debates over the validity of humanism as a moral and political framework for France's recovery.

Eleutheria provides one of Beckett's most stringent critiques of post-war Parisian life, and Dr Piouk is a composite character through which this critique is channelled. He is intimately familiar with arts and culture of contemporary

---

[10] Sartre addressed the invasion of Hungary in the first chapter of *Questions de méthode* (1957; Search for a Method) where he was particularly damning of the Soviet Union's failure to recognize the Hungarian Uprising as a worker's revolution. He broke fully with Communist thinking in 1968 after the Soviet invasion of Czechoslovakia, turning his attention to the younger generations of the French left and pursuing his anti-imperialist thinking in the wake of the Algerian conflict.

Paris, as he reveals to the Glazier and Mlle Skunk in his description of Victor's ailments: 'He was taking an interest in the inexhaustible variety of the Parisian scene, in art, in theatre, in science, in politics, in every new school of philosophy, in the –' (1996: 104). Dr Piouk is cut off by the Glazier and moves on to Victor's interest in the 'Merovingian Kings', the first Frankish dynasty whose line ushered in the end of the late-Antiquity Roman military occupation of northern Gaul and made Paris its capital.[11] Dr Piouk's comment, 'in the –', is unfinished, creating an absence in his report which is reflected in Victor's turn away from the world. However, Victor's interest in a monarchic lineage that originated in the defeat of an imperial conqueror and the founding of France's beloved capital leaves the Second World War lingering in what is afflicting Victor. Piouk's summary is a satirical version of Beckett's assessment of the cultural climate of Paris in 1945, in which '[t]he same crowd, writing & painting, tops the bills that has topped it since the liberation' (Beckett to MacGreevy, 19 August 1945, *LSB II*: 19–20). For Beckett, post-war Parisian culture was more exhausting than inexhaustible. In the play, this melancholy translates into detached apathy, even hostility. 'It's no longer the Third Republic,' remarks Dr Piouk in act 2 (1996: 119), seemingly in defiance of the Gaullist notion of Vichy as a mere 'interruption'. Earlier in the play, after being quizzed on his Communist allegiances, Dr Piouk is goaded into offering his 'solution' for 'the problem of humanity'. Echoing the medicalized language of humanity's 'condition' that Beckett uses in 'The Capital of the Ruins', Dr Piouk's solution is a curative of sorts:

> Dr PIOUK. Well, then. I would ban reproduction. I would perfect the condom and other devices and bring them into general use. I would establish teams of abortionists, controlled by the State. I would apply the death penalty to any woman guilty of giving birth. I would drown all newborn babies. I would militate in favour of homosexuality, and would myself set the example. And to speed things up, I would encourage recourse to euthanasia by all possible means, although I would not make it obligatory. Those are the broad outlines.
>
> (1996: 44)

---

[11] The Merovingian kings, like d'Aubigné in 'The Calmative' or Patrick Sarsfield and Saint Ruth in *Mercier and Camier* (see Chapter 6), are representative of Beckett's interest in French military-religious figures. The Merovingian dynasty began when Childeric I and his son, Clovis I, united the Franks under a single monarchy. It was Clovis I who oversaw the transition from the Romans to the Franks as rulers of Gaul and the establishment of Paris as the Frankish capital. He also converted to Catholicism and oversaw the First Council of Orléans. Like Beckett's Clov, Clovis I struggled to keep his house in order. Viking, Visigoth and Roman forces thwarted his attempts to expand and secure the Franks' realm.

In many ways, Dr Piouk's is that same hyperbolic fantasy of degeneration and anti-natalism which we saw in Chapter 3 through the decaying bodies of the trilogy. Piouk's 'broad outlines' are recognizably akin to the violent 'solution' of extermination expounded in Nazi and Vichy discourse. Yet his solution for the 'human' problem is not part of a bid for political power or racial superiority. Piouk will end suffering by bringing an end to the being which suffers: humanity itself. The scene is a reversal of Gaullist optimism in its proposal that unity is in fact the cause of suffering. It also inverts Vichy's campaign to promote childbirth and conservative family values, in which contraceptives and abortion were vilified. Further still, in an example of Beckett's ability to condense multiple historical markers into his texts, it is also a savage parody of the contradictory intellectualism of figures like Sartre: a philosopher who could espouse the humanistic notion of the freedom of the individual in his 'Existentialism Is a Humanism' lecture yet also find validity in the Stalinist regime. The text evinces Beckett's judgement that a language of 'humanity', no matter the context, has within it the violent potential of the 'dum-dum bullet'. In *Eleutheria*, the solution is to erase 'the human species', an end to life but, more importantly in the play's perverse humour, an end to the language of 'humanity'.

Piouk is presented as an intellectual who has solved the problem of Marxism in practice. Aspiring to this goal, Maurice Merleau-Ponty, like Sartre, sought to address the disparity between the lived reality of the Soviet Union and the emancipatory promise of Marxism. In *Humanisme et terreur, essai sur le problème communiste* (1947; *Humanism and Terror: An Essay on the Communist Problem*, trans. 1969), Merleau-Ponty followed Sartre's argument that Marxism was the basis of modern philosophy and the most accurate description of the rational processes of historical progress. Marxism is also, he claimed, the basis of common humanity in the modern age:

> Marxism is not just any hypothesis that might be replaced tomorrow by some other. It is the simple statement of those conditions without which there would be neither any humanism, in the sense of a mutual relation between men, nor any rationality in history. In this sense Marxism is not a philosophy of history; it is *the* philosophy of history and to renounce it is to dig the grave of Reason in history. (1969: 153; emphasis in original)

Those appalled by the USSR should not condemn Marxism as an ideology of violence, Merleau-Ponty argued, since 'violence is the common origin of all regimes. Life, discussion, and political choice occur only against a background of violence' (1969: 109). The misstep of Stalinism, he contended, was to forget that the proletariat were not just the resources of the revolution but those who would come to hold power. Likewise, he argued that the realities of Stalinist violence should not result in the dismissal of Marxism's achievements, above all its exposure of the colonial legacies of the West's modern liberal democracies. As such, Merleau-Ponty called for what he later termed 'une attitude d'attentisme marxiste', another version of the political 'wait-and-see' stance many citizens had adopted during the war, in which the failures of Stalin's regime were intellectually remoulded into one more step in the progression towards true revolution.[12] Merleau-Ponty asserted that while violence should not be the natural condition of the Marxist state, such a state might require violence to come into being (though not sustain it). Marxist *attentisme* therefore required the intellectual acceptance, even justification, of violence and murder as part of progression towards a proletarian state. In *Eleutheria*, having been battered by all manner of bourgeois intellectual pontifications on humanity, including the violent anti-natalism of the mock-Communist Dr Piouk, Victor ends the play asking Mme Karl for another blanket. Mme Karl comforts Victor by reassuring him that 'spring will soon be here' (1996: 169), anticipating the fantastical optimism of André Breton's 'dream of spring' that Beckett would later denigrate (*LSB II*: 196). Rather than climbing on what Breton called the 'ship of humanity', Victor finishes by shuffling in his bed, wandering around the stage, '*scrutinis*[ing] *the audience*' and, after laying down, '*turning his emaciated back on humanity*' (1996: 170). Beckett's vocabulary of emaciation recalls the concern he voiced to MacGreevy after the war, that he feared MacGreevy's work in Ireland left him 'starved'. Yet Victor's turn on 'humanity' is embodied, not spoken. On stage, the word 'humanity' would not be uttered, left as it is to the stage directions to clarify Victor's actions to a potential actor. Dialogue, mere language, cannot, it seems, do justice to Beckett's rejection of the post-war language of 'humanity'. It is left to the body, the image of a starved and exhausted body, to embody an unequivocal and weary dismissal of the violent means by which progress was imagined in the wake of the Second World War.

Post-war Marxism and the failure of humanism's promises for greater human dignity are also the objects of parody in 'La Fin' ('The End'):

> For some time past a sound had been scarifying me. I did not investigate the cause, for as I said myself, it's going to stop. But as it did not I had no choice but to find out the cause. . . . It was a man perched on the roof of a car haranguing the passers-by. That at least was my interpretation. He was bellowing so loud that snatches of his discourse reached my ears. Union . . . brothers . . . Marx . . . capital . . . bread and butter . . . love. It was all Greek to me. (*ECEF*: 51–2)

---

[12] Merleau-Ponty uses the 'attentisme' phrase in his 1955 publication *Les Aventures de la dialectique*, a development of his thought in *Humanisme et terreur*.

This section appears in the second half of the text. Famously, the early version of 'La Fin', 'Suite', was published in Sartre's *Les Tempes modernes* with the second half missing, prompting Beckett to write an irate letter to Simone de Beauvoir. He submitted the second half again, but it was not published (*LSB II*: 40–2). Blackman suggests that *Eleutheria*'s parody of Marxist intellectuals was a response to the rejection of the second half of the text (2008: 74–5).

Given the parody of Marxism in 'La Fin', it is certainly possible that *Les Tempes modernes* elided Beckett's second half on ideological grounds. The text is invested in a disruption of the very structures of Marxism as they were presented in the post-war moment.[13] Rather than a fully formed address, the narrator can only make out snippets of the man's speech: 'Union . . . brothers . . . Marx . . . capital . . . bread and butter . . . love.' Basic necessities are sandwiched between morsels of Marxist watchwords which offer zero nourishment while starvation and homelessness continue. As the man finishes his 'discourse', he directs his speech towards the impoverished narrator:

> All of a sudden he turned and pointed at me, as at an exhibit. Look at this down and out, he vociferated, this leftover. If he doesn't go down on all fours, it's for fear of being impounded. Old, lousy, rotten, ripe for the muckheap. And there are a thousand like him, worse than him, ten thousand, twenty thousand –. A voice, Thirty thousand. (*ECEF*: 52)

The orator identifies the narrator as a 'leftover', the remainder of progress and, in the post-war context, of recovery. As if 'at an exhibit', the narrator is put on display by the Marxist, who fetishizes him and the thousands of others who found themselves 'down and out' after the war.

In its language of display and exhibition, the scene recalls the recurring debates about the aesthetics and politics of representation in post-war France, and the role of Communist artists as part of France's recovery. In October 1944, to celebrate the ongoing liberation of the nation, the Salon de la Libération took place, an exhibition designed to unite France in cultural expression. In the event, the Salon of 1944 signified the deep tensions of the visual arts scene in Paris at the time. The Communist faction of the Resistance sought legitimization through the exhibition, claiming political power by way of demonstrating the contributions of Communist artists to France's recovery. The debate became all the more heated when Pablo Picasso formalized his membership of the PCF in 1944, an occasion which provoked disdain from many commentators. Picasso's

---

[13] See Smith (2017) for a close reading of this scene in terms of an Adornian sense of the 'radical politics' in the post-war moment.

alleged wealth of 600 million francs did not suggest him as a hero of Communism. The celebration of Picasso's political manoeuvre in the Communist magazine *L'Humanité* was subject to a substantial degree of mockery. Protests followed:

> When the Salon opened, traditionalists and friends of the excluded painters held a demonstration inside. 'Take them down! Take them down!' they yelled in front of Picasso's paintings. . . . Young right-wingers even went round Paris altering the chalked Communist slogans of '*Pétain au poteau*' ('Pétain for the firing squad') to '*Picasso au poteau*'. (Beevor and Cooper 2007: 181)

The battle for 'true France' raged as heavily among the makers of culture as it did in the courts of the post-war trials, and, as Laurence Bertrand Dorléac writes, 'Picasso's membership in the Communist Party established the party's reputation in France as the natural family of intellectual and artists, while bluntly reinstating an orthodox logic of political commitment, in an art scene that was having difficulty establishing its corporate image as "resisters" and its "sense of history"' (2008: 312).[14] Picasso gave his clearest rationale for joining the Communist Party in a note in the American magazine *New Masses*, published on 24 October 1944, in which he aligned himself with André Breton's earlier surrealist movement, arguing that the 'aesthetic revolution was inevitably the counterpart of a political revolution' (Bertrand Dorléac 2008: 315). Beckett distrusted Breton's 'fully realized' human and the notion of humanity 'as one', and Communism's absorption of the individual into the collective is similarly concerned with the homogenizing erasure of the self. Beckett's Marxist 'orator' – dispassionate towards the beggar-narrator, for he is not a worker – is indicative of the pervasiveness of the intellectual battles of post-war Paris. Before 1939, it was 'Germanic destiny' which brought Beckett's 'vomit' up; after the liberation, articulations of French destiny from Gaullists, Communists and lingering Pétainists alike appeared to elicit similar dismay and ridicule.

Beckett's work of the mid- and late 1940s emerges from a historical reality in which the Gaullist rhetoric of liberation, unity and anti-Communism was pitted against the juggernauts of the PCF, magazines like *L'Humanité* and the weight of celebrity commanded by Sartre and his circle, intellectuals who could both be devoted to the radical freedom of the individual and accommodate the violence of Stalinism in the hope that it might yet lead to revolution. *Eleutheria* and 'The End' deploy processes of inversion and parody that reveal the ideological frameworks which circulated in post-war Paris to have themselves been 'old,

---

[14] Bertrand Dorléac quotes from Louis Parrot's 'Picasso au Salon', published 7 October 1944, the day after the opening of the Salon.

lousy, rotten' (*ECEF*: 52), many of them espousing human unity and progress yet justifying the state violence of the USSR and the ongoing laudation of the worker in the hope that reason would prevail as a historical force. Much as the dog remains starving while Watt rationalizes the method of its feeding, people continued to suffer in the harsh reality of the post-war moment while debates raged over the kind of nation that should be rebuilt. Beckett's text registers this moral crisis in the post-war period, the Marxist orator bellowing about 'love' as he berates the homeless narrator and condemns him to the 'muckheap'.

In *The Unnamable*, the narrator puts an end (of sorts) to the notion of progress, dismissing its relevance to his individual condition: 'There will be no more from me about bodies and trajectories, sky and earth, I don't know what it all is,' the narrator declares, swapping the dialectic logic of history for stasis and ignorance (*U*: 36). This follows a larger dismissal of the 'lectures' on humanity styled as violent force-feedings.

> [W]hat they were most determined for me to swallow was my fellow-creatures. In this they were without mercy. I remember little or nothing of these lectures. I cannot have understood a great deal. But I seem to have retained certain descriptions, in spite of myself. They gave me courses on love, on intelligence, most precious, most precious. They also taught me to count, and even to reason. Some of this rubbish has come in handy on occasions, I don't deny it, on occasions which would never have arisen if they had left me in peace. I use it still, to scratch my arse with. (*U*: 8)

In the fictions Beckett produced after the war, surrounded as he was by the clamour over post-war humanism, progress and reason are little more than alleviations of an irritation. 'Love' and 'intelligence' are dismissed as mere 'courses'. The 'inestimable gift of life' and notion of 'fellow-creatures' are 'rammed ... without mercy' down the narrator's 'gullet' (*U*: 8), the gastric torture literalizing the debates of the post-war period. As Alys Moody argues, Beckett's recourse to a language of hunger and forced feeding is 'animated by the frantic impulse to purge oneself of the alien intrusion of language' (2018: 108), one energized by Beckett's 'reaction against the demand that both art and hunger be made political and made to serve the ultimate end of liberation' in the post-war period (112). But in the same way that intellectual rhetoric can conceal actual violence, the scene is also torture. In this, too, Beckett's work has stark historical resonance. We find in *The Unnamable* a powerful and disturbing evocation of the violence which haunted France's recovery: both the actual violence of the purges that followed the liberation and the discourse of violence inherent to debates over Marxism.

The purges that followed the liberation of French towns and regions saw thousands tortured, assaulted and killed for crimes of collaboration, both real and imagined. The kinds of tortures that *The Unnamable* cites were not inconceivable in the bid to force a confession of fraternizing with the enemy. Head shaving, as noted, and summary executions were the most common image of the waves of purges which took place in 1944, again in January and February 1945 (when Beckett was back in Paris), and once more in the spring of 1945 'following the shock of deportees returning' from the camps (Beevor and Cooper 2007: 88). Law was of little matter, and in turn any notion of unity or 'fellow-creatures' had to emerge out of the 'communal fury' that the purges represented: 'the fact that sleeping with a German might have been the only way for a woman to keep her children from starvation was scarcely considered when the communal fury was unleashed' (Beevor and Cooper: 77). The notion of 'communal fury' also fuelled the desire for revolution among French Marxists and Communists, and, as we have seen, Merleau-Ponty and others saw violence as the means by which human unity could ultimately be achieved.

Reflecting the violence-unity dialectic of the post-war moment in France, Beckett's work of this period repeatedly connects 'humanity' with violence. In *Molloy*, there are several violent or near-violent encounters between Molloy and his 'fellow creatures'. Early in the novel, Molloy observes 'C' walking off into 'the treacherous hills' so reminiscent of *maquis* territory:

> Yes, night was gathering, but the man was innocent, greatly innocent, he had nothing to fear, though he went in fear, he had nothing to fear, there was nothing they could do to him, or very little. But he can't have known it. I wouldn't know it myself, if I thought about it. Yes, he saw himself threatened, his body threatened, his reason threatened, and perhaps he was, perhaps they were, in spite of his innocence. What business has innocence here? What relation to the innumerable spirits of darkness? It's not clear. (*M*: 6)

While no physical violence occurs between Molloy and 'C', a 'spirit of darkness' lurks in the scene as Molloy stalks the 'threatened' body. The ironic declaration that C 'had nothing to fear' recalls Albert Camus's series of essays 'Neither Victims or Executioners' for *Combat* (1946), in which he identified the twentieth century as the 'century of fear', the moment in which fear became 'a basic element' of modern living (2002: 257–9). Camus was one of the figures who, in the light of Stalinist atrocities and the violence of the French post-war purges, revised his conviction that 'communal fury' was necessary for post-war recovery. Initially a supporter of both the purges and Merleau-Ponty's assertion that violence is the generative force of both politics and human progress, Camus subsequently saw violence itself as a threat to 'reason', and argued that the 'legitimize[d] murder' (2002: 261) of the war, the post-war purges and Stalin's regime revealed the failure of the 'language of humanity' to prevent 'lying, humiliation, killing, deportation, and torture' (2002: 599). In *Molloy*, C goes in fear despite Molloy reasoning that 'very little' would be done to him. And yet, C 'saw himself threatened' by an unnamed terror in the world. His innocence, in the end, counts for nothing, and the sinister ambiguity of Molloy's conclusions over innocence – 'it's not clear' – reflects what Camus described as the specific fear that gripped post-war France whereby 'we seek to eliminate it by means that replace one form of terror with another' (2002: 260). The novel discloses this climate of fear by leaving the violence of Molloy's description in doubt; he simply moves on to a description of the man's hat (*M*: 6).

Such a lack of resolution creates its own kind of terror in this early scene, but there is also relief that the man goes away unharmed. There is no such respite, however, when Molloy murders the charcoal-burner later in the novel. Just as Camus, like Beckett in 'La Peinture', identified the 'language of humanity' as a failed resource against violence, the scene starts with the possibility of a humanistic sentiment of fellow-feeling: 'I notably encountered a charcoal-burner. I might have loved him, I think, if I had been seventy years younger' (*M*: 84). In his old age, however, Molloy does not feel so warmly towards this stranger: 'He was all over me, begging me to share his hut, believe it or not. A total stranger. Sick with solitude probably' (*M*: 85). Concluding that 'he wanted to keep me near him', Molloy's solution is to beat him:

> I smartly freed a crutch and dealt him a good dint on the skull. That calmed him. The dirty old brute. I got up and went on. But I hadn't gone more than a few paces, and for me at this time a few paces meant something, when I turned and went back to where he lay, to examine him. Seeing he had not ceased to breathe I contented myself with giving him a few warm kicks in the ribs, with my heels. This is how I went about it. I carefully chose the most favourable position, a few paces from the body, with my back of course turned to it. Then, nicely balanced on my crutches, I began to swing, backwards, forwards, feet pressed together, or rather legs pressed together, for how could I press my feet together, with my legs in the state they were? But how could I press my legs together, in the state they were? I pressed them together, that's all I can tell. (*M*: 85–6)

Described in detailed physicality, the scene is *Godot*-esque in its slapstick nature. The reality, however, is that Molloy has beaten to death a helpless stranger:

> I rested a moment, then got up, picked up my crutches, took up my position on the other side of the body and applied myself with method to the same exercise. I always had a mania for symmetry. But I must have aimed a little low and one of my heels sank in something soft. . . . [I]f I had missed the ribs, with that heel, I had no doubt landed in the kidney, oh not hard enough to burst it, no, I fancy not. People imagine, because you are old, poor, crippled, terrified, that you can't stand up for yourself, and generally speaking that is so. But given favourable conditions, a feeble and awkward assailant, in your own class what, and a lonely place, and you have a good chance of showing what stuff you are made of. (*M*: 86–7)

Molloy not only indulges in the violence that Camus deplores but also produces chilling details of the physical suffering inflicted. The charcoal-burner goes from being referred to by 'he' and 'him' pronouns to 'the body', signifying that Molloy has not only done physical harm to a 'fellow-creature' but stripped him of any claim to humanity. The language and possibility of fellowship are thus tainted by a violence that seems prompted by the very notion of relation between Molloy and another human being. Molloy's response to the charcoal-burner's appeal to company and companionship is the infliction of physical pain, a viciousness which is saturated in the very real violence which permeated France's recovery. Appeals to humanism and fellowship functioned as a language for progress and hope in the post-war moment, yet ideological articulations of 'humanity' did little to halt the fact that, as Camus wrote of post-war France and Europe more broadly, 'men are still being killed, threatened, and deported, preparations are being made for war, and it is impossible to say a word without instantly being insulted or betrayed' (2002: 260).

Assimilation and anthropology

The revelations of varying degrees of collaboration in France and the return of those who had suffered in the Nazi camps presented significant challenges to post-war humanism. Vichy's antisemitism was apparent in its propaganda and policies, but its role in roundups and deportations to Nazi death camps were not common knowledge until after the war. Though not racially driven, nor actively exclusionary, post-war French humanism entailed its own identity politics, remaining 'quite unblushing in its assumption that the model of Man was a certain idea of the white French male' and 'leaving little space' for difference, for those who 'could not be assimilated to the dominant model' (Kelly 2004: 153).¹⁵ This language of assimilation also makes its way into Beckett's work. In 'The Expelled', the question of assimilation arises when the narrator is approached by a policeman, a representative of the state, who 'pointed out . . . that the sidewalk was for everyone, as if it was quite obvious that I could not be assimilated to that category' (*ECEF*: 8). In *The Unnamable*, we find the threat of humanist assimilation levelled at the narrator. The 'lectures they gave me on men', the narrator despairs, 'before they even began trying to assimilate me to him!' (*U*: 8). In *Molloy*, the titular character mocks 'anthropology', another 'pain in the balls' with 'its inexhaustible faculty of negation, its relentless definition of man, as though he were no better than God, in terms of what he is not' (8). In *Watt*, Beckett identifies anthropology as the process of speaking of 'man' as though 'he were a termite' (64), negated to the point of total dehumanization.¹⁶

Assimilation and anthropology were ideological keystones in wartime racial policies in France, and, while post-war French humanism did not pursue anthropological theorizing, humanism is inherently connected to attempts to define and give certain values to human identity. Assimilation also has a particular pertinence to French sociocultural history. In the first instance, as Erna Paris writes, the roots of the essentialism that accompanied life in Vichy and occupied France lay in the pre-war period:

> Prejudice against 'foreigners' deepened in the intervening years [between the two world wars]: a culture of 'Frenchness' was defined in opposition to the foreign, menacing, supposedly 'rootless' Jew. Anti-Semitism sprang, elemental and whole, from a collage that swept together the anti-Judaic heritage of traditional Christianity, the racism of the emerging anthropological sciences and populist anti-capitalism. (2002: 90–1)

As noted in Chapter 1, Vichy's anti-Jewish Statutes were conceived independently from the Nazis and came into effect in 1940 after the invasion of France; they 'implied the purification of France by defining Jews racially' (Lackerstein 2012: 256) and even expanded the definitions of 'Jewishness' beyond the Nazi's own decrees.¹⁷ Though Vichy's antisemitism was less driven by the pseudo-scientific race theories which propelled Nazism, public institutions dedicated

---

¹⁵ Such a definition failed to recognize the diversity of the French citizenry or the role of colonial forces during the war.
¹⁶ For a reading of *Watt* in the context of colonial anthropological discourse, see Bixby (2009).
¹⁷ Typically convoluted, Vichy 'further extended the Occupier's definition of Jewishness from those with three Jewish grandparents to those with two if they were also married to someone with at least three Jewish grandparents' (Lackerstein 2012: 256).

to the subject of 'Jewishness' had spread across France during the war. The Faculty of Medicine in Paris established the Institute of Hygiene early in the war, home to René Martial, an 'anthrobiologist' who claimed that 'the French race had been debased by the immigration of Asians and Jews and by the myth of racial equality' (Lackerstein 2012: 211). This was complemented by the celebrity of such figures as the previously mentioned Alexis Carrel, the Nobel Prize-winning eugenicist who decreed that what was required in Europe was nothing less than the 'systematic construction of civilized man in the totality of his corporal, social and racial activities', the results of which would allow humanity to 'reconstruct mankind according to natural laws' (qtd. in Jackson 2001: 327).[18] We might again think of Piouk's 'interest' in 'mankind'; figures like Carrel are as much detectable in Piouk as the celebrity of Sartre and other intellectuals. Indeed, the language of 'man', 'assimilation' and 'anthropology' in Beckett's writing as much evokes the racial anthropology which proliferated under Nazism and Vichy as it does the humanist rhetoric of the post-war period, and even goes so far as to indicate the shared obsession with defining 'humanity' across these ideological frameworks. Beckett's frustrations with post-war France seem in part tied to the prospect that Vichy and Gaullism, like the Nazi propaganda he encountered in the late 1930s, demanded the definition of 'man' in relation to the national vision of the state, and the recurrent parodies of such discourse in his writing suggest a keen awareness of the ideological battleground.

However, though it is presented as a threat in Beckett's work, 'assimilation' has a longer, more idealistic history in French culture and politics, especially in the aspirations of French Enlightenment culture to enrich and expand the citizenry. One of the most grievous wounds that Vichy did to France was the transformation of this aspiration into violent racial policies:

> The French doctrine of assimilation had its positive face. French language and values were deemed universal and open to all who wanted to acquire them. In a tradition leading from the honorary citizens of the 1790s through hospitality to exiles in much of the nineteenth century to warm receptivity to French-speaking African intellectuals such as Leopold Sedor Senghor in the twentieth century, French assimilationism opened the gates to anyone who wanted to be accepted. . . . Difference seemed a threat after 1940; pluralism, a form of weakness. At such times, woe to Jews or gypsies or other peoples refractory to

---

[18] For a full discussion of Carrel and his legacy in France, see Reggiani (2006).

assimilation. Deliberate, obstinate, provocative difference then seems not merely a rejection, but a menace. (Marrus and Paxton 1995: 367)

This pre-1940 doctrine rested on 'a willingness to submerge one's cultural identity totally in being French', yet also welcomed the enrichment of French society through an openness to other cultures (1995: 368). The markers of what constituted 'being French', however, were dramatically changed by Vichy and its project of national regeneration. In turn, following the liberation, French culture was charged with recouping the pluralism of this Enlightenment ideal. In one of the earliest post-Liberation texts to reflect on the war in France, Sartre published *Réflexions sur la question juive* (1944; trans. *Anti-Semite and Jew*, 1995). The text was based on his critiques of the antisemitic writings of Charles Maurras and Maurice Barrès, two figures Beckett was deeply sceptical of, and excerpted in one of the first issues of *Les Tempes modernes* (Becker, Introduction to *Anti-Semite and Jew*, 1995: vi). As a reader of, and later a published author in, *Les Tempes modernes*, Beckett was more than likely familiar with the text. *Anti-Semite and Jew* was Sartre's attempt to theorize the French tradition of 'assimilation' as a curative for, or at least a counter to, European antisemitism. He positions antisemitism in relation to bourgeois power, claiming that it was through hate that the bourgeoisie controlled the nation state. Antisemitism, Sartre argues, is a passionate rather than rational response to one's circumstances, a form of hatred capitalized on by totalitarian thinking. Throughout the essay, Sartre refers to the long-held 'doctrine of assimilation' in France as the basis for modern French identity, framed through a Marxist focus on property and ownership:

> The true Frenchman, rooted in his province, in his country, borne along by a tradition twenty centuries old, benefiting from ancestral wisdom, guided by tried customs, does not need intelligence. His virtue depends upon the assimilation of the qualities which the work of a hundred generations has lent to the objects which surround him; it depends on property. (1995: 16)

For 'the Jew', on the other hand, Sartre suggests that it is their responsibility to take 'the initiative' and try to look at themselves 'through the eyes of others' in order to be assimilated into national culture. Assimilation into society also requires, Sartre contends, the assimilation by Jews of 'all the thoughts of men' in order to acquire 'a human point of view of the universe' that will 'destroy the Jew in himself' (70); that is, 'destroy' that which makes others see 'the Jew' as different, what Sartre argues to be the true definition of 'Jewishness'. Couched in this language of 'destruction' and an emphasis on difference, the essay was met with criticism. Sartre's understanding of assimilation was premised on the erasure of Jewish subjectivity and historical difference, an assumption ill-conceived in the light of revelations about the Holocaust. As Andrew Leak writes,

> While few doubted Sartre's good will, many criticised the assumptions he made.... Jews in particular criticized him for his lack of historical perspective, but also for his failure to recognise that there existed a certain Jewish subjectivity which could not be reduced to the simple interiorization of an external judgement. (2006: 79)

Sartre's fidelity to a discourse of 'humanity' and 'the human' derived from the humanism of the post-war moment left little space to consider the extent to which a bankrupt discourse of 'man' had led to the antisemitism of Vichy and Nazism. In many ways, Sartre's essay represented one of the worst failures of the discourse of 'the human' in post-war France, recycling rather than expunging the very terms by which 'undesirables' were othered in the first place. Against this assimilating impulse, we find the narrator of *The Unnamable*, refusing to choke down the 'lectures' on 'man' which assault it on all sides, desiring a silence beyond the received wisdoms of an all but defunct liberal humanism. While Sartre saw the erasure of Jewish subjectivity as necessary for a 'true' discourse of humanity to arise, Beckett vehemently opposed, both culturally and politically, the very terms by which Sartre and others conceived the debate. 'Human' was reserved for times of 'huge slaughters', and Beckett's work during the post-war years reaffirms this point with biting and sometimes disturbing exactitude.

6

Beckett and War Writing

When Beckett wrote in 'The Capital of Ruins' that 'humanity' was a concept that should be 'thought again' in the 'universe become provisional' created by the war, he was deploying a language that not only responded to the crises of the post-war moment, but to which other twentieth-century writers have also turned when searching for a means to respond to modern warfare. The notion that the world, that humanity itself, had 'become provisional' in the wake of a global conflict was one that H. G. Wells adopted thirty years earlier, for example, in his 1916 novel *Mr Britling Sees It Through*. An intellectual and a pragmatist, the titular Mr Britling spends substantial parts of the novel revising his long-held opinions on a variety of topics as the First World War unfolds: the prospect of conflict in Europe, warmongering, empire and Irish independence. Where previously these issues had remained abstract, suitable for discussions over dinner parties and in essays, the reality of the war and its politicking is brought to Mr Britling's doorstep after the deaths in the trenches of both his son and Herr Heinrich, a German visitor to his home prior to the war:

> [He] was in a phase of imaginative release. Such a release was one of the first effects of the war upon many educated minds. Things that had seemed solid forever were visibly in flux; things that had seemed stone were alive. Every boundary, every government, was seen for the provisional thing it was. (1916: 197–8)

Despite Mr Britling's confidence in his intellectual and political convictions, the events of the war expose the insubstantial nature of the reality that surrounds him. Life at all levels, from Mr Britling's idyllic English country life to the political structures of Europe, is rendered provisional by warfare.

Many literary responses to war in the twentieth century have 'flux' at their centre, themselves provisional statements about a world in which meaning seems to always collapse. After the First World War, many writers were unsure whether language itself could capture the fractured nature of reality.

They seemed to identify that particular war as a new phase in the history of human atrocities and blood shed, one that required new modes of expression and response. T. S. Eliot's 'heap of broken images' is of a distinctly different character to poetic conceits like Rupert Brooke's foreign fields or Thomas Hardy's Drummer Hodge, for example, in which the poet reflects with patriotic melancholy on the value of dying for one's country. Concepts such as patriotic duty and heroism are, in the aftermath of total war, themselves left provisional. The scale of modern war, in both its global nature and the numbers of its dead, leaves language incapable of articulating whole truths about the experience of war. As John Sleigh Pudney wrote in 1943, 'Words will not fill the post / Of Smith, the ghost' (12). Eliot's 'compound ghost' of the *Four Quartets* comes to mind here, but 'Smith' is explicitly a soldier bearing one of the generic names used as a 'compound' for the mass, unknown dead of industrial warfare. Words fail to describe the experience of the soldier 'Smith', or account for how or why he died, and for what.

This chapter explores Beckett's work in terms of the genre of modern war writing, drawing on the various methods used by twentieth-century war writers to respond to the provisionality and flux which war creates. To do so, the chapter examines Beckett's little discussed use of military imagery and the ways in which his work explores the ethical dimensions of war and its representation. With reference to several texts of the 1940s and 1950s and through close readings of *Mercier and Camier* and the early drafts of *Fin de partie*, the chapter uncovers patterns of allusion in Beckett's writing to wars of the past, notably the First World War, the Boer War and the Jacobite-Williamite wars of religion in the seventeenth century. The chapter also examines Beckett's seldom acknowledged enthusiasm for First World War combat fiction and situates his military imagery in the 'war book' tradition of twentieth-century European war writing.

'In military fashion': Military objects in Beckett's post-war writing

Throughout Beckett's writings in the decade or so following the Second World War, there are recurrent images of soldiers and military details, some from specific conflicts, others from unknown wars. There is, for example, the soldier-turned-pauper in Beckett's post-war novella 'La Fin'/'The End', mentioned in Chapter 3, who describes the use of military practices while begging. Since 'to tip one's hat is no easy matter either', the narrator 'solve[s] the problem, always fundamental in time of adversity, by wearing a kepi and saluting in military fashion' (*ECEF*: 41). While he concludes it may in fact not have been a kepi, he is sure that he never made the mistake of wearing medals (*ECEF*: 41). Given how much weight Beckett's mid-career work put on a small collection of recurring objects – what Julie Bates describes as the author's 'art of salvage' (2017: 3) – we would do well not to overlook the hermeneutic and historical connections that items like kepis and medals suggest. While Bates does not include such objects in her analysis of Beckett's salvaging, Seán Kennedy argues that Beckett's objects, both recurrent and unusual, operate as 'a condensed expression of history in its inexpressibility' by appearing, sometimes, seemingly out of nowhere (2015: 189). In the case of the kepi and similar military objects, they are items that are so symbolically charged yet, in the surrounding dislocations of the Beckettian text, seem at first devoid of direct historical connection. By reinserting these objects into the various historical conditions they evoke, we can more fully appreciate the ways in which Beckett's work contend with the role of war in modernity.

The kepi was a staple part of French military uniform throughout the nineteenth and twentieth centuries. While most other European militaries phased it out after the First World War, the kepi remains in use in the French army to this day. For the narrator of 'The End', it is part of a half-remembered past steeped in military service. There are differences, though, between the French and English versions of the text, and each evokes slightly different historical contexts. In 'La Fin', the kepi is described as 'un vieux képi britannique' (an old British kepi; 1958: 80). In the French, the 'Britishness' of the kepi distorts the historical marker the item otherwise establishes, undermining what would be a clear link for French readers between the kepi and French military tradition. The object exists in the English version of the text without the 'British' descriptor, though, an example of Beckett's habit of shifting historical markers when working in different languages. Given the generic association of the kepi with French military history, the English text points towards a French history while the French text is, ironically, made more ambiguous with its detail. The description of the kepi in French, however, seems to suggest that the hat is somehow out of time or place, as though the previous military history that the hat signified has faded, itself a provisional signifier of power. Regardless, the object remains in both, introducing military service into the undisclosed history of the narrator – possibly a distinguished service, given the medals, or at least one recognized officially by the state.

The impoverishment of the narrator in 'The End', and his apparent exclusion from society, readily evokes the soldiers who suffered the violence and humiliation of France's 1940 defeat. The homeless veteran is a compound for the potentially (or wilfully) unnoticed outcomes of war, and the refashioned form of everyday life with which the wounded soldier is faced. The image of the narrator recalls Beckett's encounters with the defeated infantry of the French army, particularly his harrowing journey out of Toulouse in 1940 where he saw exhausted soldiers in tattered uniforms trying to escape the German invasion. The kepi, along with the rest of the soldier's uniform, became a symbol of national degeneration: 'the soldiers of 1940 were not worth those of 1914,' as we saw in Chapter 3. One refugee out of Paris in 1940 recalled an encounter with a group of soldiers during the exodus from the city:

> [We] came upon some isolated soldiers, without arms, eyes cast down, their shoes scraping the grass at the road side. They avoided a cyclist, then brushed past a stationary car without seeming to see either of them. They walked like blind men, like dishevelled ghosts. Keeping apart from the peasants on their carts, from the city people in their cars . . . they moved on alone, like beggars who have even given up begging. We were witnessing the start of the rout, but we did not yet know it. We took them for laggards, we thought their regiments were far in front. (L. Werth, qtd. in Jackson 2001: 2)

The scale and effect of such a defeat is contained within this image of the soldier-beggar, a historical weight thus impressed upon Beckett's 1946 image of the kepi-wearing, saluting narrator who dismisses the military background and record of service their medals and hat may represent. The narrator uses elements of his military experience in his begging, though he remains wary of signifiers such as medals and pieces of uniform that may elicit critical or political commentary. The narrator does not 'make the mistake' of drawing down on a history that his military objects represent, seemingly conscious that war service does not necessarily entail a straightforward or kindly response.

The kepi also contains a symbolic resonance with France's post-war recovery. Seán Kennedy connects a reference to the kepi in 'Premier amour'/'First Love' with Charles de Gaulle's celebrity in the post-war period, signifying the general's vision of collective French resistance (2015: 194). Complicating things further, we should not neglect the fact that the kepi was as much part of the image of Marshal Philippe Pétain who, like de Gaulle, was never pictured out of uniform; in public, Pétain was always connected to the military history from which he derived his power through his uniform and medals. For Jean Guéhenno and many who disdained the petty politics of Vichy, the kepi represented the corrupt and outdated notion of French patriotism that Pétain embodied, and dismissed as pageantry the weight of military history that Pétain's kepi attempted to represent:

> From now on, nobody has a right to do anything but talk about the speeches and celebrate the wisdom of a Marshal from the previous war who can't even count the number of stars above the visor of his kepi very well anymore, a very old man with a military pension, who repeats whatever his prompters tell him. (4 August 1940, *DDY*: 10)

Unlike Beckett's narrator, Pétain made sure always to wear the medals, stars and other signifiers of rank and 'duty' that he had earnt in the First World War. It was the source of his political and cultural control in wartime France and used to defend his collaboration during the post-war trials. The kepi represents the strange overlaps between Pétainism and Gaullism, identified in Chapters 3 and 5, each of them vying for visions of a 'true France' and the ideal French citizenry. Both ideologies constructed France through different interpretations of the same symbols and histories, particularly the invasion in 1940. For Pétain, the 1940 defeat symbolized the failure of the Third Republic; for de Gaulle, it was a last resistive stand before the dark years of Vichy which a unified France eventually defeated. In the case of 'First Love', the kepi (which is not 'britannique' in the French) is to be mentioned only to be dismissed: 'Kepis, for example, exist beyond a doubt, indeed there is little hope of their ever disappearing, but personally I never wore a kepi' (*ECEF*: 70). There is an odd frustration that there is 'little hope' of the kepi 'disappearing', as though war, or those who dress for war, will always 'exist beyond a doubt', the symbolic nature of the item itself eliciting dismay from the narrator. Yet the narrator's personal distaste or distrust of the kepi, for reasons undisclosed, undermines the very nature of symbol on which political rhetoric of all stripes, from Gaullism to Pétainism, depends. The symbol of the kepi in Beckett's writing, surrounded by formal conceits of rupture and narrative dismissal ('I *never* wore a kepi'), is unable to achieve its full political meaning despite its invocation in the text.

The complex intertwining of the First World War with the Second which Pétain represented – one solidified on a day-to-day level during the war by Vichy propaganda and groups like the Legion of Combatants – was reflected in the public mourning practices that took place after 1945. France's experiences of surrender and collaboration in the Second World War were difficult to situate against the near-mythic heroism of the First:

> The end of World War II brought forth no similar outpouring of grief. Of the 600,000 French dead, only a third had died weapon in hand. The rest had vanished in bombardments, executions, massacres and deportations or had fallen victim to internal combat in France or its colonies. Traditional forms of commemoration were inappropriate to such circumstances. . . . Monuments to the dead of World War II are extremely rare. Most of the memorial steles honor the victims of 'the two wars', with the names of those killed between 1939 and 1945 added to the longer as well as more prominently placed list of those killed between 1914 and 1918. (Rousso 1991: 22–4)

Public events were also indexed to the First World War. Celebrations of the German surrender on 8 May 1945 were 'relatively quiet', and the French government instead condensed 'all war commemorations past and future' into the 11 November 1945 Armistice Day ceremonies (Rousso 1991: 25). The dead of the Second World War were mingled with those of the First, subsumed into the status of 'war dead' who had fallen in the name of France rather than in the specific circumstances of the 1940 defeat, an event still in flux in French political consciousness. Such an intermingling of the dead in historical memory is replicated in the recurrence of an object like the kepi in Beckett's post-war novellas. The object spans historical conflicts, used as it was by soldiers throughout the nineteenth and twentieth century, leaving the kepi as one of the strange palimpsests in Beckett's work that contain multiple historical referents. By extension, Beckett's characters are palimpsests of history, becoming a generic trope, the beggar-veteran, an image which proved most generative to Beckett after the war, replete as his texts are with beggars, tramps and vagabonds who are often in closer proximity to war than it might first appear.

'Shitting in his puttees': Beckett and soldiers' bodies

Beckett's texts of the 1940s and 1950s regularly draw on past military conflicts, with the First World War in particular doing 'duty' for the 'horrors of the century' (Corcoran 1993: 115). Certain objects – medals, kepis, puttees – are one way that Beckett references those 'horrors' without directly representing them as the material world of conflict intrudes in what are predominantly historically dislocated texts. The body is another, not the strong body of Vichy in this case but rather the wounded, suffering bodies of soldiers we encounter explicitly in *Mercier and Camier* and the early drafts of *Fin de partie*, and suggestively in the trilogy. In Beckett's writing, war is remembered through bodies: bodies that hurt, shit and bleed. They record that war demands not the heroism or even 'boy-scout stuff' which dominate most official narratives of warfare. Rather, war demands that human bodies suffer.

During their meandering journey, Mercier and Camier encounter a 'ranger' in 'sickly green uniform' adorned with 'heroic emblems and badges' who, 'inspired by the example of the great Sarsfield', the narrator tells us, 'risked his life without success in defence of a territory which in itself must have left him cold'. The ranger, we are told, was wounded in his service:

> He suffered torment with his hip, the pain shot down his buttock and up his rectum deep into the bowels and even as far north as the pyloric valve, culminating as a matter of course in uretroscrotal spasms with quasi-incessant longing to micturate. Invalided out with a grudging pension, whence the sour looks of nearly all those, male and female, with whom his duties and remnants of bonhomie brought him daily in contact, he sometimes felt it would have been wiser on his part, during the great upheaval, to devote his energies to the domestic skirmish, the Gaelic dialect, the fortification of his faith and the treasures of a folklore beyond compare. The bodily danger would have been less and the benefits more certain. (*MC*: 8)

The soldier, it emerges, is an Irish citizen who fought for the British in the First World War, apparently 'inspired' by Patrick Sarsfield, first Earl of Lucan, who died fighting for the Jacobites in Flanders in 1693.

Following the narrator's sarcastic evaluation of Irish cultural nationalism and the country's struggle for independence, Mercier and Camier register the ranger's war service, combining the military insignias he wears with his bodily experience:

> Let us show him a little kindness, said Mercier, he's a hero of the great war. Here we were, high and dry, masturbating full pelt without fear of interruption, while he was crawling in the Flanders mud, shitting in his puttees.
>
> Conclude nothing from those idle words, Mercier and Camier were old young.
>
> It's an idea, said Camier.
>
> Will you look at that clatter of decorations, said Mercier. Do you realize the gallons of diarrhoea that represents?
>
> Darkly, said Camier, as only one so costive can. (*MC*: 10)

The scene sets the 'domestic skirmish' of the Easter Rising and Irish Civil War within the context of the 'the great war', and the pair's scathing description of that 'domestic' situation dissolves into puerile commentary with an apparent disregard for the pained body before them. The ranger's experiences in Flanders are reduced to 'crawling in the Flanders mud, shitting in his puttees', the horror of war measured not by battlefield heroics but by injuries and degradation.[1] Yet despite the scene's bitter humour and scatological obsession, it constitutes a powerful indictment of war that admonishes the very principle of measuring service experience by 'decorations', reframing the body as the record of warfare and exemplifying that, as Elaine Scarry puts it, 'the main purpose and outcome of war is injuring' (1985: 68).

Invariably, Beckett's detailed description of military suffering draws attention to the composition of the novel after the Second World War. Andrew Gibson has highlighted the interweaving of French and Irish historical markers in the text, pointing to where the English translation leans Irish, while the French version is very much of 'the France of 1946'. In particular, Gibson connects the ranger and his medals in *Mercier et Camier* to the post-war propaganda imagery of Charles de Gaulle (2013: 30). The anti-warism of the text undoubtedly enfolds multiple images of 'decorated' generals, but given that the French text is one very much 'of 1946', I suggest the always decoration-clad Pétain is another significant point of allusion, especially given his First World War legacy and the discourse of heroic martyrdom that surrounded the marshal both during and after the war. Beckett's ranger is himself a 'hero of the great war', an epithet which, from the mouths of Mercier and Camier, seems less an honorific and more a snide remark at the politicized figure of the war veteran.

The references to the Irish wars of independence in the pair's assessment of the ranger have a localizing effect on the text, yet it is difficult to place its historical setting precisely. We learn later that Mercier and Camier are also aware of the conditions of at least one other conflict. Camier connects the date their parasol was made commercially available to the 1899 Siege of Ladysmith in Natal during the Boer War:

> [The parasol] must have come out about 1900, said Camier. The year I believe of Ladysmith, on the Klip. Remember? Cloudless skies, garden parties daily. Life lay smiling before us. No hope was too high. We played at holding fort. We died like flies. Of hunger. Of cold. Of thirst. Of heat. Pom! Pom! The last rounds. Surrender! Never! We eat our dead. Drink our pee. Pom! Pom! Two more we didn't know we had. But what is that we hear? A clamour from the watch-tower! Dust on the horizon! The column at last! Our tongues are black. Hurrah none

---

[1] In another parallel with Louis MacNeice's *Autumn Journal*, mentioned earlier in Chapter 4, Beckett's turn to the battles in Flanders recalls MacNeice's description of those 'at Gallipoli or in Flanders / Caught in the end-all mud' (2007: 51–2).

the less. Rah! Rah! A craking as of crows. A quartermaster dies of joy. We are saved. The century was two months old.

Look at it now, said Mercier. (*MC*: 60)

It is uncertain whether Mercier and Camier saw combat or are reimagining second-hand accounts of it. That it may be reminiscence of lived experience of some kind rather than imagination is suggested by the drafts of *En attendant Godot*, a text which Ruby Cohn suggests developed out of the 'pairdness' and back-and-forth dialogue used by Beckett in *Mercier et Camier* (2001: 139). In the early drafts of *En attendant Godot*, the play is set more concretely in the late 1940s in the aftermath of the Second World War. When Vladimir and Estragon remember standing on the Eifel Tower, they state it was half a century ago, around 1900, the same year Mercier and Camier give for their parasol (BDMP *Godot*, MS BNF MY 440/01r; Van Hulle and Verhulst 2018: 173). Though the dialogue is revised in the later drafts of *Godot*, Estragon's recollection that he and Vladimir have been 'blathering' for 'half a century' in the published version retains a vaguened marker of the play's historical setting. Given the overlaps between the texts, it is possible Mercier's morbid 'look at it now' is also from the post-Second World War moment looking back. This is not a necessary exercise to glean the pacifist perspective on warfare that the scene entails. That said, identifying the likely historical setting of the novel in the mid-century, in the aftermath of another global conflict, lends significant weight to the anti-warism in Camier's vision of military suffering.

Camier's description of Ladysmith once more mediates military experience through the body. The living risk thirst, famine, bodily effluence, death; the dead become objects, available to the transgressions of the cannibal: 'we eat our dead.' Despite the acidic tone, such military recollections in *Mercier and Camier* represent a pacifist sentiment, one which intensifies against the backdrop of the Second World War and its aftermath.[2] Pacifism is a spectrum, one that ranges from the rejection of military institutions to opposition to all forms of violence.

---

[2] This section intersects with analyses of *Mercier et Camier/Mercier and Camier* that have interrogated the text's historical allusions, particularly Elizabeth Barry's focus on how the military details of the text reveal the politics of Beckett's translation practices and Anna Shidlo's Freudian reading of Beckettian history as a recognition of traumatic repression (1998). Though Barry briefly notes 'Beckett's characteristic penchant for the scatological' (2005: 513) in these military allusions, her work does not touch on the wounded bodies themselves. Connor (1989), Kennedy (2005c) and Gibson (2013) have also attended to the historical intersections of *Mercier and Camier*. For Beckett's 'penchant' for the scatological in a political framework, see David Lloyd's (1989) work on the author's writing in relation to postcolonial Ireland. Paul Stewart explores the recurrence of defecating horses in Beckett's work as part of the author's sexual motifs (2011: 17–28), and Andrew G. Christensen (2017) examines scatology in *Molloy* as part of Beckett's notion of language as excess.

As Jenny Teichman argues, however, all pacifisms share some degree of 'anti-warism' (1986: 1–2), and many find their articulation in the overt presentation of 'the physical immediacy of damaged human bodies' (Scarry 1985: 64), as occurs in *Mercier and Camier*. By identifying the injured body as a necessary part of warfare, this corporeal pacifism is an expression of the realities of war, an expression which stands against the reduction of conflict to historical, political and geographical abstraction and the erasure of the injuries and death war requires. Of all of Beckett's post-war work, the descriptions of Flanders and Ladysmith are the most powerful and direct confrontations with the realities of warfare, operating as moments of historical fixity in texts often governed by temporal flux. At the most basic level, *Mercier and Camier* offers a pacifistic war writing by dint of unambiguously representing what war does to soldiers' bodies.

The novel's turns to conflicts of the past raise the question as to whether the memory of warfare and its record in soldiers' bodies should have been enough to prevent further conflict. Specifically, in returning to wars of the past, wars in which Beckett himself did not participate yet which shaped the historical conditions which led to the Second World War, *Mercier and Camier*'s descriptions of combat experiences raise ethical questions concerning military violence and the demands of commitment and duty made of soldiers in combat. This process of transhistorical referentiality also suggests that a certain ambivalence towards bodily violence risked emerging with the repeated horrors of modern warfare, indicated by the rapid turn to mock empathy when Mercier and Camier encounter the ranger. The novel's engagement with military duty and patterns of historical violence through the repeated image of soldiers' bodies allows us to consider the ways in which a bodily focus – and the attendant themes of historical memory, violence and the ethics of duty – enables a transhistorical reflection on the nature of modern warfare. As we shall see, the suffering body is also a source of the chilling ambivalence that seems to inflect the pair's responses to physical suffering.

Both the encounter with the ranger and the evocation of the conditions of the Ladysmith siege at the turn of the century dwell on the body – the violated, wounded, terrified body – as a symbolic space in which the effects of military commitment and a 'high and dry' stance are placed under interrogation: Do Mercier and Camier's responses suggest an apathy caused by an oversaturation in images of conflict, in too much war, be it Irish or international? Would the ranger have been 'wiser' if he'd fought in the 'domestic skirmish'? Is one form of violence over another preferred? What does it mean to fight on 'foreign soil' for a nation that leaves one 'cold'? And will more harm be done to human bodies by not acting? This last question is acutely significant given that Beckett wrote the text in the aftermath of the Second World War. With the blanket bombings of civilians, the strafing of refugees fleeing cities and the revelations of the Nazi's 'Final Solution', the prospect that non-action could cause more harm seems much more likely. Ireland's neutrality policy shadows Mercier and Camier's reactions, though Mercier and Camier's position – 'high and dry, masturbating full pelt without fear of interruption' – is difficult to parse politically. It could imply abstention from all military and political activity, both home and abroad. Given the mockery of the 'domestic' preoccupation with 'Gaelic dialect' and 'folklore', the exchange is clearly aimed at the cultural agenda of traditionalist nationalism which emerged out of the 'domestic skirmish' of the Easter Rising and subsequent conflict that took place during and after the First World War. From this perspective, what with the mobilization of that cultural agenda to keep Ireland 'high and dry' during 'the Emergency', Irish neutrality seems to be in Beckett's sights here. However, both military service and politically motivated abstention buckle in the presence of the soldier's wounds, as the biopolitics of warfare is put front and centre in the exchange.

Beyond the direct historical markers of the text, the wounded Irish soldier remains alarmingly visceral in both the French and English versions of the novel. Such images of combat suffering draw *Mercier and Camier* into the European war writing tradition of the first half of the twentieth century, particularly the popular 'war books' generated by the First World War, as well as the poetry of Beckett's friend Thomas MacGreevy. These texts provide a compelling context for Beckett's recourse to images of wounded soldiers, one which reveals how the injured body of a soldier operates as a nexus for exploring the ethics of warfare from an anti-war position.

Beckett and the tautology of war writing

Just as the Second World War overshadowed Beckett's middle years, the First World War was a significant backdrop for his childhood. Though no conscription bill ever successfully passed in Ireland, thousands of young men volunteered for the British army, be it for the economic prospect of a soldier's pay, or because of the sense of duty and adventure encouraged by both British and Irish propaganda. Recruitment posters in Ireland used events like the sinking of the Lusitania and the invasion of small countries such as Belgium to encourage enlistment (Keitch 2017). In the event, between 200,000 and 300,000

Irish citizens volunteered for British forces (Jeffrey 2000: 5). The war years also included the 1916 Easter Rising, an event which presented pressing questions of national duty to those Irish soldiers fighting in Flanders and elsewhere. For Beckett's family and many civilians in Ireland, however, the most immediate concerns of the period were the limitations placed on daily necessities by the events of the war. Food and fuel were rationed during the war (*DF*: 22), and like in so many institutions at this time, it disrupted Beckett's schooling as male staff members went to fight (*DF*: 44).

Beckett knew many people, Irish or otherwise, who were physically or mentally injured by the war. His uncle, Howard Beckett, was deeply affected by his experiences, as Beckett recalled later in life:

> [Howard] had been in the Ambulance Corps during the First World War and witnessed horrors that were thought to have affected him deeply. Beckett could 'remember him coming home on leave. Coming to Cooldrinagh in uniform. He had a dreadful time. He was more or less pushed into it, blackmailed into it by the family. To join up.' (*DF*: 9)

The war's effects were made concrete to Beckett through figures like Howard and the veterans he encountered during his student years in Dublin, where he observed 'how wretched the lives of so many of his fellow men could be: beggars, tramps, ex-soldiers wounded or gassed in the First World War' (*DF*: 67). The 'decimation' of the Irish male population was all the starker in Dublin compared to the suburbs of his family home (*DF*: 44), a fact which, according to Knowlson, Beckett used to inform his description of the 'blind paralytic' (*MPTK*: 34) wheeled daily to the corner of Fleet Street with a placard around his neck in the story 'Ding-Dong' (*DF*: 67). Beckett's friend Thomas MacGreevy was wounded twice during the war, first on the front line of the Somme, then in Ypres (MacGreevy 1991: 97), and Beckett's psychoanalyst Wilfred Bion also served. There is no suggestion that Bion and Beckett spoke of the subject, though Bion's daughter remained adamant that the war shaped his methods as an analyst, including during the 1930s when Beckett was in his care (Jacobus 2005: 193). Like 'Ding-Dong', Beckett's critical language of 'no-man's land' and 'rupture in the lines of communication' from this time in the essay 'Recent Irish Poetry' (1934) is 'contaminated by memory of the Great War' (Campbell 2016: 73), revealing how Beckett had, even before the Second World War, internalized a military vocabulary that found its way into his writing.

Beckett's return to earlier conflicts in his writing also evokes the sense felt by many that the Second World War was a horrifying repeat or extension of the

First. In 1943, writing between his deployments in the North Africa campaigns, the poet Keith Douglas suggested that writing about the combat of the Second World War was, in effect, a tautology:

> there is nothing new, from a soldier's point of view, about this war except its mobile character. There are two reasons: hell cannot be let loose twice: it was let loose in the Great War and it is the same old hell now. The hardships, pain, and boredom; the behaviour of the living and the appearance of the dead, were so accurately described by the poets of the Great War that every day on the battlefields of the western desert – and no doubt on the Russian battlefields as well – their poems are illustrated. Almost all that a modern poet on active service would be inspired to write, would be tautological. (2000: 352)

This sense of the 'same old hell' of military violence extending itself across history is to be felt in Beckett's descriptions of combat suffering in the Boer War and the First World War in *Mercier and Camier*. It also takes up the very issue of the 'tautological' which Douglas identifies, the 'said before' which haunts the literature of the Second World War, a phenomenon Beckett represents by way of the maimed bodies which confront Mercier and Camier in their journey and in their memories.[3] Beckett's use of historical conflicts allows him to forgo direct representation of the war in the 1940s while still responding to what Gill Plain calls a 'pervasive sense of obligation' that the war generated, that in the face of another global war, 'something nonetheless had to be said' (2014: 39–40).

Beckett's peculiar tactic of historical elision takes this obligation one step further. In the aftermath of the Second World War, Beckett returned to images of soldiers from wars in which he did not participate but which, it would seem, imprinted themselves on his imagination. The injured and dead of the Second World War are unspoken in *Mercier and Camier*, yet in a reverse tautological effect, it is the military violence of the Second World War which is evoked in the description of the soldiers from earlier wars. A closer analysis of these referents reveals the degree to which, in his method of historical deferral, Beckett raises questions of duty and the ethical burdens that war creates, questions revived by the horrors of the Second World War yet unanswered in the turmoil of the post-war moment. These references show that Beckett is drawn in particular to Irish military history. *Mercier and Camier* sets evocations of the Jacobite-Williamite war, the Boer War, the Easter Rising and the First World War side by side in order to suggest a pattern of conflict in which the Irish were often both complicit

---

[3] The body is also a crucial site of expression for Douglas in his war poetry. Take, for example, the fly ridden skin and 'burst stomach' of the soldier's body in 'Vergissmeinnicht' (2011: 118).

and unwilling subjects. The novel looks to events in which Irish soldiers were particularly affected by the decisions of British military powers, be it in the violent repression of the Rising or the administration of Irish soldiers fighting in British regiments in South Africa and the trenches. Beckett's turn after the Second World War to these wars of the past defers from immediate representation to a continuum of military violence that is steeped in the political and ethical issues surrounding notions of duty and commitment. In the context of Irish military activity abroad during British colonial rule, this is fraught territory: 'Those that I fight I do not hate / Those that I guard I do not love,' as W. B. Yeats puts it in 'An Irish Airman Foresees His Death' (2008: 64). Thus, throughout the novel, Mercier and Camier remain in constant proximity to such politics, much of it framed in military language and Irish history. Before their encounter with the ranger, they find themselves in a 'public garden' containing a beech tree dedicated to 'a Field Marshal of France peacefully named Saint-Ruth' who was 'struck dead by a cannon-ball, faithful to the last to the same hopeless cause' (*MC*: 5). The scene refers to French officer Charles Chalmont who died from friendly fire in Ireland fighting against Williamite forces (Barry 2005: 508–9). In doing so, the scene foregrounds the image of the soldier left 'cold' in a war in which they appear to have only an oblique stake in the conflict.

Other moments in the text use snippets of military discourse. Early on, Camier puts their journey in tactical terms: 'It is no longer possible to advance. Retreat is equally out of the question.' Mercier subsequently observes that they cannot 'turn back' because they will 'lose ground' (*MC*: 17). In another moment of indecision, caused by a menacing barman, the pair are reported to have 'put a bold front on it . . . though [were] actually shitting with terror'; peace is only assured with 'sickly smiles and scurrilous civilities' (*MC*: 68). The feeling of 'terror' is sustained when Mercier and Camier beat the constable who arrests them, sending 'the helmet flying' with a kick and clubbing his 'defenceless skull' (*MC*: 76). The violence they inflict is remembered later in a form that evokes post-traumatic stress disorder: 'they were weary, in need of sleep, buffeted by the wind, while in their skulls, to crown their discomfiture, a pelting of insatiable blows' (*MC*: 77). Later still, they encounter the grave of a nationalist who was 'brought here in the night by the enemy and executed, or perhaps only the corpse brought here, to be dumped' (*MC*: 82). As Seán Kennedy demonstrates (2005c), this scene works through the legacy of violence in the Irish Free State via the figure of Noel Lemass, a survivor of the Easter Rising who was later abducted, likely tortured and then murdered by pro-Treaty forces; the grave is a monument to Lemass, hidden away in the

Dublin mountains. Central to the scene is the unanswered question as to what happened to Lemass's body before and after he was shot. Though Mercier and Camier claim to have forgotten the details of Lemass's murder, Kennedy observes that the pair's cultural amnesia does not simply erase the context in which the novel is set. Indeed, they display a 'gratuitous attitude to violence' which, for many, was the 'peculiar prerogative of Irishmen of all stripes in the nineteen twenties and thirties' (2005c: 127). The pair's caustic remarks towards the ranger can be read in the same vein; so saturated are they in political violence from all sides that they are simply unable, or unwilling, to offer anything other than faux 'kindness'.

It is in the invocation of the Boer War, though, that we get the most penetrating exploration of combat violence. The description of the Ladysmith siege combines a subtle reference to Irish military history with the text's broader patterning of bodily suffering. Camier recounts seeing the 'the column at last' which came to liberate Ladysmith. That column was comprised of a number of Irish units, including the 1st Battalion of the Inniskilling Fusiliers, a regiment that had suffered heavy losses at the Battle of Colenso on 15 December 1899, an earlier skirmish in the area. The Fusiliers' flank met the Boer forces head-on. In the successful liberation of the town, the Irish troops again suffered terrible casualties, and overall, it was the Irish regiments that experienced the greatest losses from the beginning to the end of the Ladysmith ordeal.[4] With the ranger scene's foreign-domestic dilemma in mind, this evocation of the Boer War draws on the tensions surrounding Irish soldiers fighting on foreign colonial soil for an imperial power – one which at the time was opposing independence for their home nation.

The Inniskilling Fusiliers are an intriguing allusion. The regiment's origin lies in the seventeenth-century wars of religion that raged in Ireland and on continental Europe:

> In 1688 the inhabitants of Enniskillen took up arms in defence of their town against the threat of occupation by the forces of James II. The troops so raised, The Inniskillingers, Foot and Dragoons, were not content to sit passively behind the walls of their town but made repeated expeditions into the surrounding district to seek out and destroy the enemy. So successful was this force it was incorporated into the army of William III. ('A Brief History')

---

[4] All details are sourced from the official regiment website: 'A Brief History'; 'Anglo–Boer War – 1899–1902'; 'Inniskillings in Dublin, 1916', http://www.inniskillingsmuseum.com/ (last retrieved 17 December 2018).

The absorption into William III's army puts the regiment in opposition to the previously mentioned Sarsfield and Chalmont, the latter who died 'faithful to the last' fighting for James II. Through the eighteenth century, the regiment formalized its tradition of 'expeditions', fighting the French in North America and the West Indies, and again during the War of Independence against French forces and American colonists seeking independence from Britain. Over the following century, prior to their participation in the Boer War, the regiment were dispatched to Egypt, Italy, Spain, Portugal and India. Beckett's time at Portora Royal School in Enniskillen makes it likely he witnessed sections of the regiment training and on duty, particularly the reserve battalions, and his school years would have likely involved a potted history of the regiment's formation.

While the Inniskilling Fusiliers are an unspoken allusion in *Mercier and Camier*, the regiment are directly referenced in the *Watt* manuscript. In the draft of *Watt*, a piano tuner, Mr Gall in the published text, describes the 'terrible years' he spent as 'lance-corporal and later simply private in ~~the Royal Inniskilling Fusiliers~~ a crack regiment' bearing 'arms in foreign lands' in 'Her and subsequently His majesty's service' (NB 1: 15r). Just prior to its involvement in both the First World War and the Irish War of Independence, the 3rd, 4th and 12th Reserve Battalions were in Ireland during the Rising, while the 1st and 2nd Battalions were sent to India and Flanders respectively. The regiment also sent troops to Gallipoli, Macedonia and Palestine, the latter of which endured its own experiences of British colonial control. The piano tuner was, like the ranger, a soldier sent to foreign soil, first under Queen Victoria, then Edward VII. Elsewhere, the *Watt* drafts include details of the lives of two manservants, Arsene and Erskine, neither of whom, like Mercier and Camier, 'had served in the Great War, nor taken any part in Ireland's fight for freedom'. They had chosen instead to remain 'faithful' to their master, Quin, who ensured they were 'well paid', though they thought him an 'old fool' (NB 1: 83r). Quin is the object of critique in the description, and, though the question of duty is bound up in the mercantile notion of 'faith' in exchange for pay, these details in the *ur-Watt* are expressed with a relatively neutral tone; they certainly do not feature the same sardonic quality found in Mercier and Camier's exchange with the ranger or in the description of Ladysmith. When Beckett came to recycle these Irish military referents in *Mercier and Camier*, it seems that the perspective lent by the aftermath of the Second World War made the neutrality of the *ur-Watt*'s descriptions impossible.

Mercier and Camier sets out Irish historical violence in a pattern that is intimately connected to the ways in which the colonial relationship governs commitment and duty. The novel also negotiates the ethics of duty and its relationship to violence more broadly, and with its repeated reference to the mutilated, bleeding, shitting bodies of war, the text is drawn into the wider sphere of war writing from the first half of the twentieth century. Specifically, the focus on the body in *Mercier and Camier* positions the text in a tradition of war writing – primarily poems and novels – which exhibit a demonstrable 'anti-warism' through representations of soldiers' bodies, most notably in terms of injury and the scatological, and often in a manner that makes apparent the alienation of soldiers from the politics of conflict. We will examine this from two perspectives: the poetry of Thomas MacGreevy, Beckett's friend and an Irishman injured fighting for the British, and the 'war books' of the late 1920s and 1930s, which often produced their own forms of bodily, scatological pacifism.

Writing soldiers' bodies

In 1934, Thomas MacGreevy published his first and only collection of poetry. Many of the pieces in MacGreevy's *Poems* combine the poet's modernist disposition with his interest in the spiritual and national possibilities of poetry as communion. Though admired by many, the collection did not receive much fanfare on publication; Brian Coffey suggests that MacGreevy's theological poetics simply was not to the taste of 'literary London' at the time (1972: 10). MacGreevy's much-neglected poetry constitutes an important literary negotiation of the First World War by an Irish combatant poet whose decision to publish on the war was, as James McNaughton argues, unusual among his republican and Catholic contemporaries (2012: 135). MacGreevy's war years rendered him somewhat estranged from the literary circles of post-Rising Ireland; he was a 'returned exile', as Anthony Cronin puts it (qtd. in Dawe 2013: 6), who had fought for the British yet remained a staunch Irish republican. Haunted with 'war-inflected traces' (Dawe 2013: 4), MacGreevy's poems deal with 'the fact of his military past as a British soldier during the Great War' and how 'the trauma of that time would not have endeared him to post-revolutionary nationalist Ireland' (Dawe 2013: 6). For MacGreevy, the feeling of having missed out on the nation's own 'great upheaval' (*MC*: 8) was as significant as his experiences abroad; indeed, with MacGreevy's injuries during the war also in mind, it is difficult not to see a trace of his experiences in the 'sour looks' experienced by Beckett's ranger.

The decade and a half that elapsed between MacGreevy's service and the composition and publication of his poems indicates the poet's struggle to come to terms with his war years. Many of these poems capture the notion of 'the spectator who *survived*' yet remain oddly detached from the war scenes they describe (Dawe 2013: 11; emphasis in original). Such a perspective is central to MacGreevy's war poem 'De Civitate Hominum', an account of seeing a scout plane shot down over the trenches. Though reminiscent of Yeats's airman, it is from a far different vantage point. The poem opens:

> The morning sky glitters
> Winter blue.
> The earth is snow-white,
> With the gleam snow-white answers to sunlight,
> Save where shell-holes are new,
> Black spots in the whiteness –
> A Matisse ensemble. (1991: 2)

Set against this cold, peaceful morning, MacGreevy describes the soldiers on watch. '[T]hose . . . / who die between peaces,' he calls them. They die wearing 'spick and span subaltern's uniform' while 'those who live between wars may not know' whether the soldiers 'die or not' (1991: 2–3). Beckett was a close reader of MacGreevy's poetry, and he marked these lines about the 'spick and span' soldiers in his 1934 copy of MacGreevy's *Poems*.[5]

The momentary peace of the poem's opening – a peace haunted by the repetitious, almost ghostly 'snow-white' of the third and fourth lines – is disrupted with the 'new' 'shell-holes' in line five, implying a suffering felt and knowable only to those soldiers witnessing the scene. Clouds – described as 'fleece-white flowers of death' – enfold 'an airman' now visible on the horizon who '[i]s taking a morning look around'. The description is banal, as though the airman's patrol is nothing more than a casual stroll. The clouds part to allow him through. The scene is still for a moment, until 'suddenly there is a tremor':

> A zigzag of lines against the blue
> And he streams down
> Into the white,
> A delicate flame,
> A stroke of orange in the morning's dress.

No body is seen, no scream heard. The poem instead ends with the anticipation of divine acknowledgement: 'My sergeant says, very low, "Holy God! / 'Tis a

---

[5] Beckett also marked the poem 'Nocturne' which MacGreevy dedicated to Second Lieutenant Geoffrey England Taylor, who, MacGreevy adds, 'died of wounds' (BDMP, *Beckett's Digital Library*); cf 'Recent Irish Poetry'.

fearful death." / Holy God makes no reply / Yet' (1991: 3). The rhythm of the line shares much with Belacqua's appeal to God in 'Dante and the Lobster', published in 1932, as the lobster is dropped into a boiling pot: 'Well, thought Belacqua, it's a quick death, God help us all. It is not' (*MPTK*: 14). Though a boiling luncheon pot and the trenches of France seem a world apart, both scenes respond to the delayed or absent notion of divine compassion. God does not reply, nor help the lobster in its time of need, and the soldiers in MacGreevy's poem are left gazing at the streak of orange left by the airman's plane, waiting for a sign from God that mercy still exists in the world.

The aestheticizing mode of the poem creates a palpable abstraction quite distinct from Beckett's treatment of conflict in a text like *Mercier and Camier*, though both writers eschew direct representation of the wars they experienced – MacGreevy by way of an imagistic vision of colour and Beckett by a historical deferral that is subsumed in scatological imagery. At first glance, both texts might appear indifferent to the suffering their describe or, in MacGreevy's case, withhold from view. They are, however, two attempts to confront the ineffable nature of war. MacGreevy's poem aestheticizes its subject (ultimately, the poet's own experiences of war) by overwhelming any sense of loss or horror with the vivid realization of the airman's death in a painterly image, leaving only the sergeant's 'very low' comment as the emotional register of the poem. The experience of the airman, presumably dead in a field far beyond the trenches, remains outside the poem's formal and referential scope. Any further emotion is that of the soldiers, those 'who die between peaces', which remains private, creating a gulf, a no man's land, between the non-combatant reader and the content of the poem.

By contrast, Beckett's scatological humour in *Mercier and Camier* draws all attention to the body and to the suffering it records, a vivid, hyperbolic description of the horror that MacGreevy's poem transmutes into the slow beauty of the 'stroke of orange' that is the mark of the airman's death, one that seems as inevitable as the sunrise. If Beckett's ranger poses the prospect of engaging with the aftermath of war, of those who survived but were changed utterly, MacGreevy's poem returns to the moment of experience only to find it distant, abstracted and ungraspable. The two texts each produce literary responses that insist on both the difficulty and necessity of bearing witness to war's suffering beyond the conventions of official rhetoric, what Adam Piette calls 'the strict sense' in which 'war makes literature ethical' (2016: 2). The imagism of MacGreevy's poem echoes his estrangement from his military experiences, and his desire to distance those experiences from political contexts which might call into question his patriotism. Meanwhile, the immediacy of the body in Beckett's novel confronts the lived experience of the suffering that inevitably accompanies war, evincing, all the while, a pacifist rejection of the very wounding it describes.

Beckett's image of the wounded soldier also brings *Mercier and Camier* into dialogue with the 'war books' of the 1920s and 1930s. Several common traits unite this genre, some of which we might now classify as modernist in style. Many of the war books of the period deployed fragmentary narratives, representative of the disorientating effects of war on time and space, as seen in Richard Aldington's *Death of a Hero* (1929) – the first major study of which was written by MacGreevy in 1931. Many also feature the rejection of 'old world' ideologies and a move towards pacifism, famously articulated in Robert Graves's *Good-bye to All That* (1929). The genre is united by visceral, experiential descriptions often focused on the physical body, as most notably found in Erich Maria Remarque's *All Quiet on the Western Front* (1929), as well as the French war books Beckett praised to MacGreevy, what he called the 'shell-shocked triangle' of *Vie des martyrs* (1917) by Georges Duhamel, *Le Feu* (1916) by Henri Barbusse and *Les Croix de bois* (1919) by Roland Dorgelès; Beckett called the three novels some of the best 'modernly' books he ever read (*LSB I*: 32). The use of the body in the poetry of the English trench poets – Owen, Rosenberg, Sassoon, among others – are also important touchstones, and Patricia Rae argues that George Orwell's writing on the Spanish Civil War carried forward the 'war books' tradition beyond the late 1920s during a period in which the genre suffered significant backlash (2009: 246). The physical realities of combatant bodies are central to the war books' cultural and social impact as a literary response to warfare, raising uncomfortable questions about duty, commitment and even the politics of criticism.

The popularity of the war books and the subsequent hostility they prompted are worth reflecting on when considering *Mercier and Camier* in this context. An article in the *Times Literary Supplement* in 1930 paints a clear picture of the anxieties around the war book 'boom' which followed the First World War:

> The recent flood of the 'literature of disillusionment' or of 'war books' – a phrase which has just acquired this special significance – differs from what has gone before only in that it is a flood in place of a trickle and that the water has grown decidedly muddier. (qtd. in Halkin 2009: 107)

A year prior, Remarque was identified as the most prevalent representative of what the British press called the 'Lavatory School', a title first used in an anonymous editorial for *London Mercury* that deplored the author's descriptions of wounded bodies and the dreadful conditions of the trenches (Eksteins 2009:

68). The focus on the suffering and futility of war also saw *All Quiet* decried as propaganda by British, French and German press alike; it was deemed 'pacifist, or allied, or German, depending on the critic' (Eksteins 2009: 68). Many critics of Remarque and Graves in particular shunned their recourse to interiority and linguistic 'vulgarity', and accused their accounts of 'the indifference and incompetence of military leaders and the complacency of jingoists on the home front' as the cause of an anti-patriotic 'Myth of War' (Rae 2009: 246). That sense of 'indifference' – captured so frequently in the image of the young man sent to die in foreign lands – is at the heart of Beckett's own description of the 'cold' foreign space in which his ranger was wounded. Likewise, Camier's memory of 'garden parties', enjoyed while 'play[ing] fort', recalls the apparent 'complacency' of the home front and the 'indifference' of military leaders.

Unsurprisingly, debates over the validity of the war books and the ways in which they could be discussed critically were heated:

> *The Daily Herald* [informed] its readers that the undiscerning fashion for war books would end in June 1930, 'when a novel will no longer be sure to sell on the mere virtue of its relation to the war.' When voices complaining of the surfeit of war books began to be heard, [the journalist] Arnold Bennett . . . insisted that nobody, except those who had fought in the war, had the right to be bored by good books about it. The subject seemed inexhaustible. (Halkin 2009: 107)

Accusations of vulgarity and 'cashing in' levelled at war-book authors abounded during the interwar period, as did questions of just who had the right to represent warfare. Who could discern what was 'true' of these experiences, and in what terms? Such questions raise significant ethical considerations for what it might mean to say one has grown 'bored' of encountering wounded bodies. If the market was saturated with 'decidedly muddier' waters, it meant readers and critics were becoming increasingly immune to the accounts of the wounded and suffering bodies these texts so often depicted. Echoing this trend, Mercier and Camier appear, as Kennedy suggests (2005c: 127), typically 'Irish' in their ambivalence towards certain kinds of violence, and are gleefully biting towards the bodily suffering they recall or encounter, suggesting they have become over-accustomed to, even overwhelmed by, the image of the wounded soldier. By implication, the text suggests that the sight of a wounded soldier had lost its affective power because of the scale and relative reoccurrence of mass mechanized warfare; it matters little whether that soldier is encountered in the street, depicted in literature or circulated in the media. The very thing that should suggest that further war is an abhorrent notion – the wounded soldier's body – seems only to elicit humour or irony, so familiar are Mercier and Camier with the grotesque bodily suffering of warfare. Yet if the novel seems to indict the pairs' caustic responses, we might also see them as ironic and comedic reformulations of that 'disillusionment' that underpins the often-extreme presentation of injured bodies in the 'war books' which followed the First World War. In its comedic hyperbole, the novel's ironic dismissal of pained soldiers' bodies confronts the eternal questions faced by war writing: How can the suffering of war be represented, and what are the ethics of doing so?

Important to understanding the relation between *Mercier and Camier* and the 'war books' is how the notions of truth and experience converged in soldiers' bodies. It was the authors themselves who most vocally defended their attempts to capture how war 'felt', to use Marjorie Perloff's term (2005: 102). Take Remarque's preface to *All Quiet on the Western Front*:

> This book is intended neither as an accusation nor as a confession, but simply as an attempt to give an account of a generation that was destroyed by the war – even those of it who survived the shelling. (1996: n.p.)

The conveyance of collective trauma – 'to give an account of a generation' – is at the heart of this venture: to offer not an evaluation or summation of the war in its entirety, but a glimpse of what the experience of the trenches meant for the individuals who witnessed them. As Sassoon wrote, 'Armageddon was too immense for my solitary understanding' (1930: 81). The acknowledgement by so many writers of the First World War that any attempt to represent their experiences would at best be partial sheds further light on Beckett's own confrontation with the tautological proposition of representing war. His solution – to turn to the wars of the past – allows him to take stock of the war of the 1940s, which he had just survived, without having to wrestle with the quandary of trying to produce mimetic fiction in the wake of a war that seemingly defied representation.

A decade after the most heated debates over the 'war books', George Orwell returned to the genre after the Spanish Civil War to explore the role of 'truth' in the experience of combat:

> The soldier advancing into a machine gun barrage or standing waist-deep in a flooded trench knew only that here was an appalling experience in which he was all but helpless. He was likelier to make a good book out of his helplessness and his ignorance than of a pretended power to see the whole thing in perspective.
>
> 'The truth' of the political situation was secondary to 'the truth about the *individual reaction*'. (Orwell 1940: 109; emphasis in original)

In his own war writing of the late 1930s and 1940s, Orwell took from the 'war book' genre both an emphasis on experience over fact and the centrality of the human body to accounts of war. He recalls, for example, the 'frightful shambles of smashed furniture and excrement' of a small Spanish village in which he fought, and that the local church shared a wall with a home turned into a lavatory; its floor, he writes, was 'inches deep in dung' (1938: 54) in which the soldiers in Spain, like Beckett's ranger, were forced to fight. Orwell makes the case that the politics of the combat – here, the fight against fascism – gets subsumed in the ordeals, the actual experience, of bodily functions during war:

> I believe it was [the] latrines that first brought home to me the thought, so often to recur: 'Here we are, soldiers of a revolutionary army, defending Democracy against Fascism, fighting a war which is *about* something, and the detail of our lives is just as sordid and degrading as it could be in prison, let alone in a bourgeois army.' ... Bullets hurt, corpses stink, men under fire are often so frightened that they wet their trousers. (1943 web.)

Beckett calls on the same kind of detail in *Mercier and Camier*, from the image of the shitting ranger to the defiled bodies of the Ladysmith siege, scenes streaked with a dark humour that nevertheless involve a serious appraisal of modernity's patterns of mass violence and the extent to which the ideology of heroism in military conflicts is a fantasy that sanitizes suffering. In turning closer attention to the physical suffering of those bodies caught up in such a cycle, Beckett's writing makes use of a scatological discourse which, as Paul Fussell suggests, disrupts the 'public language used for over a century to celebrate the idea of progress' by deploying the vocabulary which wounded soldiers needed to describe their experiences: 'blood, terror, agony, madness, shit, cruelty, murder, sell-out, pain and hoax' (2013: 184). Beckett's novel bears the imprint of war's effect on public and private language alike.

As in the descriptions of combat in the war books of authors like Remarque and Orwell, Mercier and Camier's encounter with the ranger offers a stark inversion of war, reframing the veteran not as representative of a national narrative of victory or valour, as his medals may suggest, but as a being disfigured by conflict whose body is the record of both experienced and witnessed physical suffering. Even Mercier and Camier's explications of their own views of military and political commitment are articulated through the body: so 'costive' are they that they can only 'darkly' understand the soldier's experience in Flanders.[6]

---

[6] Beckett puns on the two meanings of 'costive' – that is, constipated, and unforthcoming in speech ('costive, adj.' *OED Online*).

Camier's constipation is presented as an inhibitor to a full recognition of what military action entails. His body does not work as it 'should', and so will not suffer as it 'should' in the face of military activity, because he cannot engage in any form of 'big push'. With the injured body of the ranger still suffering before the pair, the scene demonstrates the demand that military commitment makes for bodily perfection in its combatants. The suffering of war, in this calculation, is the trauma, the 'injuring' that Scarry details, that is done to 'perfect' bodies to render them non-combative. It is the goal of bullets, gunpowder and gas to leave bodies imperfect, hence the medicalized detail of the ranger's rectal injuries. Such bodies suffer and continue to do so long after peace – so-called – arrives. They are haunted by the 'dark' sense that potentially dubious notions of national duty and commitment drove enlistment. Beckett's ranger was, we are told, 'inspired by the example of the great Sarsfield', or what Yeats called 'A lonely impulse of delight' (2008: 64). Since no Irish citizens were conscripted in the First World War, any deaths on foreign soil were those of volunteers. How voluntary they truly were, though, seem to be the question that Yeats and Beckett are both keen to raise, though the martyr-like notion of 'fate' by which Yeats's airman 'foresees his death' is revised through the body in Beckett's war writing: the absent body of Yeatsian 'fate' against the lived, and still living, experience of the wounded bodies found in *Mercier and Camier* and the 'war books'.

In *Mercier and Camier*, the prospects of duty and commitment are interrogated by the image of the defiled body: of the bullet-wounded ranger, and the corpses in the retelling of Ladysmith. The text deploys the repetitions of Irish historical violence to suggest that history has failed to teach 'us' anything about 'playing fort', and that written accounts of war can, at best, make clearer the 'flies . . . hunger . . . cold . . . thirst . . . heat' of combat experience (*MC*: 60). The novel, like the war books which precede it, operates knowing that it will likely 'do nothing to prevent conflict', but can 'at least lay bare the nature of what is at stake' (McLoughlin 2010a: 1). In the dark humour of Mercier and Camier's responses to soldiers' bodies, the lessons of history are made a topic suitable for 'garden parties' rather than battlefields, a prospect made all the starker when we acknowledge the post-Second World War position from which Beckett was writing.

Embodying war memory

Mercier and Camier's representation of modernity's violence through specific points of Irish military history intimates the way in which war appears an unavoidable refrain through time, a pattern which relies on the suffering and pain of human bodies. In the trilogy of novels that followed *Mercier and Camier*, Beckett's historical and geographical coordinates are far less determined than the earlier novel. As we have seen, though, the bodies of Beckett's trilogy have striking historical resonance in their disruption of the obsession with able-bodiedness and social value that preoccupied Vichy. Beckett's descriptions of the bodies in the trilogy, particularly certain details included in *The Unnamable*, also point to military backgrounds for his characters. As the narrator surveys itself, he notes that for clothing he can think of 'nothing for the moment' save that he is wearing 'possibly puttees' and 'perhaps a few rags' (*U*: 15).[7] Like the kepi discussed earlier, the puttee has particular resonance with the combat uniforms of nineteenth- and early-twentieth-century European militaries. Infantry and cavalry wore them alike, and though puttees ceased to feature heavily in many European uniforms, they remained a staple of French combatants until 1945 (Barnes 1972: 282). While the ranger and his medals and puttees are encountered in the external world of *Mercier and Camier*, *The Unnamable* includes such details in the narrator's small zone of existence. On their own, these puttees appear to be among the many Beckettian objects streaked with histories that the texts refuse to acknowledge. However, the specificity of the clothing – not only rags but puttees, the military association clearly intentional – and the body wearing it demands further attention. For this, we must turn to the aforementioned French war books that Beckett praised nearly two decades prior: the 'shell-shocked triangle' of *Vie des martyrs* (1917), *Le Feu* (1916) and *Les Croix de bois* (1919).

The descriptions of wounded and dying soldiers found throughout the 'shell-shocked triangle' directly anticipate the bodily forms of Beckett's writing after the Second World War. Duhamel's descriptions of the trench 'martyrs' in *Vie des martyrs* especially include many details that chime with the bodies of Beckett's post-war prose.[8] Duhamel's fifth chapter is devoted to the death of 'Mercier', a baker turned soldier whose eyes continue to weep after he is dead. The image prefigures the puttee-wearing narrator of *The Unnamable* who weeps uncontrollably: 'The tears stream down my cheeks from my unblinking eyes. What makes me weep so? From time to time. There is nothing saddening here. Perhaps it is liquefied brain' (*U*: 15). A steady, unblinking stare is a consistent symptom of shell shock, commonly known as the 1,000- or 2,000-yard stare;

---

[7] The detail is a direct translation from the French text's 'molletières', a word which survived from the first draft of *L'Innommable* through to the translation (BDMP *L'Innommable*).
[8] There is also a link to *Waiting for Godot* worth noting. One of Duhamel's injured soldiers is called Lévy, another possible source for Beckett's use of the name in the play's early drafts.

'liquified brain' is also evocative of the kind of life-limiting wounds that could be sustained in combat.[9] Elsewhere, the 'stiff' and 'distorted' legs of the injured soldiers Carre and Lerondeau in *Vie des martyrs* (2010: 19) recall Molloy's 'short stiff' right leg (*M*: 19), particularly Lerondeau's which is 'such a bad business' that it is 'permanently shorter than the other by a good twelve centimetres' (2010: 16). The deterioration continues in both Duhamel's text and across the trilogy: Lerondeau dies from his injuries while in *The Unnamable* the narrator feels it only natural that '[h]aving lost one leg, what indeed more likely' but that he should 'mislay the other?' (*U*: 43). Carre's 'black stumps' of teeth prompt the narrator to confess 'this distresses me, for a man with a fractured thigh needs good teeth' (Duhamel 2010: 18). In *The Unnamable*, the narrator snaps at flies from their jar only to wonder 'Does this mean I still have my teeth? To have lost one's limbs and preserved one's dentition, what a mockery!' (*U*: 45). The formal conceit of a character creating a series of voices through which to remember and tell stories in *The Unnamable* also replicate the kind of experiences of many wounded soldiers depicted in various war books of the 1920s and 1930, perhaps most famously in Dalton Trumbo's *Johnny Got His Gun* (1939), the harrowing fictionalization of a wounded veteran trying to tell his story while trapped inside his mutilated body. While pained bodies are visualized on stage in plays like *En attendant Godot* and, as discussed later, *Fin de partie*, *The Unnamable* is filled with bodily pain expressed through intimate description, remembrance and storytelling. With this in mind, there is much to suggest that images of wounded soldiers were generative to *The Unnamable*, particularly images found in war books like *Vie des martyrs* with its vignettes of different soldiers' pains.

Such resonance with the wounded bodies of the First World War also reasserts the trilogy's affront to Vichy-like sensibilities: the veterans of the First World War trenches to which Vichy so often compared the soldiers of 1940 are recast as decaying forms fantasizing about further degeneration. In recognizing Beckett's figures as soldier-like in their disfigurements, they are made memorials to the actual suffering that their real-life counterparts endured, refuting the narratives of heroic martyrdom that Vichy and, later, Gaullism employed and imprinted onto soldiers' bodies.

Beckett's turn to the genre of war writing is also significant for the composition of *Fin de partie*. While the trilogy focuses on debilitated bodies that are historically evocative yet dislocated from a temporal or geographical setting, Beckett uses a localized tension in the genesis of the play akin to that found

---

[9] Liquified brain might refer to the tissue necrosis caused by mustard gas use during the First World War.

in *Mercier and Camier*, returning to questions surrounding the presentation of war-wounded bodies and the ways in which such bodies – like war memorials – preserve the violence of the past. In this case, the locale is not Ireland but France.

Fin de partie has been well served by readings that see the horrors of the death camps in both its form and content (Adorno 1982), and that locate in it references to imperialist famine politics used in Ireland (Kennedy 2012) and Eastern Europe (McNaughton 2018). Beckett's early drafts of *Fin de partie* also disclose his ongoing preoccupation with the image of the wounded soldier's body. By attending to this neglected aspect of the text and its manuscripts, we can more thoroughly recognize the particular kind of war imagery which informs the figures Beckett puts on stage and which more generally circulated in his imagination in the aftermath of the Second World War.

While *Fin de partie* and its English language counterpart are taken to be Beckett's most direct creative response to the mass death of the Second World War – both the devastation of nuclear weapons and the Holocaust's 'multitude … in transports' (*E*: 20) – the text's drafts reveal the First World War to be a further source for the bodies and situations Beckett stages, all the way through to the final scene of Hamm and Clov together in their room. In one of the earliest drafts, likely written in 1952 (BDMP *Fin*, UOR MS 2932), Beckett imagines a series of characters entering and exit the stage to the strokes of a gong.[10] They include one 'Camier', who leaves early in the text, and 'L'Anonyme'; both are described as wearing medals. In the next undated draft, held in the Harvard Theatre Collection in Houghton Library, the scene features a dialogue between B and L, during which B explicitly remarks on the Médaille de la Reconnaissance Française (Medal of French Gratitude) worn by L (BDMP *Fin*, MS HTC THR 70/3/01r). Such medals were awarded from 1917 to non-combatant personnel; Beckett received one for his services in Gloria (*DF*: 320). As in the references to Roussillon in *En attendant Godot*, Beckett introduces and subsequently elides his wartime experiences in a text which, in retrospect, was part of the genesis of *Fin de partie*. As in Beckett's use of military objects elsewhere, the Médaille de la Reconnaissance Française spans the French experience of two world wars, compressing the linked histories the medal represents into the object itself, an effect which is then made visible on the imagined stage.

The next draft, another undated typescript (BDMP *Fin*, UOR MS 1227/7/16/2), features two figures, 'Ernest' and 'Alice', who begin the play with handkerchiefs over their faces, anticipating Hamm on stage in the final version

---

[10] Throughout this chapter, I follow Van Hulle and Weller's (2018) ordering of the drafts.

of *Fin de partie*. While Ruby Cohn suggests that the draft is 'unrelated to *Fin de partie*' because it does not intimate a 'master/slave relationship' (2001: 220), there is enough in the play for Dirk Van Hulle and Shane Weller (2018) to include it in their study of the genesis of the play. One of the through-lines which link this draft and those preceding to the later published text is the pool of war images from which they draw. In the 'Ernest & Alice' draft, it is not a chair but a cross on which the shrouded Hamm-like character Ernest sleeps, and he is snoring with a champagne bucket tied around his neck (BDMP *Fin*, UOR MS 1227/7/16/2/01r). For this draft, Beckett switches the reference to war from objects such as medals to the tableau of the scene itself. Ernest's cross literalizes the setting of another of the 'shell-shocked triangle', Roland Dorgelès's *Les Crois de bois* (Wooden Crosses). The novel tells the harrowing story of Demarchy, who enlists in 1914 and is sent to the trenches in Champagne, France, where he watches as ever-increasing numbers of wooden crosses are erected to mark the dead French and German soldiers. Beckett puts the symbol of the Champagne dead on stage and lays on top of it a sleeping figure who is loudly, even comically, snoring. On the page's drafts, Beckett doodles in heavy pen marks a coffin with a well-defined cross on its lid, drafting the scene around the picture as though the wooden cross is at the heart of the text (BDMP *Fin*, UOR MS 1227/7/16/2/09v). The snoring Ernest on the cross prefigures Hamm's yawn amid his discourse on suffering in a disturbing reimagination of Vladimir's haunting line 'was I sleeping while the other suffered?' (*CDW*: 84).

In the Ernest and Alice draft, Ernest elliptically evokes the waste of life caused by war as he stares into the contents of his champagne bucket each evening and declares 'voilà ce que tu as perdu aujourd'hui dans le gouffre du rachat universel' (this is what you have lost today, in the abyss of universal redemption) (BDMP *Fin*, UOR MS 1227/7/16/2/06r; trans. Van Hulle and Weller 2018: 157). The line laments the 'redemption' of the mass at the expense of the individual, a sentiment that resoundingly decries the humanistic collectivism of post-war France, and rejects the erasure of the subjective experiences of individuals in favour of national 'redemption'. In Beckett's hands, indifference to the pain of 'multitudes' and individuals alike is put into mouths of characters such as Hamm, a vicious and cruel creature, pitiable in his circumstances, and before that in the image of Ernest asleep. Hamm is the apparent master of his domain, just as Ernest is served by Alice. The masters are indifferent, able to sleep through the clatter of life ending en masse.

The next undated draft later referred to by Beckett as *Avant fin de partie* (BDMP *Fin*, UOR MS 1227/7/16/7) is set in a region of France which saw some of the fiercest fighting during the First World War. The characters, here X and F, introduce the locale of the play:

> F. Nous sommes dans la Picardie, à quelque dix jours de marche bon train de Paris, et plus précisément dans le Boulonnais – ...
>
> F. Je dirais même aux alentours de Wissant. ...
>
> F. Votre habitation, édifiée sur la falaise, comporte un living room ... et un ... couloir transformé en cuisine. ... Détruite progressivement dans l'automne de 1914, le printemps de 1918 et l'automne suivant, dans des circonstances mystérieuses – ...
>
> F. ... De la grande baie de la salle de séjour ..., avant qu'elle ne fût aveuglée, dans des circonstances mystérieuses – ...
>
> F. On voyait par temps clair, par-delà la Manche, les falaises d'Albion
>
> (F. We're in Picardie, about ten days walking at a steady pace from Paris, and more exactly in the Boulonnais – ...
>
> F. I could even say, not far from Wissant. ...
>
> F. Your house, built on the cliffs, consists of a living-room ... and a ... corridor made into a kitchen. ... Destroyed steadily in the autumn of 1914, the spring of 1918 and the following autumn, in mysterious circumstances – ...
>
> F. ... From the big bay window in the sitting-room ..., before it was bricked up, in mysterious circumstances – ...
>
> F. One could see, in clear weather, the cliffs of Albion across the Channel.)
>
> (BDMP *Fin*, UOR MS 1227/7/16/7; qtd. and trans. in Rákóczy 2017: 43)

S. E. Gontarski acknowledges that 'the protagonists are obviously survivors of a World War I battle' and that 'the devastation in the Picardy/Normandy area was familiar to Beckett'. However, Gontarski sees the First World War allusion as 'not a very subtle means of deflecting the play's autobiographical level away from his World War II experiences in the region' (1985: 33). Given the importance traced so far of the First World War to the drafts of *Fin de partie*, I suggest that the 'more exactly' (UOR MS 1227/7/16/7) defined geography of *Avant fin de partie* confirms the importance of the symbolic power of the wounded veteran in Beckett's creative process for this text. Staging characters that are tied, sometimes implicitly, sometimes literally, to sites of specific war memory provides Beckett with the means to stage a form of suffering intimately connected to soldiers' experiences. In the Picardy setting, the physical limitations of the characters X and F, who like Hamm and Clov struggle to walk or sit, are more explicitly those of combat veterans. In the final text of *Fin de partie*, the setting is delocalized from specific geographical and historical spaces, and objects like medals and crosses are expunged. However, the characters retain the physical limitations which suggest the wounded soldier: one struggling to stand, one struggling to sit, both attempting to deal with their situation and the situation of their bodies.

As we have noted, the First World War was a particularly important conceptual space for mourning in France after 1945. The setting in Picardy and various characters implicitly debilitated by the battles of 1914–18 in the early *Fin de partie* drafts evokes what Henry Rousso calls the 'symbolic embodiment' and 'universally admired archetype' of the combat veteran which came to mass consciousness in France after the First World War:

> World War I, a cataclysm without precedent, had claimed nearly a million and a half lives and left millions of others maimed – visible walking reminders of the slaughter . . . the principal message bequeathed by the survivors of that conflict was one that spoke to the senses; it was a message first of physical suffering and then of mental anguish. . . . After this national sacrifice, which had gone virtually uncontested until 1917, the French were joined in mourning. (1991: 22)

By contrast, 1945 saw the French divided, sometimes violently, faced as the nation was by the military collapse of 1940, the realities of collaboration and deportations, and the return of the victims of the camps. As Rousso demonstrates, the politicization of mourning the dead of the Second World War began in France as early as the 1940 defeat, and a succession of narratives took hold. The dead of the Nazi invasion were declared casualties of the 'decadence' of the Third Republic. Pétain and Laval refused responsibility for the deportation of Jews and others to the death camps. De Gaulle saw all deaths of 1939–45 as a sacrificial part of the liberation narrative. The French war dead of the Second World War were retroactively subsumed into the dead of the First. In the process, the sense of lives lost was rendered ever more superficial in its numerical presentations. To say 600,000 French people were killed during the Second World War is to offer only a macroscopic view. The reality of the situation was vastly different. Of that 600,000:

> [a] majority of the 170,000 soldiers who died in action were killed in the spring of 1940. . . . They had been mourned discreetly and with attenuated pride. Some

80,000 Free French and Resistance casualties died in the successful campaigns of 1944-1945. . . . Civilian causalities were almost as high as total military losses. Both groups were outnumbered by those who died in prisons and camps, between 70,000 – 100,000 Jews who were France's shameful contribution to the Holocaust. These different groups called for different types of mourning and commemoration. (Kelly 2004: 80)

For de Gaulle's government, and for de Gaulle himself, to engage in 'different types of mourning' risked acknowledging the deep divisions that existed before, during and after the occupation.

The manuscripts of *Fin de partie* demonstrate that Beckett did away with most of the geographical and historical markers as he revised and refined the text. In doing so, he shifts greater attention not only to the physical conditions of the figures on stage but also to the mental anguish they express. Traces of the war remain in these elements, but the history to which they are indexed fades from view. This begins in Beckett's work after *Avant fin de partie*, when the war setting disappears in the subsequent draft. However, war lingers through the presence of two mysterious explosions which feature in the draft labelled *A&B* (BDMP *Fin*, UOR MS 1660; Rákóczy 2017: 47). Nevertheless, the state of physical and mental suffering that the historical and geographical surrounds of Picardy imprint on the characters remains palpable despite the text's delocalized setting.

War does not entirely recede from view in the final text, however. It is retained through Nell and Nagg who, as noted in Chapter 1, keep with them the marks of the war memory associated with the Ardennes region of France:

NAGG. Tu te rappelles—

NELL. Non.

NAGG. L'accident de tandem où nous laissâmes nos guibolles.

(*Ils rient.*)

NELL. C'était dans les Ardennes.

(*Ils rient moins fort.*)

NAGG. À la sortie de Sedan. (*Ils rient encore moins fort. Un temps.*)

(1978: 156–7)

NAGG. Do you remember—

NELL. No.

NAGG.   When we crashed on our tandem and lost our shanks.

[*They laugh heartily.*]

NELL.   It was in the Ardennes.

[*They laugh less heartily.*]

NAGG.   On the road to Sedan. [*They laugh still less heartily.*]

(*E*: 13)

For English-speaking audiences, the significance of the particular geographical space invoked is indicated by the pair's declining laughter: their mirth subsides not on the memory of losing their legs but at mention of the Ardennes. In the French, though, the specific defeat at Sedan is suggested with a bilingual pun: the sortie ('exit' in French; attack or battle in English) of Sedan. Sedan was, as we have noted, the site of a 'major French defeat during the First World War and the war against Prussia' (Morin 2009: 115). Yet the location just as readily (and more so in the post-war context of the play's composition) evokes the fall of France in 1940. The failures of French and Allied forces at Sedan against German blitzkrieg and their forced retreat (or *sortie*) directly led to the catastrophe of Dunkirk, the collapse of the French military and the conditions that allowed the Nazis to take Paris (Horne 2019: web). The bilingual nature of the pun is compounded by the transhistorical implications of the reference, with 'Ardennes' further invoking the last major Nazi offensive during the Battle of the Bulge in 1944 (McNaughton 2018: 158). The pair's hearty laugh over their lost limbs confuses any direct sense of trauma in their memories. However, though we do not see Nagg and Nell's bodies on stage, they nevertheless register as the corporeal memorials of war like that of the ranger in *Mercier and Camier*, the bodies of the trilogy and both the image of Ernest on the cross and the Picardy veterans of the *Fin de partie* drafts. The combat nature of the wounds suffered by these bodies indicates that Beckett's image of war was shaped by the literature and descriptions of the First World War. Likewise, it is apparent that these images haunted his writing after the Second World War, returning as part of an extended creative exploration of the aesthetics of physical suffering that is steeped in the very real conditions of military violence.

Beckett's impulse through the drafts of *Fin de partie* to put on stage a war memory located in the First World War calls back to the implicit concern of so many war books written after 1918, including that of the 'shell-shocked triangle' which he applauded: that is, that war requires some kind of record, even if it is futile to presume future wars can be prevented. We can also discern the effect of not one but two world wars on Beckett's staging and descriptions of war memory in his consistent use of characters bored or indifferent to suffering. The play's drafts, particularly *Avant fin de partie*, make use of the specific conditions of the mourning that occurred in France after 1945, notably how the First World War's mythologized heroism and communal memory had been politicized by Pétain during his trials and in the physical structures of war memorials. Beckett stages the superseding of mourning, one conflict replaced by another in political discourse, yet in his hands the heroism of official war memory is replaced by the actuality of war's suffering. While the drafts and published play address the question of 'rachat universel' in the face of war, as raised by Ernest, and *Fin de partie* is most often treated as a play directed towards the universal condition of humanity after the war, the image of the wounded soldier and the political implications of its representation in a French context remain palpable in certain objects and details which seemed to capture Beckett's imagination throughout the play's drafts. From the French medals of the early drafts, to Ernest's wooden cross, to F's description of the surrounding French region in which he and X are situated, each one stages a version of Beckett's closing comment in 'The Capital of the Ruins' on the function of the local and the particular in war memory: this kind of pain and memory 'will have been in France'. The play derives from, and so has in its theatrical fabric, Beckett's specific negotiations of the ongoing war memory which saturated contemporary French society and culture alike.

'No more tide': Beckett's statement on history

Beckett's war-wounded characters evince a deep suspicion of rhetoric built around heroism and duty. While we can continue to see Beckett's cautious dismissal of his Resistance work as 'boy scout stuff' to be part of his guarded treatment of his own biography, it is useful to consider his apprehension within the context of the problematic rewriting of Resistance history after the war. Beckett made it clear that the France of the late 1940s presented many challenges to the conception of the nation that he 'clung to'. The de Gaulle government could not simply erect monuments to the recent dead, for only some fell in the service of the de Gaulle cause. This was compounded ever further by the unbreakable relation between Pétain, the First World War and a tradition of heroism – the 'poor old misled man' was not saved from his folly because he was a 'hero of Verdun'.

Many of the texts discussed in this chapter and across this book involve a focus on the fleshy aspects of war's suffering. They also mark out the cultural and political landscape that surrounded their composition, chiefly by way of intimating that the official declarations of peace did not necessarily replicate peace in everyday life. While governments and national cultures may plead 'rachat universel', individuals who were left 'shitting in their puttees' were faced with 'costive' communities, some of whom yawned with indifference once the initial shock of the war was over. Beckett compresses these political dimensions into objects (puttees and medals), motifs (sleeping and yawning) and in the physical forms that he describes or puts on stage.

Indeed, as the analysis of Beckett's enthusiasm for First World War fiction here demonstrates, Beckett's private language and pool of warfare images were generated by the literature and imagery of the First World War, yet crystalized when he came to write after the Second. While the image of Ernest, the proto-Hamm, draped over a white cross with a bucket around his neck is hardly subtle once we recognize the allusion to *Les Crois de bois*, the repeated references to the First World War in Beckett's works of the late 1940s and 1950s indicate that the conflict of 1914–18 and its literature were significant in shaping how Beckett thought about war. Encounters with veterans, reports of warfront conditions and the 'shell-shocked triangle' of war books were another set of 'obsessional images' (*DF*: xxi) which Beckett used in the creation of a war writing preoccupied with the aesthetics of suffering and the ethics of its representation. The associative aspects of the injured or dead soldier motif – memory, pain, bearing witness – are intrinsic to the tableaus Beckett drafts in the texts from which *Fin de partie* emerged. This is also true of the inclusion of the puttee and the specific injuries described in *The Unnamable*. The meaning creation in such texts is bound up in the affective potential of staging or describing objects or people linked to war, and the affective possibilities therein are invariably informed by the historical conditions of their creation and reception.

In Joyce's *Ulysses*, Stephen Dedalus declares that 'history is a nightmare from which I am trying to awake' (2000: 42). Beckett's historical statement is found in the empty idealism of *Endgame*'s Hamm who yearns for the 'sands of time' as comfort against the tide of history: 'If I could drag myself down to the sea! I'd make a pillow of the sand for my head and the tide would come' (*E*: 37). Short of telling Hamm there's nothing left of time, nor history, nor anything, Clov can only wearily utter 'there's no more tide' (*E*: 38). In *Waiting for Godot*, 'everything oozes', Estragon remarks (*CDW*: 56), a Beckettian version of the Heraclitan river of time. By *Endgame*, the flow of time has come to an end. Macroscopic and microscopic finality alike prevail in the text. Hamm proclaims, 'to hell with the universe' (*E*: 29), provisional as it is. Meanwhile, humanity, that watchword of post-war French recovery, is such a repugnant notion to Hamm that even a flea must be killed just in case humanity 'might start from there all over again' (*E*: 22).[11] However, such defiant anti-humanism cannot entirely stave off the reality of post-war mourning from imprinting itself on the text. We experience a brief moment of the truth of existence after the Second World War when Nell dies – to mourn is to live:

HAMM.   Go and see is she dead.

[CLOV *goes to bins, raises the lid of* NELL's, *stoops, looks into it. Pause.*]

CLOV.   Looks like it.

[*He closes the lid, straightens up.* HAMM *raises his toque. Pause. He puts it on again.*]

HAMM.   [*With his hand to his toque.*] And Nagg?

[CLOV *raises lid of* NAGG's *bin, stoops, looks into it. Pause.*]

CLOV.   Doesn't look like it.

[*He closes the lid, straightens up.*]

HAMM.   [*Letting go his toque.*] What's he doing?

[CLOV *raises lid of* NAGG's *bin, stoops, looks into it. Pause.*]

CLOV.   He's crying.

[*He closes the lid, straightens up.*]

HAMM.   Then he's living. (*E*: 38)

In *Endgame*, mourning is a condition of living. To confront that mourning, though – to resist the yawn, to open the dustbin lid himself – is something that Hamm refuses to do. Mourning is staged, though we do not see it. The process of grief is removed from sight, a replication of the practices across post-war France as the nation struggled to confront the realities of the war and the dead and injured that suffuse Beckett's form of war writing.

---

[11] Van Hulle and Weller (2018) suggest that Beckett developed a renewed disgruntlement with the post-war culture of 'humanity' when writing the play because of his work translating Ponget's *L'Homme*, a text he repudiated for its optimism (2018: 151–3).

Epilogue

This book has explored how Beckett's works negotiated the political nature of the war, particularly the organizing myths and ideologies behind so much of its propaganda. Yet we must also recognize that the war and the years which followed involved profound grief and loss for Beckett. It is this combination – the political potential of his writing in conjunction with the grim, sad, sometimes bitter treatment of the reality that it refers to or defers from – which makes Beckett's work and the history that surrounds it so endlessly compelling. War is not always visible in the work of the 1940s and 1950s, but it is there. The war underlies the images of destitution and pain, and the language of indecision and comic indifference, a current in the writing that is not undone by Beckett's vaguening but woven into the creative fabric as a way to respond to a 'universe become provisional'. In 1956, Beckett observed to Israel Shenker that 'I think anyone nowadays who pays the slightest attention to his own experience finds it the experience of a non-knower, a non-can-er' (Graver and Federman 2005: 162). That 'experience', that being-in-the-world, takes place in the shadow of war. Beckett's own experience of the war and its aftermath was one filled with not knowing and not being able, from not knowing where friends were and how much help they needed to not being able to access food or travel freely. The inability, the non-can-ing, which recurs in Beckett's work – the inability to speak, to move, to be at peace – is a trace of the war.

Beckett's texts beyond the trilogy and *Endgame* often describe smaller and smaller spaces – the inside of a skull, say, or geometrically defined chambers – and historical and geographical references appear with increasing rarity. When they do appear, references to a world outside these texts' confining spaces can be strangely disorientating. In the opening of *All Strange Away*, published in 1964, war returns to Beckett's literary world, only to be dismissed:

> Imagination dead imagine. A place, that again. Never another question. A place, then someone in it, that again. Crawl out of the frowsy deathbed and drag it to a place to die in. Out of the door and down the road in the old hat and coat like after the war, no, not that again. Five foot square, six high, no way in, none out, try for him there. (*TFN*: 73)

'Which war?', we might ask. As we have seen, Beckett uses wars of the past to do 'duty' for those more immediate. But it is the Second World War that is the catalyst, the one which presses upon the text the desire to say 'no, not that again' – to reject an obsession with a past steeped in conflicts both physical and political. In the sixth text of *Texts for Nothing*, the narrator recalls those Dantean souls obsessed with history, personal or otherwise, condemned to say, 'I was, I was' in 'Purgatory, in Hell too' (*TFN*: 27). Despite such a warning, Beckett's writing remains disturbed by the past, unable to prevent it seeping into texts, to shake the sense of a world fractured anew that the author felt after 1945.

The memory of the war and the post-war years of French political instability also materialize in *How It Is* through its images of torture and violence, explored so powerfully by Emilie Morin with reference to the Algerian War (2017). The novel's biblical setting 'in the mud' also has the historical correlative of the dreadful conditions Beckett faced in Saint-Lô: 'past moments old dreams back again or fresh like those that pass or things things always and memories I say them as I hear them murmur them in the mud' (*HII*: 3). As Erna Paris writes, 'the mud' was a significant concept used throughout the aftermath of the Second World War in relation to the Gaullist narratives of liberation and the Resistance:

> The French have a term for the fake history they adopted long ago and were teaching their children; they call it *la boue* (the mud), and anyone who tries to 'stir it up' is publicly pounced upon. Buried with 'the mud' are tiny handfuls of undisputed facts about France's wartime experience. (2002: 80)

The core of *How It Is* is the 'murmur' in the mud. It is foreshadowed by the 'nostalgie de cette boue' (nostalgia for that slime) in *Text for Nothing* VI (1958: 156), which acutely registers the kind of historical burden to which Paris refers, where 'words can be blotted' and 'all you have to do is say you said nothing' (*TFN*: 26). Keeping silent, blotting the words: this is not only how to survive in the mud but also how to deny or rewrite past activity, saying you said nothing when the case may in fact be otherwise, concealing the past for the sake of the present. The mud of *How It Is* is not that which Beckett's ranger suffered through in Flanders, but it cannot be separated from it either. With distance from the events of the 1940s, the more immediate war memory of *Mercier and Camier* and *Fin de partie* with their direct allusions to historical violence (as embodied by Nell and Nagg, and discoverable through the manuscripts) is substituted in *How It Is* for present violence, the torture of one by another to reveal something about themselves or the past. Yet this happens in 'la boue', in the surrounds of opaque historical memory. In *How It Is* and the other torture texts like *Rough for Radio II* or the earlier draft story 'On le tortura bien' (*PI*: 235), words are brought forth by physical violence, with tin opener and bullwhip, and it is in this, in the violent elicitation of speaking and remembering, that the shadow of the war and its immediate aftermath seem to linger in Beckett's writings, between the desire to utter 'no, not that again' and the inability to forgo 'stirring it up'.

Interviews and correspondence make clear that the war and 'the horrors of that hateful time' (*LSB IV*: 460) never left Beckett. As far as Beckett's writing openly reveals, Saint-Lô left its mark on him most of all. Beckett's work in Saint-Lô signified many changes in the author's life: it was the end of the war for Beckett; the end of a life spent relocating as he secured his place in Paris; and it was a farewell of sorts to a working life associated with Ireland. From then on Ireland was at a remove, a place to visit to see friends, family and for funerals. However, after 'The Capital of the Ruins', and the poems 'Saint-Lô' and 'Antipepsis' (written the same year as 'Saint-Lô'), Beckett revisited Saint-Lô in his writing through the recurring spectre of his friend Arthur Darley, the Irish Red Cross surgeon who died in December 1948 from the tuberculosis he had been treating. Beckett wrote the poem 'Mort de A.D.' in tribute to Darley, and his name appears later in a draft of 'For to end yet again' and Beckett's final piece, *Stirrings Still*.

While Beckett and Darley spent much of their time together in Saint-Lô and met on several occasions after Beckett finished with the Irish Red Cross (*LSB II*: 105), Seán Lawlor and John Pilling suggest that they were not 'particularly close' (*CP*: 391), though Ernest Keegan thought Beckett's elegy a 'perfect' picture of Darley (JEK C/1/32). Recalling Beckett's fascination with the psychology and personality of Samuel Johnson that underpinned his research for the play fragment 'Human Wishes', Beckett found in Darley a man defined by his turmoil. Knowlson describes Darley as 'an interesting case study for a writer' who 'after a couple of drinks ... would change completely' (*DF*: 349). Beckett was also perhaps interested in Darley because, as he commented to Gottfried Büttner, Darley 'belonged to a Catholicism converted branch ... of a well-known Irish protestant family and was deeply concerned with his religion' (17 March 1970, *LSB III*: 226). Though devoutly religious, he was also plagued by 'carnal desire' (*DF*: 349). Punning on the 'Saint' of Saint-Lô, Beckett records this in his elegy for Darley: 'Devouring the lives of the Saints a / Life a day reviving in the night his black sins' (trans. in *DF*: 349). The poem suggests that Darley's death spurred some form of reflection on Beckett's part about the very personal nature of faith and its conflict with the cravings of the body. Yet Darley's name appears in Beckett's later works at odd moments, haunting texts which seem otherwise unconcerned with the historical moment of Beckett's time in Saint-Lô.[1]

---

[1] It is unknown whether Beckett discussed with Darley the fact that Beckett was reasonably familiar with the poetry of Arthur's ancestor George Darley (1795–1846). Beckett knew George Darley's

Darley's name appears twice in Beckett's later writing, first in an early draft of 'Pour finir encore' ('For to end yet again'): 'manière de support mais moins la vieille planche de la mort d'A. D. témoin des départs d'alors' (qtd. in *CP*: 399). Indeed, the final version of 'For to end yet again' has a recurring refrain of a figure 'amidst his ruins the expelled' (*TFN*: 151) that is as much an evocation of the singular image of Ozymandias surrounded by 'dust indeed deep to engulf the haughtiest monuments' (*TFN*: 151) as it is another vision of 'humanity in ruins'.

In Beckett's last prose piece *Stirrings Still*, a corrupted 'Darly' and the day he 'died and left him' appears in the published text (*CIWS*: 108). As Dirk Van Hulle shows, Beckett began with the name 'Magee' in the manuscripts (recalling favoured actor Patrick Magee). The name is then 'McKee' in later drafts before becoming 'Darley' and then 'Darly', and Van Hulle is surely right to suggest that this 'McKee' is Frederick F. McKee, another staff member of Saint-Lô whose widow Beckett visited and corresponded with for a number of years after his return to Paris (Van Hulle 2011: 81). The deaths of Darley and McKee are recalled by Beckett in one of his 1989 interviews with James Knowlson (Knowlson and Knowlson 2007: 90–2). In the same interview, Beckett remarks on the deaths of Tommy Dunne and James Gaffney, both Saint-Lô staff members. Gaffney died in 1952 in an Aer Lingus plane crash, which Beckett knew of at the time, but he did not know of Dunne's passing until Eoin O'Brien told him in 1989. *Stirrings Still* was written over the period Knowlson began to work with Beckett, towards the end of his life, on what would be the foundation for the authorized biography. A kind of renewed grief over personal recollection seems present in Beckett's accounts of Saint-Lô, and this lingering memory manifests in the names which appear in the drafts and final version of his last prose piece. Like the medals and puttees of the mid-career writing, a name like Darley (or 'Darly') registers both the memory of 'that hateful time' of war and ruins and the connections Beckett forged as a result of the war. Yet the distance of age and time and the transformation of grief into remembrance leave Darley as 'Darly', one letter short of the complete name, like a fading memory.

The use of 'Darly' in *Stirrings Still* also evokes the loss of friends who died early in life. With the shifting choice of names in the manuscripts it is clear that, though Darley is the name referenced in the publication, the memory as much stands in for the various figures whose early deaths affected Beckett as it does

poetry well enough at least to mark the unnamed poem 'It Is Not Beauty I Demand' as Darley's in his copy of Francis Palgrave's *The Golden Treasury* (1862) (BDMP Library). Beckett also had in his library a copy of A. J. Leventhal's 1950 collected lectures on George Darley, published as part of Leventhal's short-lived attempt to revive public interest in Darley's poetry (BDMP Library).

pay tribute to Darley: Péron, lost to the cruelties of a Nazi concentration camp; Paul Léon, too; Gaffney, and Dunne, whom Beckett had known as a young man when he was Beckett's assistant in Saint-Lô. The reference, in this instance the name of a friend who passed some forty years prior, does duty for the representation of all those lost, the weight of history becoming in the late work the weight of memory. With 'Darly' and 'others too in their turn before and since' (*CIWS*: 108), this 'self so-called' stretches out across 'time' and is marked by 'grief' such that death itself is the end of not just the 'self so-called' but the 'others too' who dwell within memory. The text cycles through this process of grief throughout its three parts with an appeal to ending that does not come: 'No matter how no matter where. Time and grief and self so-called. Oh all to end' (*CIWS*: 115). The appeal for all to end takes in self, grief and time itself, as though the facticity of death might become the end of grief. These intersections of memory and grief in *Stirrings Still* in turn bring Lawlor and Pilling's sense of 'Mort de A.D.' into focus: 'the poem can also be read as something more than a response to the death of a friend, as a desperate reaction to the fact of death itself' (*CP*: 398). Crucially, though, it is in his return late in life to the period immediately following the war which allowed Beckett to think again on the nature of 'time' and its relationship to 'grief'. Possibly provoked by the critical and biographical interest in his life that was unavoidably linked to his ageing, to an approaching 'end', Beckett in his old age seems drawn to memories of Saint-Lô, a time amid the ruins in which the provisionality of life was made starkly apparent.

Although even Beckett's later texts start from the conception of a provisional 'universe' that Beckett documented in 1946, it is ultimately the works of the 1940s and 1950s that are most profoundly underpinned by the provisional, from the physical conditions of the characters and the locales to the nature of knowledge and thought. The contemporaneous methods of propaganda are paramount to understanding these textual conditions: the creation of double-meanings, indecision and false thought. Vital too is the image of the wounded soldier, their body distorted by the machine of industrial warfare. Beckett's texts are also infused with a deep suspicion of any rhetoric which weaponizes suffering for political means, be it the image of one soldier 'shitting in his puttees' (*MC*: 10) or the 'acres of corpses' described in 'First Love' (*ECEF*: 62). In Beckett's work after the Second World War, the strategies of the political machines which plunged Europe into chaos are disrupted, and their organizing impulses are replaced by the provisionality that Beckett identified in the war's wake, from the provisionality of the body to the provisionality of meaning itself. It is the work's very insistence on the provisional which creates what Herbert Blau identifies as Beckett's 'political immediacy' (qtd. in Ben-Zvi and Moorjani 2008: 7). Beckett's is a war writing of provisionality. By recognizing his work as such we open up his texts to new spheres of understanding. In doing so, we can continue to explore more thoroughly the profound ways that his work illuminates the transformative effects of the Second World War on both the concept of 'humanity' and the day-to-day conditions of everyday life.

Bibliography

Archival material

Beckett archival material

Avant fin de partie. Undated, unpublished typescript. Beckett International Foundation, University of Reading, MS 1227/7/16/7.
Beckett Digital Library, The Beckett Digital Manuscript Project, ed. D. Van Hulle, M. Nixon and V. Neyt: https://www.beckettarchive.org/library
En attendant Godot/Waiting for Godot, digital genetic edn (The Beckett Digital Manuscript Project, module 6), ed. D. Van Hulle, P. Verhulst and V. Neyt, Brussels: University Press Antwerp, 2017, http://beckettarchive.org
Fin de partie/Endgame, digital genetic edn (The Beckett Digital Manuscript Project, module 7), ed. D. Van Hulle, S. Weller and V. Neyt, Brussels: University Press Antwerp, 2018, http://beckettarchive.org Accessed through the BDMP *Fin de partie/Endgame* module: https://www.beckettarchive.org/findepartie/about/catalogue
'German Diaries', Beckett International Foundation, University of Reading.
L'Innommable/The Unnamable, digital genetic edn. (The Beckett Digital Manuscript Project, module 2), ed. D. Van Hulle, S. Weller and V. Neyt, Brussels: University Press Antwerp, 2013, http://beckettarchive.org
Malone meurt/Malone Dies, digital genetic edn. (The Beckett Digital Manuscript Project, module 5), ed. D. Van Hulle, P. Verhulst and V. Neyt, Brussels: University Press Antwerp, 2017, http://beckettarchive.org
Molloy, digital genetic edn. (The Beckett Digital Manuscript Project, module 4), ed. D. Van Hulle, S. Weller and V. Neyt, Brussels: University Press Antwerp, 2018, http://beckettarchive.org
'The Capital of the Ruins', typescript, Beckett International Foundation, University of Reading, MS 2905.
Watt notebooks, Harry Ransom Humanities Research Centre, University of Texas at Austin, Box 6.5–7 and Box 7.1–4. (c) The Estate of Samuel Beckett 2020.
Watt typescripts, Harry Ransom Humanities Research Centre, University of Texas at Austin, Box 7.5–6. (c) The Estate of Samuel Beckett 2020.

Archival material about Beckett

'Interview with Mary Crowley', 1972, Deirdre Bair Papers, Harry Ransom Humanities Research Centre, University of Texas at Austin, MS 5124, Container 1.6.

'Gabrielle Cecile Martinez PICABIA', Records of the Security Service, National Archives, KV 2/1313.
'Resistance – correspondence', Research Files, James and Elizabeth Knowlson Collection, University of Reading, JEK A/3/77/5.
'Resistance – Jeannine Picabia', Research Files, James and Elizabeth Knowlson Collection, University of Reading, JEK A/3/77/10.
'Resistance – Samuel Beckett', Research Files, James and Elizabeth Knowlson Collection, University of Reading, JEK A/3/77/13.
'Transcript of interview with Belmont, Georges', Interviews, James and Elizabeth Knowlson Collection, University of Reading, JEK A/7/13.
'Transcript of interview with McKee, Simone', Interviews, James and Elizabeth Knowlson Collection, University of Reading, JEK A/7/57.
'Transcript of interview with Stuart, Francis', Interviews, James and Elizabeth Knowlson Collection, University of Reading, JEK A/7/74.
'Interview with Ernest Keegan', Interviews, James and Elizabeth Knowlson Collection, University of Reading, JEK C/1/32

Other archival material

Air Ministry and Successors: Operations Record Books, Squadrons, National Archives, KEW AIR 27/2142.
Mission reports 1942–1944, National Archives, KEW AIR 40/2559.
Records of the Security Service, National Archives, KV.
Special Operations Executive: Personnel Files, SOE Records, National Archives, KEW HS9/597/5.

Publications by Beckett

(1990), *As The Story Was Told*, ed. D. McMillan, New York: Grove Press.
(2012), *Collected Poems of Samuel Beckett*, ed. S. Lawlor and J. Pilling, London: Faber & Faber.
(2009), *Company / Ill Seen Ill Said / Worstward Ho / Stirrings Still*, ed. D. Van Hulle, London: Faber & Faber.
(1986), *The Complete Dramatic Works*, London: Faber & Faber.
(1995), *The Complete Short Prose 1929–1989*, ed. S. E. Gontarski, New York: Grove Press.
(1983), *Disjecta: Miscellaneous Writings and a Dramatic Fragment*, ed. R. Cohn, London: John Calder.
(1993), *Dream of Fair to Middling Women*, London: John Calder.
(1996), *Eleutheria*, trans. B. Wright, London: Faber & Faber.
(1952), *En attendant Godot*, Paris: Les Éditions de Minuit.

(2009), *Endgame*, preface by R. McDonald, London: Faber & Faber.
(2009), *The Expelled / The Calmative / The End & First Love*, ed. C. Ricks, London: Faber & Faber.
(1978), *Fin de partie*, Paris: Les Éditions de Minuit.
(2009), *How It Is*, ed. M. O'Reilly, London: Faber & Faber.
(2004), *L'Innommable*, Paris: Les Éditions de Minuit.
(2009), *The Letters of Samuel Beckett, vol. 1: 1929–1940*, ed. M. Dow Fehsenfeld and L. More Overbeck, Cambridge: Cambridge University Press.
(2011), *The Letters of Samuel Beckett, vol. 2: 1941–1956*, ed. G. Craig, M. Dow Fehsenfeld, D. Gunn and L. More Overbeck, Cambridge: Cambridge University Press.
(2014), *The Letters of Samuel Beckett, vol. 3: 1957–1965*, ed. G. Craig, M. Dow Fehsenfeld, D. Gunn and L. More Overbeck, Cambridge: Cambridge University Press.
(2016), *The Letters of Samuel Beckett, vol. 4: 1966–1989*, ed. G. Craig, M. Dow Fehsenfeld, D. Gunn and L. More Overbeck, Cambridge: Cambridge University Press.
(2010), *Malone Dies*, ed. P. Boxall, London: Faber & Faber.
(2010), *Mercier and Camier*, ed. S. Kennedy, London: Faber & Faber.
(2009), *Molloy*, ed. S. Weller, London: Faber & Faber.
(2010), *More Pricks Than Kicks*, ed. C. Nelson, London: Faber & Faber.
(2009), *Murphy*, ed. J. C. C. Mays, London: Faber & Faber.
(1958), *Nouvelles et Textes pour rien*, Paris: Les Éditions de Minuit.
(2010), *Texts for Nothing and Other Shorter Prose 1950–1976*, ed. M. Nixon, London: Faber & Faber.
(2010), *The Unnamable*, ed. S. Connor, London: Faber & Faber.
(2009), *Watt*, ed. C. J. Ackerley, London: Faber & Faber.

Publications about Beckett

Ackerley, C. J. (2004), *Obscure Locks, Simple Keys: The Annotated* Watt, *Journal of Beckett Studies*, 14 (1–2): 24–213.
Ackerley, C. J. and S. E. Gontarski, eds (2006), *The Faber Companion to Samuel Beckett*, London: Faber & Faber.
Adorno, T. (1982), 'Trying to Understand Endgame', trans. M. T. Jones, *New German Critique*, 26: 119–50.
Anderton, J. (2016), *Beckett's Creatures: Art of Failure After the Holocaust*, London: Bloomsbury.
Atik, A. (2006), 'Beckett's Thesaurus', *Fulcrum*, 6: 456.
Badiou, A. (2003), *On Beckett*, eds A. Toscano and N. Power, Manchester: Clinamen.
Bair, D. (1980), *Samuel Beckett*, London: Picador.
Barry, E. (2005), 'Translating Nationalism: Ireland, France and Military History in Beckett's *Mercier et Camier*', *Irish Studies Review*, 13 (4): 505–15.

Bates, J. (2017), *Beckett's Art of Salvage*, Cambridge: Cambridge University Press.

Beloborodova, O., D. Van Hulle, and P. Verhulst, eds (2018), *Beckett and Modernism*, Basingstoke: Palgrave.

Ben-Zvi, Linda and Angela Moorjani, eds (2008), *Beckett 100: Revolving It All*, Oxford: Oxford University Press.

Bixby, P. (2009), *Samuel Beckett and the Postcolonial Novel*, Cambridge: Cambridge University Press.

Blackman, J. (2008), 'Postwar Beckett: Resistance, Commitment, or Communist Krap?', in R. Smith (ed.), *Beckett and Ethics*, 68–85, London: Bloomsbury.

Bowles, P. (1994), 'How to Fail', *PN Review*, 20 (4), March–April 1994. Available online: https://www.pnreview.co.uk/cgi-bin/scribe?item_id=3022 (last retrieved 2 March 2019).

Brazil, K. (2013), 'Beckett, Painting and the Question of "the Human"', *Journal of Modern Literature*, 36 (3): 81–99.

Carville, C. (2018), *Samuel Beckett and the Visual Arts*, Cambridge: Cambridge University Press.

Christensen, A. G. (2017), '"Tis My Muse Will Have It So": Four Dimensions of Scatology in *Molloy*', *Journal of Modern Literature*, 40 (4): 90–104.

Clifton, G. (2011), '"Pain Without Incarnation": *The Unnamable*, Derrida and the Book of Job', *Journal of Beckett Studies*, 20 (2): 149–71.

Cohn, R. (2001), *A Beckett Canon*, Ann Arbor: University of Michigan Press.

Connor, S. (1989), '"Traduttore, Traditore": Samuel Beckett's Translation of *Mercier et Camier*', *Journal of Beckett Studies*, 11–12: 27–46.

Cronin, A. (1999), *Samuel Beckett: The Last Modernist*, New York: Da Capo Press.

Davies, W. (2017), 'A Text Become Provisional: Revisiting "The Capital of the Ruins"', *Journal of Beckett Studies*, 26 (2): 169–87.

Davies, W. (2020), 'Realist Fiction and the Politics of Form in *Watt*', in S. Kennedy (ed.), *Beckett Beyond the Normal*, Edinburgh: Edinburgh University Press.

Dowd, G. (2013), 'France: 1928–1939', in A. Uhlmann (ed.), *Samuel Beckett in Context*, 65–97, Cambridge: Cambridge University Press.

Eagleton, T. (2006), 'Political Beckett?', *New Left Review*, 40: 67–74.

Einarsson, C. P. (2017), *A Theatre of Affect: The Corporeal Turn in Samuel Beckett's Drama*, Stuttgart: Ibidem.

Gaffney, P. (1999a), 'Dante, Manzoni, De Valera, Beckett…? Circumlocutions of a Storekeeper: Beckett and Saint-Lô', *Irish University Review*, 29 (2): 256–88.

Gibson, A. (2010a), *Samuel Beckett*, London: Reaktion.

Gibson, A. (2010b), 'Beckett, de Gaulle and the Fourth Republic 1944–49: *L'Innommable* and *En attendant Godot*', *Limit(e) Beckett*, 1: 1–26. Available online: http://www.limitebeckett.paris-sorbonne.fr/one/gibson.html (last retrieved 14 May 2019).

Gibson, A. (2013), 'Franco-Irish Beckett: *Mercier et Camier* in 1945–6', in P. Fifield and D. Addyman (eds), *Samuel Beckett: Debts and Legacies: New Critical Essays*, 19–38, London: Bloomsbury.

Gibson, A. (2014), 'French Beckett and French Literary Politics', in S. E. Gontarski (ed.), *The Edinburgh Companion to Samuel Beckett and the Arts*, 103–16, Edinburgh: Edinburgh University Press.

Gibson, A. (2015), 'Beckett, Vichy, Maurras, and the Body: *Premier amour* and *Nouvelles*', *Irish University Review*, 45 (2): 281–301.

Gierow, K. R. (1969), '1969 Nobel Award Ceremony Speech'. Available online: https://www.nobelprize.org/nobel_prizes/literature/laureates/1969/press.html (last retrieved 5 May 2019).

Golden, S. (1981), 'Familiars in a Ruinstrewn Land: *Endgame* as Political Allegory', *Contemporary Literature*, 22 (4): 425–55.

Gontarski, S. E. (1985), *The Intent of Undoing in Samuel Beckett's Dramatic Texts*, Bloomington: Indiana University Press.

Gordon, L. (1998), *The World of Samuel Beckett, 1906–1946*, New Haven: Yale University Press.

Gordon, L. (2013), 'France: World War Two', in A. Uhlmann (ed.), *Samuel Beckett in Context*, 109–25, Cambridge: Cambridge University Press.

Gouvard, J. M. (2019), 'Beckett and French War Propaganda: A New Source for *Waiting for Godot*', *Journal of Romance Studies*, 19 (1): 1–22.

Graver, L. and R. Federman (2005), *Samuel Beckett: The Critical Heritage*, London and New York: Routledge.

Gribben, D. (2008), 'Beckett's Other Revelation: "The Capital of the Ruins"', *Irish University Review*, 38 (2): 263–73.

Houston Jones, D. (2012), *Samuel Beckett and Testimony*, Basingstoke: Palgrave Macmillan.

Juliet, C. (2009), *Conversations with Samuel Beckett and Bram Van Velde*, Champaign, IL: Dalkey Archive Press.

Katz, D. (1999), *Saying I No More: Subjectivity and Consciousness in the Prose of Samuel Beckett*, Evanston, IL: Northwestern University Press.

Kennedy, S. (2004), '"The Artist Who Stakes His Being Is from Nowhere": Beckett and Thomas MacGreevy on the Art of Jack B. Yeats', *Samuel Beckett Today / Aujourd'hui*, 14: 61–74.

Kennedy, S. (2005a), 'Beckett Reviewing MacGreevy: A Reconsideration', *Irish University Review*, 35 (2): 273–87.

Kennedy, S. (2005b), 'Introduction to "Historicising Beckett"', *Samuel Beckett Today / Aujourd'hui*, 15: 21–7.

Kennedy, S. (2005c), 'Cultural Memory in *Mercier and Camier*: The Fate of Noel Lemass', *Samuel Beckett Today/Aujourd'hui*, 15: 117–31.

Kennedy, S. (2010), '"In the Street I Was Lost": Cultural Dislocation in Samuel Beckett's 'The End'', in S. Kennedy (ed.), *Beckett and Ireland*, 96–113, Cambridge: Cambridge University Press.

Kennedy, S. (2012), 'Spenser, Famine Memory and the Discontents of Humanism in *Endgame*', *Samuel Beckett Today / Aujourd'hui*, 24: 105–20.

Kennedy, S. (2014), 'Beckett and the Irish Big House', in S. E. Gontarski (ed.), *The Edinburgh Companion to Samuel Beckett and the Arts*, 222–36, Edinburgh: Edinburgh University Press.

Kennedy, S. (2015), '"Humanity in Ruins": Beckett and History', in D. Van Hulle (ed.), *The New Cambridge Companion to Samuel Beckett*, 185–200, Cambridge: Cambridge University Press.

Kennedy, S. (2019), 'Beckett, Censorship and the Problem of Parody', *Estudios Irlandeses*, 14 (2): 104–14.

Kennedy, S. (2020), 'Beckett, Evangelicalism and the Biopolitics of Famine', in S. Kennedy (ed.), *Beckett Beyond the Normal*, forthcoming, Edinburgh: Edinburgh University Press.

Kiberd, D. (2019), 'Samuel Beckett: European Irishman?', *The Irish Times*, 25 May, accessed online: https://www.irishtimes.com/culture/books/samuel-beckett-european-irishman-1.3887546. Accessed online: (last retrieved 16 October 2019).

Knowlson, J. (1996), *Damned to Fame: The Life of Samuel Beckett*, London: Bloomsbury.

Knowlson, J. and E. Knowlson (2007), *Beckett Remembering, Remembering Beckett*, London: Bloomsbury.

Lloyd, D. (1989), 'Writing in the Shit', *Modern Fiction Studies*, 35 (1): 69–85.

Maude, U. (2009), *Beckett, Technology, and the Body*, Cambridge: Cambridge University Press.

McMullan, A. (2010), *Performing Embodiment in Samuel Beckett's Drama*, New York: Routledge.

McNaughton, J. (2005), 'Beckett, German Fascism, and History: The Futility of Protest', *Samuel Beckett Today/Aujourd'hui*, 15: 101–16.

McNaughton, J. (2018), *Samuel Beckett and the Politics of Aftermath*, Oxford: Oxford University Press.

Moorjani, A. (2013), 'Beckett's *Molloy* in the French Context', *Beckett in the Cultural Field / Beckett dans le champ culturel, Samuel Beckett Today / Aujourd'hui*, 25: 91–108.

Moorjani, A. (2015), 'Molloy, Malone Dies, The Unnamable: The Novel Reshaped', in D. Van Hulle (ed.), *The New Cambridge Companion to Samuel Beckett*, 19–32, Cambridge: Cambridge University Press.

Morin, E. (2009), *Samuel Beckett and the Problem of Irishness*, Basingstoke: Palgrave Macmillan.

Morin, E. (2017), *Beckett's Political Imagination*, Cambridge: Cambridge University Press.

Morin, E. (2019), 'Beckett, War Memory, and the State of Exception', *Journal of Modern Literature*, 42 (4): 129–45.

Moynahan, J. (1995), *Anglo-Irish: The Literary Imagination in a Hyphenated Culture*, Princeton: Princeton University Press.

Nixon, M. (2011), *Samuel Beckett's German Diaries: 1936–1937*, London: Continuum.

Nixon, M. (2019), 'Introduction', *Journal of Beckett Studies*, 28 (1): 1–4.

O'Brien, E. (1986), *The Beckett Country*, London: Black Cat Press/Faber & Faber.

Perloff, M. (2005), 'In Love with Hiding: Samuel Beckett's War', *The Iowa Review*, 35 (1): 76–103.

Pilling, J. (1994), 'Beckett's English Fiction' in J. Pilling (ed.), *The Cambridge Companion to Beckett*, 17–42, Cambridge: Cambridge University Press.

Pilling, J. (2006), *A Samuel Beckett Chronology*, Basingstoke: Palgrave Macmillan.

Pountney, R. (1988), *Theatre of Shadows: Samuel Beckett's Drama 1956–76*, Gerrards Cross: Colin Smythe.

Rabaté, J. M. (2013), 'Paris, Roussillon, Ussy', in Anthony Uhlmann (ed.), *Samuel Beckett in Context*, 52–64, Cambridge: Cambridge University Press.

Rabaté, J. M. (2016), *Think Pig!: Beckett at the Limit of the Human*, New York: Fordham University Press.

Rákóczy, A. (2017), 'In Search of Space and Locale in the Genesis of Samuel Beckett's *Fin de partie*', in M. Bariselli, N. M. Bowe and W. Davies (eds), *Samuel Beckett and Europe: History, Culture, Tradition*, 41–54, Newcastle: Cambridge Scholars.

Reid, A. (1968), *All I Can Manage, More Than I Could: An Approach to the Plays of Samuel Beckett*, New York: Grove Press.

Ricks, C. (1993), *Beckett's Dying Words*, Oxford: Oxford University Press.

Salisbury, L. (2013), 'Resistances: Beckett's Language of Power in War and Peace', *Times Literary Supplement*. Accessed online: https://www.the-tls.co.uk/articles/private/resistances/ (last retrieved 5 September 2019).

Salisbury, L. (2014), 'Gloria SMH and Beckett's Linguistic Encryptions', in S. E. Gontarski (ed.), *The Edinburgh Companion to Samuel Beckett and the Arts*, 153–69, Edinburgh: Edinburgh University Press.

Shidlo, A. (1998), '"The Horror of Existence": A Labyrinth of Evasions in *Mercier et Camier*', *Samuel Beckett Today/Aujourd'hui*, 7: 231–44.

Simpson, H. (2020a), '"We're Not in Form": *Waiting for Godot* and the Fascist Aesthetics of the Body', in W. Davies and H. Bailey (eds), *Beckett and Politics*, forthcoming, Basingstoke: Palgrave Macmillan.

Simpson, H. (2020b), '"Hurts! He Wants to Know If It Hurts!": Suffering Beyond Redemption in *Waiting for Godot*', in S. Kennedy (ed.), *Beckett Beyond the Normal*, Edinburgh: Edinburgh University Press.

Smith, R. (2017), 'Radical Sensibility in "The End"', *Journal of Beckett Studies*, 26 (1): 69–86.

Stewart, P. (2011), *Sex and Aesthetics in Samuel Beckett's Work*, Basingstoke: Palgrave Macmillan.

Tajiri, Y. (2007), *Samuel Beckett and the Prosthetic Body*, Basingstoke: Palgrave Macmillan.

Teekell, A. (2016), 'Beckett in Purgatory: "Unspeakable" *Watt* and the Second World War', *Twentieth-Century Literature*, 62 (3): 247–70.

Teekell, A. (2018), *Emergency Literature: Irish Literature, Neutrality, and the Second World War*, Evanston, IL: Northwestern University Press.

Tonning, E. (2007), *Samuel Beckett's Abstract Drama*, Bern: Peter Lang.
Van Hulle, D. (2011), *The Making of Samuel Beckett's Stirrings Still / Soubresauts and Comment dire / what is the word*, Antwerp: University of Antwerp Press.
Van Hulle, D. and P. Verhulst (2018), *The Making of Samuel Beckett's En attendant Godot/Waiting for Godot*, London: Bloomsbury.
Van Hulle, D. and S. Weller (2018), *The Making of Samuel Beckett's Fin de partie/ Endgame*, London: Bloomsbury.
Weiss, K. (2009), '"…Humanity in Ruins…": The Historical Body in Samuel Beckett's Fiction', in S. Kennedy and K. Weiss (eds), *Samuel Beckett: History, Memory, Archive*, 151–68, Basingstoke: Palgrave Macmillan.
Weller, S. (2013), 'Post-World War Two Paris', in Anthony Uhlmann (ed.), *Samuel Beckett in Context*, 160–72, Cambridge: Cambridge University Press.
Weller, S. (2015), 'Beckett and Late Modernism', in Dirk Van Hulle (ed.), *The New Cambridge Companion to Samuel Beckett*, 89–102, Cambridge: Cambridge University Press.
Weller, S. (2019), *Language and Negativity in European Modernism*, Cambridge: Cambridge University Press.
White, K. (2011), *Beckett and Decay*, London: Bloomsbury.
Will, B. (2014), 'The Resistance Syndrome: Alain Badiou on Samuel Beckett', *South Central Review*, 31 (1): 114–29.
Wimbush, A. (2014), 'Humility, Self-Awareness, and Religious Ambivalence: Another Look at Beckett's "Humanistic Quietism"', *Journal of Beckett Studies*, 23 (2): 202–21.
Wimbush, A. (2015), 'The Pretty Quietist Pater: Samuel Beckett's *Molloy* and the Aesthetics of Quietism', *Literature and Theology*, 30 (4): 439–55.

General bibliography

Albanese, R. (2008), 'Republican School Discourse and the Construction of French Cultural Identity: La Fontaine and Corneille as Case Studies', in G. D. Chaitin (ed.), *Culture Wars and Literature in the French Third Republic*, 65–82, Newcastle: Cambridge Scholars.
Anon. (1945), 'Pétain Trial Opens Today', *The Guardian Archive Online*, 2009. Available online: https://www.theguardian.com/theguardian/2009/jul/23/petain-trial-from-the-archive (last retrieved 5 December 2019).
Asher, K. (1998), 'T. S. Eliot and Charles Maurras', *ANQ: A Quarterly Journal of Short Articles, Notes and Reviews*, 11 (3): 20–9.
Atkin, N. (1998), *Pétain*, Harlow: Longman.
Bach, R. (1999), 'Identifying Jews: The Legacy of the 1941 Exhibition, "Le Juif et la France"', *Studies in 20th Century Literature*, 23 (1): 30–92.
Barbusse, H. (1916), *Le Feu*, Paris: Flammarion.

Barnes, R. M. (1972), *A History of the Regiments & Uniforms of the British Army*, London: Sphere.
Beevor, A. and A. Cooper (2007), *Paris: After the Liberation, 1944–1949*, London: Penguin.
Berstein, S. (2001), 'Gaullism', in J. Krieger (ed.), *The Oxford Companion to Politics of the World*, Oxford: Oxford University Press. Available online: https://www.oxfordreference.com/view/10.1093/acref/9780195117394.001.0001/acref-9780195117394-e-0272 (last retrieved 4 August 2019).
Bertrand Dorléac, L. (2008), *Art of Defeat, France 1940–1944*, trans. J. M. Todd, Los Angeles: Getty Publications.
Bialas W. and A. Rabinbach, eds (2007), *Nazi Germany and the Humanities: How German Academics Embraced Nazism*, London: Oneworld.
Blanton, C. D. (2015), *Epic Negation*, Oxford: Oxford University Press.
Bolton, J. (2016), '"Lucid Song": The Poetry of the Second World War', in A. Piette and M. Rawlinson (eds), *The Edinburgh Companion to Twentieth-Century British and American War Literature*, 85–93, Edinburgh: Edinburgh University Press.
Bowen, E. (1978), *The Heat of the Day*, London: Penguin.
Brouillette, S. (2019), *UNESCO and the Fate of the Literary*, Bloomington, IN: Stanford University Press.
Brown, T. (2015), *The Irish Times: 150 Years of Influence*, London: Bloomsbury.
Bruller, J. (1991), *The Silence of the Sea / La silence de la mer*, ed. J. W. Brown and L. D. Stokes, Oxford: Berg.
Callil, C. (2007), *Bad Faith: A Story of Family and Fatherland*, London: Vintage.
Campbell, M. (2016), 'Irish Writing of Insurrection and Civil War', in A. Piette and M. Rawlinson (eds), *The Edinburgh Companion to Twentieth-Century British and American War Literature*, 64–74, Edinburgh: Edinburgh University Press.
Camus, A. (2002), *Camus at Combat: Writing 1944–1947*, ed. J. Lévi-Valensi, trans. A. Goldhammer, Princeton, NJ: Princeton University Press.
Chambrun, R de (1984), *Pierre Laval, Traitor or Patriot?*, trans. E. Stein, New York: Charles Scribner's Sons.
Childers, K. S. (2003), *Fathers, Families and the State in France, 1914–1945*, Ithaca, NY: Cornell University Press.
Christofferson, T. and M. Christofferson (2006). *France During World War II: From Defeat to Liberation*, New York: Fordham University Press.
Cleary, J. (2014), 'Introduction', in Joe Cleary (ed.), *The Cambridge Companion to Irish Modernism*, 1–20, Cambridge: Cambridge University Press.
Coffey, B. (1972), 'Thomas MacGreevy: A Singularly Perfect Poet', *Hibernia Review of Books*, 4: 10.
Cole, R. (2006), *Propaganda, Censorship and Irish Neutrality in the Second World War*, Edinburgh: Edinburgh University Press.
Corcoran, N. (1993), *English Poetry Since 1940*, London: Routledge.
Cot, P. (1941), 'Morale in France During the War', *American Journal of Sociology*, 47 (3): 429–51.

Creswell, M. and M. Trachtenberg (2003), 'France and the German Question 1945–1955', *Journal of Cold War Studies*, 5 (3): 5–28.
Crowdy, T. (2007), *French Resistance Fighter: France's Secret Army*, Oxford: Osprey Publishing.
Curtis, M. (2002), *Verdict on Vichy: Power and Prejudice in the Vichy France Regime*, London: Weidenfeld & Nicolson.
D'Aubigné, A. (1972), *Printemps*, Genève: Librairie Droz.
Dagnino, J. (2016), 'The Myth of the New Man in Italian Fascist Ideology', *Fascism*, 5 (2): 130–48.
Davis, T. S. (2016), *The Extinction Scene: Late Modernism and Everyday Life*, New York: Columbia University Press.
Dawe, G. (2013), 'Nocturnes: Thomas MacGreevy and World War One', in S. Schreibman (ed.), *The Life and Works of Thomas MacGreevy*, 3–16, London: Bloomsbury.
De Gaulle, C. (1944), Speech at the Hôtel de Ville in Paris, *World War II Database*. Accessed online: https://ww2db.com/battle_spec.php?battle_id=115 (last retrieved 20 February 2019).
Dorgelès, R. (1919), *Les Croix de bois*, Paris: Éditions Albin Michel.
Douglas, K. (2000), 'Poets in This War, 1943', in D. Graham (ed.), *The Letters of Keith Douglas*, Manchester: Carcanet Press.
Douglas, K. (2000), *Complete Poems*, ed. D. Graham, London: Faber & Faber.
Duhamel, G. (1917; 2010), *Vie des martyrs/The New Book of Martyrs*, trans. F. Simmonds, London: Aterna.
Duthuit, G. (1948), 'Introduction', *Transition Forty-Eight*, 1: 5.
Eksteins, E. (2009), 'Memory', in H. Bloom (ed.), *All Quiet on the Western Front: New Edition*, 57–80, New York: Bloom's Literary Criticism, InfoBase Publishing.
Ellul, P. (1973), *Propaganda: The Formation of Men's Attitudes*, New York: Vintage Books.
Eliot, T. S. (1944), 'Preface', in *France Remembered*, trans. J. G. Weightman, London: Sylvan Press.
Eliot, T. S. (2004), *The Complete Poems & Plays*, London: Faber & Faber.
Elliott, G. (2017), *A Forgotten Man: The Life and Death of John Lodwick*, London: I. B. Tauris.
Evans, B. (2014), *Ireland in the Second World War: Farewell to Plato's Cave*, Manchester: Manchester University Press.
Evleth, D. (1999), *The Authorized Press in Vichy and German-Occupied France, 1940–1944: A Bibliography*, Westport, CT: Greenwood.
Feldman, M. (2013), *Ezra Pound's Fascist Propaganda, 1935–45*, Basingstoke: Palgrave Macmillan.
Fisk, R. (1996), *In Time of War: Ireland, Ulster, and the Price of Neutrality*, Philadelphia: University of Pennsylvania Press.
Flood, C. (2000), 'Pétain and de Gaulle: Making the Meanings of the Occupation', in V. Holman and D. Kelly (eds), *France at War in the Twentieth Century; Propaganda, Myth, and Metaphor*, 88–110, New York: Berghahn.

Fogg, S. L. (2009), *The Politics of Everyday Life in Vichy France*, Cambridge: Cambridge University Press.

Fontaine T. (2007), *Chronology of Repression and Persecution in Occupied France, 1940–44, Online Encyclopaedia of Mass Violence*. Accessed online: https://www.sciencespo.fr/mass-violence-war-massacre-resistance/en/document/chronology-repression-and-persecution-occupied-france-1940-44 (last retrieved 14 August 2019).

Fouché, J. J. (2004), *Massacre at Oradour: France, 1944: Coming to Grips with Terror*, Dekalb, IL: Northern Illinois University Press.

Fussell, P. (2013), *The Great War and Modern Memory*, Oxford: Oxford University Press.

Gaffney, P. (1999b), *Healing Amid the Ruins*, Dublin: A.& A. Farmar.

Galtung, J. (1969), 'Violence, Peace, and Peace Research', *Journal of Peace Research*, 6 (3): 167–91.

Gerber, M. (2018), 'Vichy's New Man: National Regeneration and Historical Revisionism in French Education, 1940–1944', PhD Diss., Ohio University.

Gildea, R. (1996), *France Since 1945*, Oxford: Oxford University Press.

Gildea, R. (2015), *Fighters in the Shadows*, London: Faber & Faber.

Giroud, V. (2000), 'Transition to Vichy: The Case of Georges Pelorson', *Modernism/modernity*, 7 (2): 221–48.

Greene, T. M. (2002), *Calling from Diffusion: Hermeneutics of the Promenade*, Northampton, MA: University of Massachusetts Press.

Golsan, R. J. (2000), *Vichy's Afterlife: History and Counterhistory in Postwar France*, Lincoln and London: University of Nebraska Press.

Guéhenno, J. (2014), *Diary of the Dark Years: 1940–1944*, trans. D. Ball, Oxford: Oxford University Press.

Halkin, A. (2009), 'The Flood', in H. Bloom (ed.), *All Quiet on the Western Front: New Edition*, 107–26, New York: Bloom's Literary Criticism, InfoBase Publishing.

Hazareesingh, S. (2012), *In the Shadow of the General*, Oxford: Oxford University Press.

Holman, V. and D. Kelly, eds (2000), *France at War in the Twentieth Century*, Oxford: Berghahn Books.

Horne, H. (2019), 'France, Fall Of', in I. Dear (ed.), *The Oxford Companion to World War II*, Oxford: Oxford University Press. Accessed online: https://www.oxfordreference.com/view/10.1093/acref/9780198604464.001.0001/acref-9780198604464-e-638?rskey=SXXrgF&result=644 (last retrieved 13 August 2019).

Humbert, A. (2009), *Résistance: Memoirs of Occupied France*, trans. B. Mellor, London: Bloomsbury.

Jackson, J. (2001), *France: The Dark Years 1940–1944*, Oxford: Oxford University Press.

Jackson, J. (2004), *The Fall of France: The Nazi Invasion of 1940*, Oxford: Oxford University Press.

Jacobus, M. (2005), *The Poetics of Psychoanalysis*, Oxford: Oxford University Press.

Jeffrey, K. (2000), *Ireland and the Great War*, Cambridge: Cambridge University Press.

Joyce, J. (2000), *Ulysses*, London: Penguin.

Junyk, I. (2013), *Foreign Modernism: Cosmopolitanism, Identity, and Style in Paris*, Toronto: University of Toronto Press.

Kaczerginski, S. (1948), *Songs of the Ghettos and Concentration Camps*, New York: Congress for Jewish Culture.

Kedward, H. R. (1993), *In Search of the Maquis*, Oxford: Oxford University Press.

Kedward, H. R. (2005), 'France', in I. C. B. Dear and M. R. D. Foot (eds), *The Oxford Companion to World War II*, 308–22, Oxford: Oxford University Press.

Keitch, C. (2017), 'First World War Recruitment Posters', *Imperial War Museum*. Accessed online: https://www.iwm.org.uk/learning/resources/first-world-war-recruitment-posters (last retrieved 5 September 2019).

Kelly, M. (2004), *The Cultural and Intellectual Rebuilding of France after the Second World War*, Basingstoke: Palgrave Macmillan.

Kelly, A. (2008), *Twentieth-Century Irish Literature*, Basingstoke: Palgrave Macmillan.

Koonz, C. (2003), *The Nazi Conscience*, Cambridge MA and London: The Belknap Press of Harvard University Press.

Labarthe, A. (1945), 'Enough!' in J. G. Weightman (ed. and trans.), *French Writing on English Soil*, 19–21, London: Sylvan Press.

Lackerstein, D. (2012), *National Regeneration in Vichy France: Ideas and Policies, 1930–1944*, London: Ashgate.

Leak, A. (2006), *Jean-Paul Sartre*, London: Reaktion.

Lukács G. (1971), *The Theory of the Novel: A Historico-Philosophical Essay on the Forms of Great Epic Literature*, trans. A. Bostock, Cambridge, MA: The MIT Press.

MacGreevy, T. (1931), *T.S. Eliot: A Study*, London: Chatto & Windus. Accessed online: http://www.macgreevy.org/style?style=text&source=book.eliot.xml&action=show (last retrieved 23 February 2019).

MacGreevy, T. (1943), 'Exhibition of Living Art Revisited', *The Irish Times*, 1 October. Accessed online: http://www.macgreevy.org/style?style=text&source=rev.irt.058.xml&action=show (last retrieved 4 December 2019).

MacGreevy, T. (1945), *Jack B. Yeats An Appreciation and an Interpretation*. Accessed online: http://www.macgreevy.org/style?style=text&source=mon.jby.001.xml&action=show (last retrieved 16 December 2019).

MacGreevy, T. (1948), 'Dante and Modern Ireland', *The Father Mathew Record*, Dublin, January 1948. Accessed online: http://www.macgreevy.org/style?style=text&source=art.fmr.060.xml&action=show (last retrieved 16 December 2019).

MacGreevy, T. (1991), *Collected Poems: An Annotated Edition*, ed. S. Schreibman, Dun Laoghaire: Anna Livia Press.

MacKay, M. (2007), *Modernism and World War Two*, Cambridge: Cambridge University Press.

MacKay, M. (2009), 'Introduction', in M. MacKay (ed.), *The Cambridge Companion to the Literature of World War II*, 1–12, Cambridge: Cambridge University Press.

MacKay, M. (2017), *Modernism, Violence, and War*, London: Bloomsbury.

MacNeice, L. (2007), *Collected Poems*, ed. P. McDonald, London: Faber & Faber.

Marrus, M. R. and R. O. Paxton (1995), *Vichy France and the Jews*, Stanford: Stanford University Press.

Mathis, U. (1988), 'La Chanson de la BBC dans le Contexte de la Production Chansonnière de l'Occupation et de la Résistance', *La chanson française et son histoire*, Guneter Narr Verlag.

McLoughlin, K. (2010a), 'Introduction', in K. McLoughlin (ed.), *The Cambridge Companion to War Writing*, 1–4, Cambridge: Cambridge University Press.

McLoughlin, K. (2010b), 'War in Print Journalism', in K. McLoughlin (ed.), *The Cambridge Companion to War Writing*, 47–58, Cambridge: Cambridge University Press.

McNaughton, J. (2012), 'Thomas MacGreevy's Poetics of Loss: War, Sexuality and Archive', *Journal of Modern Literature*, 35 (4): 130–50.

Merleau-Ponty, M. (1969), *Humanism and Terror*, trans. J. O'Neil, Boston: Beacon Press.

Moody, A. (2018), *The Art of Hunger: Aesthetic Autonomy and the Afterlives of Modernism*, Oxford: Oxford University Press.

Morgan, E. (2001), 'Question Time: Radio and the Liberalisation of Irish Public Discourse after World War II', *History Ireland*, 9 (4). Available online: https://www.historyireland.com/20th-century-contemporary-history/question-time-radio-and-the-liberalisation-of-irish-public-discourse-after-world-war-ii/ (last retrieved 4 June 2019).

Mott, F. W. (1916), 'Special Discussion on Shell Shock without Visible Signs of Injury', *Proceedings of the Royal Society of Medicine*, 9: i–xliv.

Mouré, K. (2010), 'Food Rationing and the Black Market in France (1940–1944)', *French History*, 24 (2): 262–82.

Munholland, K. (1994), 'Wartime France: Remembering Vichy', *French Historical Studies*, 18 (3): 801–20.

Ó Drisceoil, D. (1996), *Censorship in Ireland 1939–1945: Neutrality, Politics and Society*, Cork: Cork University Press.

O'Dwyer, G. (2017), *Charles de Gaulle, the International System, and the Existential Difference*, London: Routledge.

O'Grady, S. (1878), *History of Ireland: The Heroic Period*, London: Sampson Low, Searle, Marston & Rivington. Accessed online: https://archive.org/details/historyirelandh01gragoog (last retrieved 1 February 2019).

Orwell, G. (1938), *Homage to Catalonia*, in *The Complete Works of George Orwell*, ed. P. Davison, 1987, vol. 6, London: Secker & Warburg.

Orwell, G. (1940), *Inside the Whale*, in *The Complete Works of George Orwell*, ed. P. Davison, 1987, vol. 12, London: Secker & Warburg.

Orwell, G. (1943), 'Looking back on the Spanish War', *New Road*. Available online: https://orwell.ru/library/essays/Spanish_War/english/esw_1 (last retrieved 30 July 2020).

Orwell, G. (1957), 'Politics and the English Language', *Selected Essays*, London: Penguin, 1957.

Ousby, I. (2000), *Occupation: The Ordeal of France, 1940–1944*, New York: Cooper Square Press.
Oxford English Dictionary Online, https://www.oed.com
Paris, E. (2002), *Long Shadow: Truth, Lies and History*, London: Bloomsbury.
Paxton, R. O. (1966), *Parades and Politics at Vichy*, Princeton, NJ: Princeton University Press.
Paxton, R. O. (1972), *Vichy France: Old Guard and New Order –1940–1944*, New York: Columbia University Press.
Paxton, R. O. (2004), *The Anatomy of Fascism*, New York: Alfred A. Knopf.
Pearson, C. (2008), *Scarred Landscapes: War and Nature in Vichy France*, Basingstoke: Palgrave Macmillan.
Piette, A. (1995), *Imagination at War*, London: Papermac.
Piette, A. (2009), 'War Poetry in Britain', in M. MacKay (ed.), *The Cambridge Companion to the Literature of World War II*, 13–25, Cambridge: Cambridge University Press.
Piette, A. (2016), 'Introduction: The Wars of the Twentieth Century', in A. Piette and M Rawlinson (eds), *The Edinburgh Companion to Twentieth-Century British and American War Literature*, 1–7, Edinburgh: Edinburgh University Press.
Piette, A. (2019), 'Poetry, the Early Cold War and the Idea of Europe', in G. Plain (ed.), *British Literature in Transition, 1940–1960: Postwar*, 161–75, Cambridge: Cambridge University Press.
Plain, G. (2015), *Literature of the 1940s: War, Postwar and 'Peace'*, Edinburgh: Edinburgh University Press.
Plain, G., ed. (2019), *British Literature in Transition, 1940–160: Postwar*, Cambridge: Cambridge University Press.
Procter, J. (2006), 'The Postcolonial Everyday', *New Formations*, 58: 62–80.
Pudney, J. (1943), *Beyond This Disregard: Poems*, London: John Lane.
Quinn, J. (2007), 'Shared Sacrifice and the Return of the French Deportees in 1945', *Journal of the Western Society for French History*, 35: 277–88. Available online: http://hdl.handle.net/2027/spo.0642292.0035.018 (last retrieved 13 June 2019).
Rae, P. (2009), 'Orwell, World War I Modernism and the Spanish Civil War', *Journal of War and Culture Studies*, 2 (3): 245–58.
Ramsay, K. W. (2017), 'Information, Uncertainty, and War', *Annual Review of Political Science*, 20: 505–27.
Rawlinson, M. (2019), 'Narrating Transitions to Peace: Fiction and Film after War', in G. Plain (ed.), *British Literature in Transition: 1940–1960*, 143–60, Cambridge: Cambridge University Press.
Reggiani, A. H. (2006), *God's Eugenicist: Alexis Carrel and the Sociobiology of Decline*, Oxford: Berghahn Books.
Remarque, E. M. (1996), *All Quiet on the Western Front*, London: Vintage.
Riding, A. (2011), *And the Show Went On: Cultural Life in Nazi-Occupied Paris*, New York: Knopf.

Ross, K. (2008), 'French Quotidian', in S. Johnstone (ed.), *The Everyday: Documents of Contemporary Art*, 42–7, Cambridge, MA: The MIT Press.

Rousso, H. (1991), *The Vichy Syndrome: History and Memory in France Since 1944*, trans. A. Goldhammer, Cambridge, MA: Harvard University Press.

Russell, R. (2000), 'Ethical Bodies', in P. Hancock, B. Hughes, E. Jagger, K. Paterson, R. Russell, R. Tulle-Winton and M. Tyler (eds), *The Body, Culture and Society: An Introduction*, 101–16, Buckingham: Open University Press.

Salisbury, L. (2020), '"Between-Time Stories": Waiting, War and the Temporalities of Care', *Medical Humanities*. Published Online First: 27 April 2020. doi: 10.1136/medhum-2019-011810 (last retrieved 5 May 2020).

Sartre, J.-P. (1945), 'Paris Under the Occupation', in J. G. Weightman (ed. and trans.), *French Writing on English Soil*, 122–32, London: Sylvan Press.

Sartre, J.-P. (1957), *Questions de méthode*, Paris: Éditions Gallimard.

Sartre, J.-P. (1980a), 'Existentialism Is a Humanism', in W. A. Kaufmann (ed.), *Existentialism: From Dostoevsky to Sartre*, 345–69, New York: New American Library.

Sartre, J.-P. (1980b), 'Marxism and Existentialism', in W. A. Kaufmann (ed.), *Existentialism: From Dostoevsky to Sartre*, 369–74, New York: New American Library.

Sartre, J.-P. (1995), *Anti-Semite and Jew: An Exploration of the Etiology of Hate*, trans. G. J. Becker, New York: Schoken Books.

Sassoon, S. (1930), *Memoirs of an Infantry Officer*, London: Faber & Faber.

Scarry, E. (1985), *The Body in Pain: The Making and Unmaking of the World*, Oxford: Oxford University Press.

Schreibman, S. (1999a), 'Introduction to *The Capuchin Annual*', *The Thomas MacGreevy Archive*. Available online: http://www.macgreevy.org/style?style=text&source=com.cpa.xml&action=show/ (last retrieved 16 December 2019).

Schreibman, S. (1999b), 'Introduction to *The Father Mathew Record*', *The Thomas MacGreevy Archive*. Available online: http://www.macgreevy.org/style?style=text&source=com.cpa.xml&action=show/ (last retrieved 16 December 2019).

Shennan, A. (2000), *The Fall of France, 1940*, London: Longman.

Slavkova, I. (2003), 'Surviving the Collapse of Humanism after World War II: The "Abhumanist" Response of J. Audiberti And C. Bryen', *Contemporary French and Francophone Studies*, 17 (3): 318–27.

Slaughter, J. R. (2007), *Human Rights, Inc*, New York: Fordham University Press.

Smith, J. (2019), 'Covert Legacies in Postwar British Fiction', in G. Plain (ed.), *British Literature in Transition: Postwar*, 337–52, Cambridge: Cambridge University Press.

Sowerwine, C. (2001), *France Since 1870: Culture, Politics and Society*, Basingstoke: Palgrave Macmillan.

Spender, S. (1941), 'The Creative Arts in Our Time', in *Penguin New Writing*, Autumn: 125–37.

Stanfield, P. S. (1988), *Yeats and Politics in the 1930s*, London: Macmillan.
Stein, G. (1996), 'Introduction to the Speeches of Maréchal Pétain', *Modernism/Modernity*, 3 (3): 93–6.
Stuart, F. (1976), 'Selections from a Berlin Diary, 1942', *Journal of Irish Literature*, 5 (1), 75–96.
Stuart, F. (1986), 'The Back Room of Davy Bryne's', *The Inflight Magazine of Aer Lingus*, January/February, 37–9.
Teichman, J. (1986), *Pacifism and the Just War: A Study in Applied Philosophy*, New York: Basil Blackwell.
Trumbo, T. (1939), *Johnny Got His Gun*, Philadelphia: J. B. Lippincott.
Tucker, W. R. (1965), 'Fascism and Individualism: The Political Thought of Pierre Drieu La Rochelle', *The Journal of Politics*, 27 (1): 153–77.
Tumblety, J. (2012), *Remaking the Male Body: Masculinity and the Uses of Physical Culture in Interwar and Vichy France*, Oxford: Oxford University Press.
Van Dusen, W. (1996), '"Portrait of a National Fetish": Gertrude Stein's "Introduction to the Speeches of Maréchal Pétain" (1942)', *Modernism/modernity*, 3 (3), 69–92.
Vinen, R. (2007), *The Unfree French: Life Under the Occupation*, London: Penguin.
Wells, H. G. (1916), *Mr Britling Sees It Through*, London: Cassell.
White, H. (1990), *The Content of the Form*, Baltimore, MD: Johns Hopkins University Press.
Wieviorka, O. (2016), *The French Resistance*, trans. J. M. Todd, London and Cambridge, MA: The Belknap Press.
Will, B. (2004), 'Lost in Translation: Stein's Vichy Collaboration', *Modernism/modernity*, 11 (4): 651–68.
Wills, C. (2008), *That Neutral Island*, London: Faber & Faber.
Wilson, J. M. (2013), 'The Augustinian Imagination of Thomas MacGreevy', in. S. Schreibman, *The Life and Works of Thomas MacGreevy*, 79–92, London: Bloomsbury.
Yeats, W. B. (1888), *Folk and Fairy Tales of the Irish Peasantry*, London: Walter Scott Pub.
Yeats, W. B. (1893), *The Celtic Twilight*, London: Lawrence and Bullen.
Yeats, W. B. (1998), *Mythologies*, New York: Touchstone.
Yeats, W. B. (2008), *W. B. Yeats: The Major Works*, ed. E. Larrissy, Oxford: Oxford University Press.

Index

Ackerley, C. J.   89
Adorno, Theodor   2
Albanese, Ralph   110
Aldington, Richard   192
Alesch, Robert   38
Anderton, Joseph   3
Arnaud, Marthe   19
Astor, W. H.   32, 49–50
Atik, Anne   59
d'Aubigné, Agrippa   98–101
Audiberti, Jacques   155
Aulard, Ernest   60

Bair, Deirdre   12, 134
Barbusse, Henri   192
Barrès, Maurice   84
Baudoin, Paul   104
Beauvoir, Simone de   163
Beckett, Frank   49, 117
Beckett, Howard   184
Beckett, Samuel
  and the Fall of France   15–21
  and the First World War   183–205
  and Irish neutrality   122–3
  and the *maquis*   46–8
  and the *Relève*   44–5
  and the Resistance   31–41, 117
  in Roussillon   41–9
  and RTÉ   133
  in Saint-Lô   131–46, 211
Beckett, Samuel – texts
  All Strange Away   209–10
  All That Fall   144
  'Antipepsis'   211
  'Le Calmant'/'The Calmative'   53, 98–102
  'The Capital of the Ruins'   1, 13, 119, 133–46, 160, 173, 205, 211
  'Censorship in the Saorstat'   118, 142
  Dream of Fair to Middling Women   92, 94
  Eleuthéria   31, 66–7, 159–62, 170

En attendant Godot/Wating for Godot
   12, 41, 45–6, 66–75, 102, 106, 136, 181, 206
'L'Expulsé'/'The Expelled'   55, 59, 63, 144
Fin de partie/Endgame   2, 11, 17, 31, 102, 174, 178, 198–207, 210
'La Fin'/'Suite'/'The End'   41, 55–6, 62–3, 110–11, 151, 159, 162–5, 169, 174–5
'German Diaries'   4–5, 73, 78–9, 93–4, 139
How It Is   210
'Humanistic Quietism'   128
'Human Wishes'   18, 211
L'Innommable/The Unnamable   54, 56–8, 59, 95, 103, 112–15, 154, 165, 169, 197
'MacGreevy on Yeats'   119
Malone meurt/Malone Dies   39, 45, 53, 103, 109–12
Mercier et/and Camier   101, 174, 178–89, 191–7, 213
Molloy   62, 95–7, 103, 107–9, 158, 166–8, 169
More Pricks Than Kicks   135, 138 n.10, 184
'Mort de A. D.'   211–13
Murphy   15, 18–20, 22
'La Peinture des Van Velde ou Le monde et le pantalon'   129–30, 154–5
Pochade radiophonique/Rough for Radio II   35, 210
'Pour finir encore'/'For to end yet again'   145, 211–12
'Premier amour'/'First Love'   176–7, 213
'Recent Irish Poetry'   85 n.3, 118, 144, 184
Rough for Theatre II   40
'Saint-Lô'   145–6, 211
Stirrings Still   211–13

Index

Texts for Nothing   60, 61, 210
Watt   12, 23–26, 34–5, 40, 49, 50,
    64–6, 85–92, 101, 169, 188
Belmont, Georges, *see* Pelorson, Georges
Bion, Wilfred   184
Bixby, Patrick   3, 103 n.11
Blanton, C. D.   8
Blau, Herbert   214
Blitz, The   51–2
Boer War   180, 185–8
Bowen, Elizabeth   88, 120–1
Boyle, Kay   3, 70
Brault, Michel   46–7
Breton, André   156–8, 162
Brooke, Rupert   174
Bruller, Jean   60–1
Bryen, Camille   155

Camus, Albert   36, 166–8
Carton, Paul   106
Carrel, Alexis   82, 113, 170
Cassou, Jean   149
Chalmont, Charles   186
Chevalier, Jacques   98
Churchill, Winston   123
Coffey, Brian   189
Cohn, Ruby   181, 200
Combat   158, 166
Communism
   and French culture   164–6
   and the Resistance   37, 159–60
Corneille, Pierre   110
Cot, Pierre   105
Cremin, Cornelius   42
Cronin, Anthony   12, 43, 46, 189
Crowley, Mary   134
Curtis, Michael   150

The Daily Herald   193
Darley, Arthur   132, 211–12
Darley, George   211 n.1
Davis, Thomas S.   73
Déchevaux-Dumesnil, Suzanne   10, 15,
    19–21, 25–7, 37–41, 72
   and Communism   26–7, 37, 40,
       44 n.23
   role in Gloria SMH   32–3
Desbonnet, Edmond   106
Dorgelès, Roland   192, 200, 206
Doriot, Jacques   28

Dorléac, Laurence Bertrand   164
Douglas, Keith   185
Drieu La Rochelle, Pierre   22, 61
Duchamp, Marcel   21
Duhamel, Georges   192, 197–8
Dunne, Tommy   133, 212
Duthuit, Georges   121, 156, 157–8

Eagleton, Terry   33
Easter Rising   179
Eliot, T. S.   84 n.2, 123, 174
Ellis, J. W.   35
Ellul, Jacques   3, 100
Estienne, Yvonne   98

The Father Mathew Record   121
First World War   105, 110, 150, 173–205
   and Ireland   183
Fogg, Shannon L.   6, 72–3
France
   and the black market   72–4
   Fall of   17–20, 79
   and the First World War   177–8,
       202–5
   and food   63–7, 69–75
   liberation of   48–9, 51
   occupation of   17–20, 52–3
   and physical culture   105–6
Franco, Francisco   16
Fussell, Paul   195

Gaffney, James   212
Gaffney, Phyllis   134–5
Gaulle, Charles de   19, 37–8, 78, 148–9,
    150, 176, 202, 205
Gaullism   151–2, 156
   and humanism   151–3
   and the Resistance   35–8
   and returnees   57
   and Vichy   55, 149, 152
Gibson, Andrew   3, 8–9, 12, 68, 84, 86,
    103, 151, 180
Gid, Raymond   53
Gildea, Robert   36
Gloria SMH   10, 31–3, 38–41, 49–50
Goebbels, Joseph   17
Goering, Hermann   155
Goldsmith, John   34
Gontarski, S. E.   133–5, 141, 201
Gordon, Lois   12, 117, 136

Index

Gouvard, Jean-Michel 72
Graves, Robert 192–3
Gribben, Darren 135–6
Griffin, Gerald 91–2
Guéhenno, Jean 7, 18 n.4, 22, 28–9, 37, 56, 59–60, 63–4, 66, 69, 75, 148, 176–7

Hardy, Thomas 174
Hébert, Georges 106–7
Heidegger, Martin 154
Hessel, Stéphane 16 n.1
Hitler, Adolf 28, 50
Horizon 155
Hotel Lutetia 49, 54
Houston Jones, David 3
Humbert, Agnès 18, 20, 36, 38, 59

Irish Civil War 179
Irish Free State 85–6, 92, 186
  and neutrality 117–21, 122, 139–44
The Irish Times 121, 140–1, 145

Jabri, Vivienne 6
Jackson, Julian 20 n.6, 78 n.1, 153
Jellet, Mainie 121
Joan of Arc 85–6, 101
Joyce, James 15, 20, 22, 206

Katz, Daniel 54
Kedward, H. R. 93
Kelly, Michael 153
Kennedy, Seán 3, 8, 85–6, 88, 106 n.12, 186, 193
Kennedy, Sighle 23
Knowlson, James 12, 28, 33, 48, 72, 184

Lackerstein, Debbie 52, 80
La Nouvelle Revue Française 22, 61
Larbaud, Valery 20
Laval, Pierre 44, 59, 77, 202
Lawlor, Seán 211–13
Lefebvre, Henri 62
Legrand, Jacques 31
Léon, Paul 33, 53, 213
Les Éditions de Minuit 60–1
Le Silence de la mer 60–1
Les Tempes modernes 55, 162–3, 171
Leventhal, A. J. (Con) 120
L'Humanité 164

Lodwick, John 34–5
London Mercury 192

MacGreevy, Thomas 6, 15, 78, 92, 121, 132, 141, 148, 158, 162, 189–91
  'De Civitate Hominum' 190–1
  'Nocturne' 190 n.5
MacKay, Marina 8 n.4, 9, 11, 138
McKee, Frederick 212
McLoughlin, Kate 137–8
McMillan, Dougald 133, 135, 136–9, 141
McMullan, Anna 102 n.9
McNaughton, James 3, 57, 103 n.11, 117, 189
MacNeice, Louis 126, 180 n.1
Maude, Ulrika 102 n.9
Maurras, Charles 77, 81–4, 149, 171
Merleau-Ponty, Maurice 154, 161–2
Moorjani, Angela 155–6
Morin, Emilie 3, 12, 35, 53, 55
Moynahan, Julian 88
Murphy, Seán 42, 132

New Masses 164
Nixon, Mark 24, 73
Nordau, Max 106 n.12
Noyer, Philippe 73

O'Brien, Eoin 132, 212
O'Brien, Kate 120
O'Dwyer, Graham 154 n.4
Ó Faracháin, Roibeard 135
O'Grady, Standish 144
Orwell, George 155, 192
  Homage to Catalonia 195
  Inside the Whale 194
  'Looking back on the Spanish War' 195
  Nineteen Eighty-Four 44
  'Politics and the English Language' 8 n.4
Oudeville, Georges 60
Owen, Wilfred 192

Paraf, Yvonne 60–1
Paris
  liberation of 49, 147
  occupation of 22, 26
Paris, Erna 169, 210
Paulhan, Jean 22

Index

Paz, Ocatvio   157
Péguy, Charles   101
Pelorson, Georges   15, 20, 28, 35, 46, 100
Perloff, Marjorie   4, 100, 194
Péron, Alfred   15, 22, 31–3, 37, 39, 46, 50, 213
Péron, Mania   39–40
Pétain, Phillippe   19–20, 23, 28–9, 51, 59, 105, 176–7, 180, 202, 205
   and the Catholic Church   94–5
   cult of   78–102, 109–12
   and the forest   97–102
   and the Legion of Combatants   110
   trial of   77–8, 147–8, 150
Picabia, Gabrielle   32, 34
Picabia, Jeannine   31, 38–9, 50
Picasso, Pablo   163–4
Piette, Adam   4, 5, 10, 191
Pilling, John   211–13
Plain, Gill   9–10, 59
Procter, James   6
Pudney, John Sleigh   174

Quinn, James   57

Reavey, George   21, 148, 158
Remarque, Erich Maria   192–4
Révolution nationale (National Revolution)   20, 27–8, 48, 78–116
Reynaud, Paul   19
Reynolds, Mary   21
Ricks, Christopher   103 n.10
Robert, Fernand   157
Rosenberg, Isaac   192
Ross, Kristin   55, 62
Rosset, Barney   134
Rossi, Tino   68
Roussillon   23–4, 41–9
Rousso, Henry   36, 149
Russell, Rachel   103

Sablon, Jean   68
Saint-Lô   130–
   bombing of   1, 48–9
Salisbury, Laura   2 n.2, 3, 34
Sarsfield, Patrick   179
Sartre, Jean-Paul   153–4, 156
   'L'Existentialisme est un humanisme'   153–4
   French Writing on English Soil   51–3, 58

Questions de méthode   159
Réflexions sur la question juive/ Anti-Semite and Jew   13, 171–2
Sassoon, Siegfried   192
Scarry, Elaine   180
Shaw, Herbert   121
Shenker, Israel   157, 209
Simpson, Hannah   69, 93 n.6
Spender, Stephen   4
Stein, Gertrude   79
Stieve, Friedrich   4–5
Stromberg Childers, Kristen   100
Stuart, Francis   25, 35

Tajiri, Yoshiki   103 n.10
Teichman, Jenny   182
Thompson, Alan   131
Teekell, Anna   3, 9–10
Temps présent   154
Thomason, Gilbert   38
Tillion, Germaine   38
Times Literary Supplement   192
Trumbo, Dalton   198
Tumblety, Joan   105

Ugeux, William   34
UNESCO   148–9, 157
Ussher, Arland   55, 149

Valera, Éamon de   118
Vallat, Xavier   110
Van Dusen, Wanda   79
Van Hulle, Dirk   212
Vichy
   and antisemitism   26–31, 81–3, 169–70
   and deportations   41

Weller, Shane   103
Wells, H. G.   173
White, Kathryn   103 n.10, 113
Wieviorka, Olivier   36
Will, Barbara   79
Wills, Clair   120
Wimbush, Andy   96–7

Yeats, Jack B.   6
Yeats, W. B.   24, 84 n.3, 88, 91–2, 106 n.12, 186, 196

www.ingramcontent.com/pod-product-compliance
Lightning Source LLC
Chambersburg PA
CBHW072145290426
44111CB00012B/1975